A

OR

FLAVOR

OTTOLENGHI
FLAVOR

Yotam Ottolenghi   Ixta Belfrage

with Tara Wigley
Photographs by Jonathan Lovekin

TEN SPEED PRESS
California | New York

CONTENTS

INTRODUCTION

I have never been shy about my love of vegetables. I have been singing the praises of cauliflowers, tomatoes, lemons, and my old friend the mighty eggplant for over a decade. I have done this on my own—in cooking demos, on book tours, and in the pages of books and magazines—and I have done this in a group, in lively discussions with colleagues in my restaurants, and in the test kitchen. It's become my mission to present vegetables in new and exciting ways and I have embraced it with nothing but enthusiasm.

Still, in the spirit of openness, I must confess to a small niggling doubt that creeps in now and then. How many more ways are there to fry an eggplant, to slice a tomato, to squeeze a lemon, or to roast a cauliflower? How many more secrets are there to be discovered in a handful of lentils or a bowl of polenta?

The answer, I am delighted to report, is many. My journey of discovery into the world of vegetables—by which I mean anything, really, that originates from a plant—has taken me in all sorts of directions that I simply hadn't imagined. If my first vegetable book, *Plenty*, was the honeymoon period, a great big party where certain vegetables—peppers, tomatoes, eggplants, mushrooms—got a whole chapter to themselves, *Plenty More* was all about process; recipes were divided into the ways in which the vegetables were treated: mashed or tossed or grilled and so forth. *Flavor* is the third book in the series, it's about understanding what makes vegetables distinct and, accordingly, devising ways in which their flavors can be ramped up and tasted afresh; it's about creating flavor bombs, especially designed for veg. This is done in three ways.

PROCESS, PAIRING, PRODUCE

The first step has to do with some *processes* that happen to vegetables when they are cooked, or to some key ingredients with which they are cooked. The second is about *pairing*; what you match a vegetable with to draw out one of its distinct qualities. The third deals with the *produce* itself: the sheer depth of flavor that certain ingredients naturally possess that allows them to play a starring role in a dish, more or less by themselves, or to prop up and brightly illuminate other vegetables.

So, after *Plenty* and *Plenty More*, *Flavor* is "*Plenty 3*," if you like, or *P3*, with the three P's (process, pairing, and produce) being the key concepts for explaining what makes certain vegetable dishes taste so good. Let me give you some examples to illustrate this, using some of my favorite ingredients: celery root (to demonstrate process), tamarind and lime (to think about pairing), and mushrooms (to show how it can be just the produce itself doing the work).

First, *process*. Three recipes in this book involve cooking celery root whole for more than two hours, then dressing and serving it in different ways. During the initial cooking of the celery root, and before any other ingredient is added, something truly magical happens. Much of the water in the celery root evaporates, its flesh turns from white to golden brown, and it becomes sweeter and richer. This browning and caramelizing, which happens to many veg (and non-veg) when they are cooked in a certain way, is a key process that teases out flavor from them. Whatever you choose to do to the celery root after this is less important. Indeed, you don't need to do anything more to it at all, if you don't want to; the browning process is such a flavor bomb

HOW MANY MORE WAYS ARE THERE TO FRY AN EGGPLANT? THE ANSWER, I AM DELIGHTED TO REPORT, IS MANY.

that it's heavenly when eaten at this stage, cut into wedges and served with a squeeze of lemon or a dollop of crème fraîche. Other processes that have a similarly terrific effect are charring, infusing, and aging (which is mostly done to ingredients well before they reach your kitchen), all of which transform and elevate vegetables to great heights.

Illustrating my concept of *pairing* is a little less straightforward because, every time you cook, you obviously pair ingredients together. What I have done, though, is identify four basic pairings—sweetness, fat, acidity, and chile heat (as in spicy heat)—that are fundamental. Introducing one or more of these key pairings to a dish has the effect of showing the vegetables (or fruit) with which they are partnered in a completely new light. The ASPARAGUS SALAD WITH TAMARIND AND LIME (PAGE 171) is a great example. Many argue that asparagus is so magnificent—with a subtle, yet refined flavor—that it doesn't need to be paired with anything, really, except some oil or butter and possibly a poached egg. I have made this same point myself in the not-so-distant past. What I have learned more recently, though, is that asparagus can actually stand its ground when paired with robust and purportedly dominant ingredients. It does this particularly well when the paired element is complex and multilayered. In the salad I mentioned, raw asparagus is paired with three sources of acidity: lime juice, vinegar, and tamarind, each with its own particular characteristics. All these layers and iterations of sour come together in a single harmony that heightens and alters the taste of raw asparagus in a way that really opens your eyes to the vegetables.

The third concept has to do with *produce*. Vegetables, famously, are not as good at imparting flavor as are meat and fish, because of their high water content and the low levels of fat and protein they contain. Some, though, are absolutely brilliant at it. Our SPICY MUSHROOM LASAGNE (PAGE 228) is proof of the power of this particular veg to carry the weight of a whole complex dish on its own little shoulders, giving any meat a good run for its money. Not many vegetables can do this, delicious as they may be, but since mushrooms are bursting with umami—that satisfying savory flavor that makes tomatoes, soy sauce, cheese, and many other ingredients so impactful—they are perfectly capable of providing ample flavor and some serious texture to give vegetarian dishes a very solid core. Other plant-based ingredients that show similarly impressive skills are alliums (onions and garlic), nuts and seeds, and fruit. All four are the types of produce that you can rely on to do some seriously hard work in your kitchen.

While making a delicious recipe can be simple, great cooking is never the result of one element in isolation—it is the interplay of different types of *processes*, *pairings*, and *produce* in one dish that elevates and makes it exquisite. Using the lasagne example again, this dish clearly relies heavily on mushroom umami (produce), but it also benefits greatly from an interplay of different fats (pairing) and the complex art of aging cheese (process). The structure of this book, in which each chapter highlights one particular kind of process, pairing, or produce, is, therefore, not to undermine or deny the existence of any other elements in a recipe; its purpose is to highlight the USP (unique selling point) of a dish, a particular element at the core that makes it particularly delicious or special.

FLEXITARIANISM

With the challenge to ramp up flavor in vegetables and take it to new heights, I've used every possible tool available in the kitchen. For me, and the way I cook and eat, this includes ingredients such as anchovies, fish sauce, and Parmesan that are not, of course, often used in recipe books in which vegetables play the starring role. Though I totally understand why that is the case, with many people following an exact vegetarian or vegan diet, I have decided to appeal to the widest group of vegetable lovers possible.

I find that more and more people are looking to brand their own individual kind of vegetable eating. Yes, many define themselves as vegetarian or vegan, but there is also a certain fluidity that characterizes the current approach to how we feed ourselves. You find vegans who eat eggs, those who eat seafood but won't touch milk because of the predicament of dairy cows, some who

IF YOU WANT TO WIN MORE PEOPLE OVER TO THE VEG CAMP, THERE IS NO WORSE WAY TO GO ABOUT IT THAN DEMAND THAT THEY GO COLD TURKEY.

exclude only proteins that are particularly harmful to the environment; there are pescatarians, beegans (vegans who eat honey), and lacto-vegetarians (abstaining from meat and eggs). There are also "lapsed" vegans or vegetarians: those who have given up a strict regime but have taken away with them the joys and skills of cooking a great meat-free meal.

My own approach to vegetables has always been pragmatic and inclusive. If you want to win more people over to the veg camp, there is no worse way to go about it than demand that they go cold turkey (excuse the pun). If an animal-based aromatic ingredient (we are not talking prime cuts of meat here, or a bluefin tuna steak) does an outstanding job at helping a vegetable taste particularly delicious, I will definitely use it for the benefit of those who are happy to eat it. At the same time, I will also offer various alternatives to animal products (and dairy products, whenever I can) so that everyone can join in.

This flexitarian approach to cooking and eating acknowledges the diversity of the people we are and the variety of choices we make. Of the 100 recipes in this book, 45 are strictly vegan and another 17 are easily "veganized." Whatever your own preference might be, I feel confident that you will find good reasons to join in my celebration of all the flavors that vegetables have to offer.

My confidence here is based on my knowledge of vegetables after years of cooking and writing about them, during which I have never ceased to be surprised. It is grounded in my love of vegetables and my understanding of how versatile they are, how receptive they are to different cooking practices, how chameleon-like their ability is to take on flavor and metamorphose themselves from one dish to the next.

And thus, a simple cauliflower, to use a favorite example, can reinvent itself across books and in many chapters, showing up as a seductive Levantine fritter, or grilled and engaged with saffron and raisins, only to return disguised

SIMPLY "MAGICAL," TO BORROW A TERM FAVORED BY MY FIVE-YEAR-OLD SON.

as bulgur in a modern take on tabbouleh, followed by an incarnation as a glamorous savory cake, a meaty steak, dressed as (coronation) chicken, or simply served whole, grilled yet totally unadorned, with only its natural splendor to call out its virtues. This is how wide the range and how wondrous the potential of every single vegetable. Simply "magical," to borrow a term favored by my five-year-old son.

IXTA

Much as vegetables have this supernatural ability to be turned into an endless smörgåsbord of delicious food, it takes a focused creative effort to unravel this potential. In other words, the umpteenth way to cook the beloved cauliflower didn't just present itself out of thin air. It was a result of trial and (many an) error, mixing and matching cauliflower with other components on the plate, of constantly looking for exciting new ingredients for it to be paired with, and, generally, being super-sensitive to the processes that happen in the pan, or in the roasting dish, or on the serving platter.

The people leading this creative process are, naturally, crucial to the particular route it will take. So, if you have already managed to spot a lime or two in places where lemons would appear in previous Ottolenghi books, or noticed a range of Mexican and other chiles peppered all over these pages, or if you came across quick pickles and infused oils used to give dishes a finishing touch—you have identified the fingerprints of Ixta Belfrage, who's had those same fingers on the vegetable pulse for the last couple of years and helped shape the recipes in this book in a particular way.

Ixta is one of the most detail-obsessed chefs I know (and I have met a few of those over the years), with an unusual talent both for making the most spectacular versions of familiar dishes (see that LASAGNE again, PAGE 228) and for putting together an unusual set of components and effortlessly creating a totally new masterpiece (see, or rather, go make, the SWEET AND SOUR SPROUTS WITH CHESTNUTS AND GRAPES, PAGE 93).

THE UMPTEENTH WAY TO COOK THE BELOVED CAULIFLOWER DIDN'T JUST PRESENT ITSELF OUT OF THIN AIR.

Ixta's journey into the world of food, which is evident in so many of the dishes here, was, a bit like mine, anything but straightforward. Despite growing up mostly in London, she spent much of her early years in different corners of the globe, eating, observing, and just soaking up some wonderful food traditions and flavors.

If you talked to Ixta, she'd be happy to tell you about her friend's grandfather, Ferruccio—who, in a corner of Tuscany, makes the best lasagne in the world, and passed a few secrets on to her. She would talk about her own grandfather's

home, near Mexico City, where she keenly watched chiles rellenos (stuffed peppers) being prepared. She'd mention Brazil, where her mother is from and where she fell for pirão (cassava-flour porridge), mocequa (fish stew), and fried cassava chips, and she'd definitely tell you about Christmas holidays in France and that most glorious of apple pies, pastis Gascon.

After all that, you'd be right to assume that cooking would be Ixta's first port of call in her professional life. Yet on her way there, she managed, among other things, to start a foundation course in art, go to university in Rio, move to Australia for three years and work as a door-to-door power-and-gas sales-person, become a travel agent, and come back to London and study design.

SHE TEACHES ME SOMETHING NEW EVERY SINGLE DAY. AND FOR THIS, I AM UTTERLY GRATEFUL.

It took Ixta's sister finally asking the obvious question one day—"Why the f*** aren't you a chef?"—for the penny to finally drop, which it did with a loud bang. After that, this self-taught, highly observant person, who spent her childhood, adolescence, and young adulthood absorbing techniques and flavors like a sponge, set out on an accelerated route that included running her own small catering operation; setting up a market stall in London, where she sold tacos (of course); and, finally, applying for a job at NOPI.

When, less than a year later, she arrived in my test kitchen—with no formal training and a modest amount of experience, but with a mountain of knowledge, creativity, and talent—I soon understood that I could more or less leave Ixta to her own devices. Cooking her own food, which is deeply rooted in the cultures she has soaked up over the years, while also brilliantly incorporating the language of contemporary cooking, she teaches me something new every single day. And for this, I am utterly grateful.

TARA

The power of a good recipe to expose the hidden potential in an ingredient and show it in a new and wonderful light is the greatest joy of my profession. It's what keeps Ixta and me going, trying to explore further, to look at every possible iteration, to wrack our brains until we finally hit on something that is both delicious and truly special.

Good cookbooks do the same thing with a set of recipes. They take them, just like raw ingredients, and piece together a narrative; they give a compelling account that makes sense and hits the spot, like a perfectly balanced stew or a trifle with just the right proportions of creamy to fruity to boozy.

Telling a story in such a way is a difficult task that takes a particular and rare talent. Tara Wigley, who has worked on all but two of the eight cookbooks that have come out of the Ottolenghi family, has this talent in ladlefuls. With her deep insight into both the human palate and the Ottolenghi flavor palette, she has always managed to turn our recipes into much more than a set of instructions for re-creating dishes at home. She has given them a context and put ideas behind them; she has assembled them in particular ways that made them make sense and made people want to prepare them.

In this book, Tara took one short look at the recipes and instantly isolated and identified what Ixta and I struggled hopelessly to figure out. She gave our vague ideas names, helped us structure the book, and then she put together the introductions to the three main sections, which provide the book with its theoretical basis. To that effect, the story that is unearthed here, through recipes, has been brought to light thanks to Tara.

YOTAM OTTOLENGHI

FLAVOR'S 20 INGREDIENTS

We conclude this introductory section with a list of *Flavor*'s essential ingredients. By "essential," we don't suggest that you necessarily need to go out and buy them all before you start cooking, or that you just can't do without them. In fact, you will be able to reproduce many of the dishes here without a single one of these ingredients. What we mean is that the twenty ingredients we highlight, as well as popping up regularly on the pages alongside our beloved vegetables, capture the essence of this book, its particular spirit. If you open a jar or a bag of any of these ingredients, edge your nose close and have a little sniff, you should be able to smell *flavor*.

Since we champion veg and the numerous ways in which you can dial up their flavor that one extra notch, it is no surprise that many of our essentials are aged or fermented. In fact, there is a whole section dedicated to dishes that rely on aged ingredients to make them as delicious and special as they are. There is also a long introduction explaining the superpower of aging and how it generates layers of flavor. Aged ingredients are shortcuts to jars of flavor that, we believe, should sit on every kitchen shelf.

Chiles, as well as umami-rich ferments, form another strong grouping on our list of essentials. Though celebrated for their spiciness (see CHILE HEAT, PAGE 127, and recipes, PAGES 196–211), our chiles do much more than that. They bring to the table a whole set of sub-flavors and fine aromas that you simply can't find elsewhere, a different kind of sweet, smoky, leathery, chocolatey, or tart. They also have an incredible ability to marry together with other flavors to create a new, singular harmony. We always think of the combination of garlic, ginger, and chile, which sits at the heart of so many dishes, and try to imagine it without the chile. Impossible.

Chiles, like ferments, run across cultures like busy diplomats. Practically every region in the world to which we are drawn has its own unique take on chile sauce, or oil, or marinade. A little bottle or jar with deep-scarlet liquid inside signifies a flavor bomb of a very particular kind.

In *Flavor*, Mexico is where we frequently go for our fix of chile heat. This has as much to do with the incredible range of chiles that come out of this country as it does with Ixta's childhood memories of Mexico and her infatuation with its food.

Chiles, as well as masa harina, hibiscus flowers, and all the clever feasts that you can create with them, are the latest additions to the ever-expanding Ottolenghi pantry. We urge you to try them out, but please don't ditch the old favorites. Some of them—rose harissa, black garlic, Aleppo chile—are on this list; others—tahini, za'atar, preserved lemons, pomegranate molasses—aren't, but they are dotted throughout the recipes, busily doing their now-familiar magic.

Aleppo chile (aka pul biber) is a dried and flaked chile, common in Turkey and Syria, named after the city of Aleppo. While the flakes themselves are dark red, they impart a bright red color when infused. We use Aleppo chile to add medium heat to lots of sauces and marinades, such as our NAM JIM (see PAGE 202), NAM PRIK (see PAGE 44), RAYU see (PAGE 237), and CHAMOY (see PAGE 187). It's also great in salad sprinkles (see KOHLRABI "NOODLE" SALAD, PAGE 260). You can find Aleppo chile in some supermarkets, but better yet, visit a Middle Eastern grocery store; you can find it under the name "pul biber" for a fraction of the price. Use the same amount of Gochugaru Korean hot pepper flakes, or half the amount of regular chile flakes, as a substitute.

Ancho chile is the dried version of the poblano chile. Poblanos are green when fresh, and become very dark red when dried, developing fruity and sweet notes with mild to medium levels of heat. We use them in both sweet and savory contexts here—see TANGERINE AND ANCHO CHILE FLAN (PAGE 278) and BLACK BEANS WITH COCONUT, CHILE, AND LIME (PAGE 86).

Anchovies don't need much of an introduction, but we should note that we do mean those that have been aged in salt, rather than marinated or pickled, and we would urge you to get anchovies kept in olive oil, rather than sunflower oil. Anchovies give a savory depth to the dishes you add them to. They are only particularly fishy if you use a fair amount. We are aware that vegetarians and vegans don't eat anchovies, so they are optional in all the recipes. They can be substituted with extra seasoning, and by that we mean anything from salt, miso, and soy sauce to finely chopped olives and capers.

Black garlic is garlic that has been gently heated for 2–3 weeks, causing the Maillard reaction (see PAGE 28) to render it black and a bit licorice-y, with notes of balsamic vinegar. It brings a distinctive sweetness to OLIVE OIL FLATBREADS (see PAGE 246) and DIRTY RICE (PAGE 252). You can find it online.

Black lime is a lime that has been sun-dried until it has lost all its water and turned rock-hard. Popular in the Persian Gulf, it is intensely sour and gives dishes a uniquely earthy and slightly bitter type of acidity. There are different versions across the region, with different names, such as Omani limes, Iranian limes, and noomi basra, and they can range in color from blond to dark brown to black. You can use any of them in our recipes, but we prefer the small black one. You can harness the lime's flavor in different ways: pierce holes in it and add it to a broth or stew to impart milder flavor, grind to a powder, or soak and finely chop the whole lot to add an intense hit of earthy acidity. You can find them online or in Middle Eastern grocers. If you can't find them, regular fresh lime zest and juice can be used as a substitute.

Cascabel chiles are, we think, the best dried chiles out there. We've used them in countless dishes in our restaurant, ROVI—the BUTTER BEANS IN SMOKED CASCABEL OIL (PAGE 41), for one, and in the rub for OYSTER MUSHROOM TACOS (see PAGE 238). On first inspection they are black, but if you hold them up to the light, they are in fact a deep and seductive red. They are nutty and mildly chocolatey, which makes them work wonderfully in both sweet and savory contexts. However, if you can't find them, anchos make a fine substitute.

Chipotle chile is the dried and smoked version of the jalapeño chile. It gives medium heat and is, unsurprisingly, smoky. We steep chipotle flakes in warm oil for a very quick but extremely effective chile oil to drizzle over CHEESE TAMALES (see PAGE 158), and blitz them into a coating for peanuts, which play a starring role in RADISH AND CUCUMBER SALAD (see PAGE 263). To make chipotle chile flakes, mince a whole chipotle chile using a sharp knife or blitz it in a spice grinder or clean coffee grinder.

Fish sauce is a Southeast Asian condiment made from fermented fish. It is extremely funky, and although we love it, we can appreciate that not everyone does. Squid Brand (which interestingly contains no squid) is very good, and is readily available in any Asian supermarket. Fish sauce is totally optional in all recipes. It's comparable in salt levels to light soy sauce, which can be used in its place. You may want to add less light soy sauce, however, if the recipe already contains soy sauce.

Gochujang chile paste is a Korean fermented paste made from chiles, glutinous rice, and soybeans, making it complex, hot, sweet, and savory all at once. Try to get Korean brands (O'food, for example), which have a serious depth to them. Gochujang is available in most Asian supermarkets, but if you can only get the supermarket stuff, taste before you add—you may need to double the amount if it's lacking in color, body, or flavor.

Ground cardamom has been an Ottolenghi pantry staple for a while because we love using it in both sweet and savory contexts. We sell it in our webstore. You can make your own, however, by starting with whole cardamom pods, discarding the papery shells, and grinding the seeds to a fine powder. You'll be happy to have it when making our CARDAMOM TOFU (see PAGE 172), though, as it requires a fair amount.

Hibiscus flowers are used widely in Mexico to flavor all sorts of foods and drinks. They are floral and tart, comparable in taste to cranberries, and impart an almost instant bright-pink hue to anything they infuse. Dried hibiscus flowers are available in many health food shops and online, although we tend to use hibiscus tea bags, as they are more readily available. We use hibiscus to add an extra level of face-puckering acidity to our LEMON SORBET (see PAGE 289), and to add tartness and vibrant color to our PICKLED ONIONS (see PAGE 158).

Jarred butter beans, specifically Brindisa Navarrico butter beans, prove that not all pre-cooked butter beans are created equal. If you are not going to cook butter beans from scratch, these "judiónes"—*giant* butter beans—are just as soft, creamy, and *perfectly* seasoned. Do try to source them to use in BKEILA, POTATO, AND BUTTER BEAN STEW (PAGE 75), or to steep in a wonderfully smoky CASCABEL OIL (see PAGE 41). Canned butter beans are, of course, a fine alternative.

Mango pickle is a hot, sharp, and textured pickle, the dominant spice of which is fenugreek, used widely in South and Southeast Asia. It shouldn't be confused with mango chutney, which is often cloyingly sweet. We use a hot Indian variety in our STUFFED EGGPLANT (see PAGE 152) and CHICKPEA PANCAKES WITH MANGO PICKLE YOGURT (PAGE 91). It can be found in the international aisles of some supermarkets, and in Indian grocery stores.

Masa harina is a flour made from nixtamalized corn. Nixtamalization is an ancient Aztec process by which corn is soaked and cooked in an alkaline solution before being washed and hulled. This helps with turning it into flour and boosts its nutritional value. Masa harina is used in Mexico and other parts of Central and South America to make tortillas (try our OYSTER MUSHROOM TACOS, see PAGE 238) and tamales (try our CHEESE TAMALES, see PAGE 158), among other things. It's important to remember that it is not interchangeable with polenta. You can find it at gourmet groceries, most health food shops, and online.

Miso is a Japanese seasoning made by fermenting soybeans (but also sometimes rice or barley) with salt and koji, which is rice that has been inoculated with mold spores, making it sound far less delicious than it actually is. Miso is the embodiment of umami (see PAGE 35); it's sweet, salty, and meaty all at once, and can single-handedly give an incredible depth of flavor to anything you add it to. We use white miso paste in our recipes because it has the perfect balance of sweet, salty, and savory that we're after, but you can use whatever color miso is available. Try to avoid using sweet white miso paste; it is, unsurprisingly, much too *sweet* for savory recipes.

Red bell pepper flakes are the dried flakes of what Americans would call "bell peppers," Australians would call "capsicums," and the British would simply (or rather confusingly) call "peppers." They are not to be confused with "crushed red pepper" or "red pepper flakes," which are made from hot red chiles. Red bell pepper flakes are mild and sweet and impart a bright red color when soaked. You can buy red bell pepper flakes online and on the Ottolenghi webstore. If you can't get them, see individual recipes for substitutions.

Rice vinegar is made from fermented rice grains, and is widely used in China, Japan, and Southeast Asia. It is milder, sweeter, and less acidic than distilled Western vinegars, so we often use it in situations that call for a more subtle and rounded hit of acidity. Our TAHINI AND SOY DRESSING (see PAGE 113), for example, benefits from the use of rice vinegar, as does the dressing in our TOMATO AND PLUM SALAD (see PAGE 267).

Rose harissa is a version of the popular North African chile paste that contains rose petals. We use a fantastic, richly spiced but not terribly hot version by Belazu. It's not available everywhere, though, and store-brand varieties tend not to be very good. As an alternative, use the French variety by DEA or the Tunisian variety by Le Phare du Cap Bon (which you're likely to find internationally in a yellow-and-blue tube or can). It won't have the rose flavor but this wouldn't really disrupt any of our recipes. The only things to watch are the level of heat, which is much higher in Tunisian products, and the fact that they don't contain as much oil. Our advice is to taste your harissa before you add it, increasing or decreasing the amount you use depending on how hot and strong you like things, and to add a bit of olive oil if you think the dish needs it. As a general rule, when substituting for rose harissa, you'll want to use about half that amount of French harissa, or a third of that amount of Tunisian chile paste.

Shaoxing wine is fermented from rice. It is mildly sweet and subtly funky, similar in taste to pale dry sherry, which can be used in its place if necessary. It's quite easy to get hold of in Asian supermarkets. It adds a particularly wonderful musty aroma to CAPONATA (see PAGE 135), SWEET AND SOUR SPROUTS WITH CHESTNUTS AND GRAPES (PAGE 93), and GRILLED FIGS (see PAGE 110).

Tamarind paste is extracted from the sweet-sour pulp of the pod-like tamarind fruit. It's indigenous to tropical Africa but popular throughout Asia, South America, and the Middle East. Commercial versions can be a bit tricky for home cooks because they vary greatly in concentration. Generally, they are sharper and more intense than the paste you extract yourself from a block of tamarind because they have citric acid added to them, so you'll have to double the amount of paste the recipe calls for when making it yourself. To do that, mix a lemon-size piece—roughly 4¼ oz/120g—with about ¼ cup/60ml lukewarm water. After a few minutes, use your hands to mix everything together, adding a little more water if needed, so that the pulp falls away from the seeds and fiber. Pass it through a fine-mesh sieve, discarding the seeds and fiber, and store the thick paste in the fridge for up to 1 month.

A NOTE ON INGREDIENTS

Unless otherwise specified, all eggs are large, all butter is unsalted, all olive oil is extra-virgin. Vegetables are trimmed, and onions, garlic, and shallots are peeled (keep the trimmings and peelings to make stock). Onions are yellow. Garlic cloves are regular in size. Chiles have their stems removed and are used with their seeds, although of course you can remove the seeds if you prefer less heat.

Salt is non-iodized table salt such as Morton's, but we often also call for flaked sea salt, especially when finishing dishes.

Black pepper is freshly cracked (never pre-ground).

Curry leaves and makrut lime leaves are fresh, rather than dried. They are available in specialty Asian supermarkets and online.

Yogurt, crème fraîche, and cream are all plain and full-fat, and can always be replaced by dairy-free alternatives, to keep things vegan.

Coconut cream can be found near the canned coconut milk in stores; it is thicker than canned coconut milk.

A NOTE ON TOASTING NUTS AND SEEDS

We toast nuts and seeds in an oven preheated to 325°F/165°C fan, spread out on a baking sheet and stirred halfway through. Flaked almonds and sesame seeds take 6–7 minutes. Pine nuts, walnuts, and pistachios take around 8 minutes, and whole almonds and hazelnuts take 8–10 minutes.

A NOTE ON TEMPERATURES AND MEASUREMENTS

All recipes have been tested in a fan-assisted (convection) oven using Celsius temperatures. For North American cooks, we've also given the equivalent Fahrenheit temperature for conventional ovens. Ovens all vary, so look for visual descriptions in the method, rather than relying only on timings, to achieve desired results.

Teaspoon and tablespoon measurements vary by country. In this book, 1 tsp = 5ml, and 1 tbsp = 15ml.

A NOTE ON PLASTIC WRAP, PARCHMENT PAPER, AND ALUMINUM FOIL

All efforts have been made to minimize our use of single-use materials. Parchment paper and aluminum foil can often be reused, rather than discarded, and reusable food wraps can be used in place of plastic wrap.

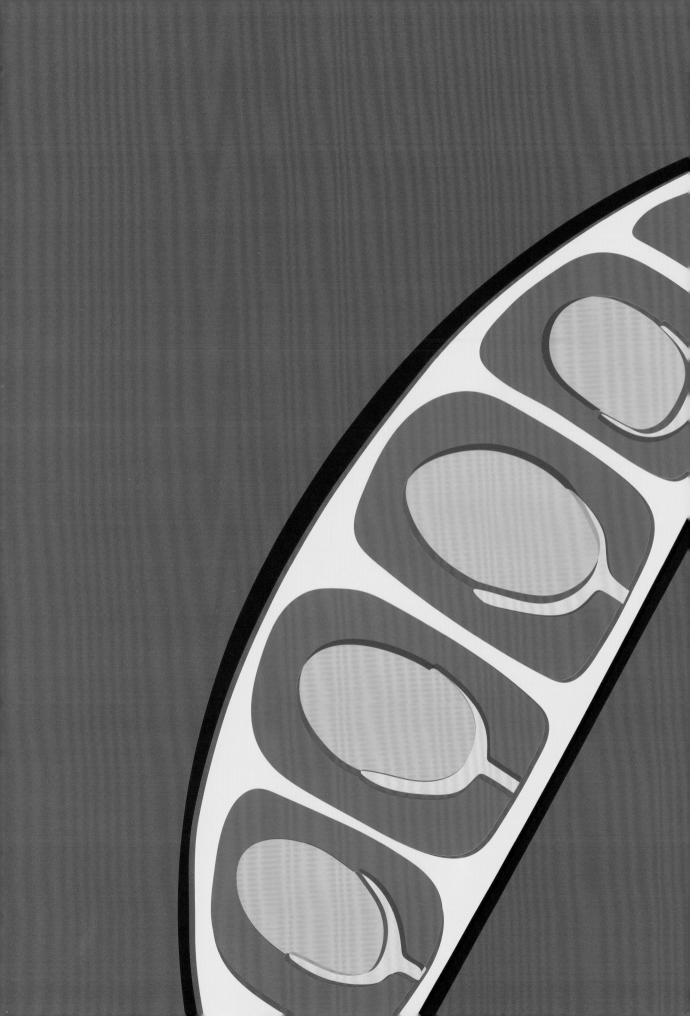

PROCESS

One of the ways to ramp up flavor in a vegetable is to subject it to a "process" before or during cooking. In *Flavor*, we've homed in on four processes: *charring*, *browning*, *infusing*, and *aging*. These demonstrate how the application of heat, smoke, or the passage of time to a vegetable or other ingredient can dramatically change, draw out, or intensify its flavor. They show, in short, how flavor can be dialed up to make things even more tasty.

Recipes have been grouped according to the main process undertaken, but there's often more than one thing going on in the same dish. Although the oil and beans in BUTTER BEANS IN SMOKED CASCABEL OIL (PAGE 41), as just one example, are *infused* by a pack of punchy aromatics, it's the deep *charring* of these aromatics in the first place that makes the dish stand out. Such is the very nature of vegetables; varied, versatile, brilliant vegetables that come in all shapes and sizes, and can be prepared in a huge variety of ways. Nevertheless, it's useful—when thinking about how flavor can get ramped up in a vegetable—to have a look at each process, one at a time.

CHARRING

In the beginning, there was fire. We are not talking about the dawn of time. We're thinking, for now, about Yotam's first memory of "cooking." It was a potato, tossed into a bonfire along with a few onions, on the Jewish holiday of Lag BaOmer, when spiritual light is celebrated by setting real lights across the land. Despite *his* best intentions, though, his spiritual awakening wasn't ignited by the lights but by the humble potato: a little ball of char, singeing his eight-year-old fingers as he peeled away its thick black skin. The steamy flesh, soft and billowy, speckled with black and tasting deep and sweet and smoky, was worth every blister on both his thumbs. This was an epic revelation.

SUCH IS THE POWER OF HEAT, SMOKE, AND NEAT BLACK STRIPES.

Another big "first," cooking-wise, was during the early days of Ottolenghi, when a simple salad of grilled broccoli, with slivers of garlic and red chile, swiftly and firmly embedded itself on the menu. More than a decade later, it's still there. Our customers—many of whom tell us that they didn't really eat broccoli until they started charring it—won't let us take it off. For some, the experience of what broccoli *can* taste like is a revelation. Such is the power of heat, smoke, and neat black stripes.

So, what's the secret behind this charring process?

The science is relatively simple to understand. The direct application of heat to the outside of the ingredient is creating a chemical change. On a cellular level, amino acids and sugars are rearranging themselves nicely. This leads to a concentration of flavors that, in turn, imparts a delicious complexity, bitterness, and sweetness. On top of that, there's a "bonus" aroma that comes from the smoke that's emitted as the skin singes and that is impossible to resist.

The degree to which these things are all imparted depends on the nature of what is being charred (its size, its water content, its sugar levels), how long it is left on the heat, and how much cooking it gets elsewhere before or after it hits the grill. Some vegetables, like the "famous" broccoli—but also cauliflower and Brussels sprouts, for example—need a bit of pre-grilling help, cooking-wise. We like boiling them quickly in water to allow heat to get to the core, before drying them well and throwing them on the grill with a bit of oil. Other vegetables benefit from being charred in the pan first and then finished off in the oven. These tend to be the more robust, hard vegetables, such as pumpkins, sweet potatoes, beets, and some cabbages.

At the other end of the scale, things such as snow peas and other green peas and beans (see SLOW-COOKED CHARRED GREEN BEANS, PAGE 49), thin slices of fennel, tomatoes, or ribbons of zucchini don't need anything beyond the charring. They can just get a lick of oil and go straight into the pan for a few seconds with no further cooking. As a general rule of thumb, things that can be eaten as they are, uncooked, just need this kiss from the pan to reach their full smoky potential without any additional cooking or marinating. Sweet firm fruit also work well, as in CALVIN'S GRILLED PEACHES AND RUNNER BEANS (PAGE 37).

Post-grill, it's very effective to throw the still-hot charred vegetables into a bath of aromatics and oil, where the smokiness will infuse the oil that will, in turn, become a more potent dressing as a result of this interaction. At the same time, the vegetable itself is more prone to absorb the aromas of garlic, lime, or whatever it happens to sit with in the liquid while it's fresh off the pan. This double win is what happens to the mushrooms in CONFIT GARLIC HUMMUS WITH GRILLED MUSHROOMS (PAGE 234).

A grill pan is brilliant at charring and burning vegetables that sit at the center of a dish—the char marks as badges of honor for an ingredient well initiated—but it is also a useful tool in infusing aromatics and other highly flavored components with a smoky scent that they carry with them wherever they are applied. Many sauces, flavored oils, and marinades will start with the charring of ingredients such as chiles, ginger, garlic, citrus zest, hard herbs, and spices before utilizing them to spread their smoky goodness all around. A Marie Rose Sauce used for dipping ROMANO PEPPER SCHNITZELS (PAGE 146), for example, escapes the fate of becoming the cloying sweet mayo of the famous prawn cocktail by the addition of well-scorched, deeply smoked tomatoes and chiles.

Equipment-wise, the magical effects of charring can be brought about fairly modestly. You can use a simple frying or sauté pan to achieve some great basic charring, which we often do when neat char marks aren't called for and the cooking carries on after this initial stage. In most cases, though, and if you don't have a barbecue on hand, investing in a heavy, cast-iron, ridged grill pan is highly recommended. This will hold heat well and allow you to scorch your vegetables at temperatures that aren't easily reached in home kitchens. It will stand the test of time and shouldn't warp or break under intense heat.

Beyond the pan, though, you just need some long-handled tongs, making it much easier to handle and turn whatever is on the grill. Good ventilation is also key: Open the windows! Open the doors! Turn on the fan!

Finally, one other method worth mentioning if you want to get a deep-charred and smoky aroma into your food, and doing it "as nature intended," is simply sitting your vegetables directly on the flame of the stove itself. Though we don't call for this method outright in any of our recipes (it involves a fair bit of stove-scrubbing when it's time to clean up), it works really well with some vegetables, saving you time and achieving an even deeper flavor than when

GOOD VENTILATION IS ALSO KEY: OPEN THE WINDOWS! OPEN THE DOORS! TURN ON THE FAN!

using a pan. Peppers can benefit from this treatment (see CHARRED PEPPERS AND FRESH CORN POLENTA WITH SOY-CURED YOLK, PAGE 140), but eggplants are where you really want to experiment with a 15-minute lie-down over an open flame. Your HERB AND CHARRED EGGPLANT SOUP (PAGE 42), your ICEBERG WEDGES WITH SMOKY EGGPLANT CREAM (PAGE 38), and every baba ganoush you make from here on will thank you for it.

BROWNING

If charring is brought about by applying direct heat to the outside of an ingredient, then how is browning different? The clue is in the name. The instruction to "roast a celery root until its skin is golden brown" will conjure a certain image, an enticing one. "Char a pepper until its skin is black all over and collapsing," on the other hand, and the image is different. But then, these skins are used for different things. You'll want to snack on the golden brown, crusty skin of the celery root. The charred skin of the pepper, meanwhile, can be peeled off and thrown away.

Browning is the name we give to the process that happens when we cook our celery root. It's the same transformation, really, that takes place every time we toast bread, roast coffee beans, or brown butter. As with charring, the science is pretty easy to understand. It has to do with the effect of heat on the sugars, proteins, and amino acids in the food. Once cooking starts and temperature

WHAT BROWNING MEANS, FOR THE HOME COOK, IS THAT THINGS SMELL BETTER, TASTE MORE COMPLEX.

increases, these sugars, proteins, and amino acids don't keep to themselves. Rather, they all react to produce a huge array of flavor chemicals, aromas, and colors. What browning means, for the home cook, is that things smell better, taste more complex, and change color, often from pale to golden brown. Bread becomes malty, crunchy, and darker; coffee beans become richer, more robust, and deeper in color; butter becomes nutty, rich, and golden brown.

In order for browning to take place, the temperature needs to be higher than the boiling point of water. The process generally starts happening around 230°F/110°C. A little bit of acidity and low-to-average water content are also conducive. When a vegetable is steamed or boiled, the conditions needed for browning will never occur. Steamed or boiled cauliflower florets will never taste like more than hot cauliflower florets. Roast the same florets in a hot oven, however, and they will undergo a transformation. Complex flavors that didn't exist are now there; notes that are nutty, creamy, sweet, and nuanced.

What cooks call browning, food scientists call the Maillard reaction. It's called Maillard after early-twentieth-century French scientist Louis-Camille Maillard, who discovered it. It's called a reaction because, in addition to requiring heat to get started, the process also produces heat. In this intense heat, the building blocks of proteins, in the presence of carbohydrates, keep rearranging themselves. The process becomes more complex as the products of each reaction get involved in their own reactions, creating thousands of different flavor and aroma molecules. The aromas you smell when cooking—deep, savory aromas that don't exist in the food's raw state—is the Maillard reaction at work.

Sweet vegetables, like beet and celery root or rutabaga and plantain, benefit particularly well from this process. The application of heat to them intensifies the sugars even further. The result can be something crusty and sweet on the outside and then almost caramel-like on the inside, tender and delicious. Yotam will never forget the first time a celery root was roasted whole at work, testing recipes for the NOPI restaurant cookbook. Coming

FLAVOR EXPLODES WHEN IT'S BROWNED, THOUGH, FLYING INTO ALL SORTS OF NEW PLACES.

out of the oven after three hours of roasting, it was cut into twelve wedges and served with a squeeze of lemon. It was devoured whole in mere minutes! We've had similar "complaints" from people who have, for the same sweet reason, been known to demolish an entire cauliflower or rutabaga by themselves. In cauliflower's raw form, one person would be hard pressed to snack on a whole head. Flavor explodes when it's browned, though, flying into all sorts of new places.

When cutting up vegetables to roast, rather than roasting them whole, there are a couple of practical things to keep in mind. The first is not to overcrowd the baking sheet; if things are crammed too close together there will be no space for steam to escape and the vegetables will "weep." Spread them out nice and evenly, and the conditions will be perfect for browning. Keep an eye on them in the oven, rotate the baking sheet halfway through cooking, and give everything a gentle stir. Also, don't combine vegetables with very different sugar levels (or starch or water content) on the same baking sheet; you don't want to be roasting slices of watery zucchini, for example, with cubes of sugary squash. This will lead to uneven cooking—some veg will steam, others will weep, others will burn; none will be happy.

It's not just vegetables, sweet or otherwise, that can be transformed by the Maillard reaction. So can any ingredient that contains a combination of sugar, protein, and carbohydrates. All these elements need to be there for the reaction to take place. The reason olive oil does not caramelize or brown in the way that butter does (as in HASSELBACK BEETS WITH LIME LEAF BUTTER, PAGE 50), is that the oil is a pure fat. Butter, on the other hand, also contains water, milk protein, and whey solids. It's these solids that brown when unsalted butter is heated gently and whose color and flavor change. These are the "brown bits" that lead to the creation of nutty, sweet, toasty brown butter. The flavor is wonderful; caramel-like and rich—just what a dish of steamed (and therefore *not* browned) CURRIED CARROT MASH (see PAGE 67) needs to elevate it to the flavor-bomb world we're spending time in.

Apart from roasting vegetables, as we have discussed, other cooking methods that will bring about the Maillard reaction are sautéing, pan-frying, searing, grilling, baking, toasting, and so on. Anything stewed, steamed, or simmered won't reach 230°F/100°C-plus and so, will never be Maillard. Anything fried, on the other hand, always will be.

Two practical notes to end on. The first has to do with taking things off the heat before they're fully done. The second is putting things on the heat before you're fully ready.

First, things such as slivers of garlic or chile that are frying, or nuts and seeds that are toasting, need to come away from the heat slightly before they are done if you are leaving them in the oil, or on the baking sheet, in the case of the nuts. The residual heat from the oil in the pan or on the sheet will

IT'S NO LONGER JUST AN ONION; IT'S THE SAVORY, SWEET PROMISE OF A DELICIOUS MEAL *JUST* AROUND THE CORNER.

continue to cook what's in or on it. If you have taken things as far as you want them to go, then just make sure you transfer them somewhere else to cool—a paper towel–lined plate, in the case of the garlic (using a slotted spoon), or to a separate baking sheet in the case of the nuts.

The second thing is perhaps more of a secret than a practical tip. Either way, if you are ever running late getting a meal to the table and the crowds are rousing, never forget that the raw onion sitting on your counter is your ultimate weapon in deception. A raw onion will only ever look, smell, and taste like a raw onion. Quickly chop it up, though, put it into a hot pan with some oil, let it take on some color, and it becomes something else entirely. It's no longer just an onion; it's the savory, sweet promise of a delicious meal *just* around the corner.

INFUSING

If browning is a fairly complex chemical process, and charring is a bold one, then infusing—by contrast—is all rather gentle and straightforward. It's what takes place when an aromatic is added to a liquid, and heat and time are applied. We do it every morning when we make a cup of tea. The aromatic can take all sorts of forms—hard herbs, dried spices, fresh botanicals, alliums—as can the type of liquid, degree of heat, and length of time things are left to steep. Vegetable oil, olive oil, high heat, low heat, two minutes on the heat, two hours off the heat—these are all variables that can be adjusted, depending on what level of infusion you're after.

THE COMBINATION OF INGREDIENTS IN AN INFUSION CAN TAKE A DISH ALL OVER THE WORLD.

Beyond the morning cup of tea, infusions are a wonderfully useful, economic, and effective process to lean on in the kitchen throughout the day. For one thing, they can quickly root a dish in a specific area and cuisine. Just as tea leaves have the power to transport us to Darjeeling, Ceylon, Assam, and beyond, the combination of ingredients in an infusion can take a dish all over the world. The garlic, onion, rosemary, thyme, green chile, and olive oil used in WHITE BEAN MASH (see PAGE 76) take the dish straight to the Mediterranean. The curry leaves, mustard seeds, and chiles of PAPPA AL POMODORO WITH LIME AND MUSTARD SEEDS (PAGE 85), on the other hand, evoke the warmth of the Indian subcontinent.

As well as taking a dish to far-flung lands, infusions are also an economical way of getting there. The equipment is simple: a saucepan, a source of heat, a wooden spoon to stir, a slotted spoon to lift things out. The ingredients are often humble: garlic, onions, dried spices, lemon peel, fresh or dried chiles. There's something nice and democratic about the fact that infusions travel in packs. This is not about the elevation of one ingredient—as with the mighty eggplant that, once charred, gets to steal the show—but about the coming together, mingling, and exchange of flavor between groups of everyday ingredients. It's about the sum being greater than the individual parts, and about the magical transformation ingredients can go through with a bit of time, heat, and oil.

The type of oil you use to heat the aromatics depends on what you want. Vegetable oil, with its neutral taste and higher smoking point, is what you need when you don't want the identity of the oil itself to impact too much on a dish, flavor- or body-wise. This is what you want when you are making a mayonnaise (see PAGE 89), for example. More often than not, though, we go for olive oil because it tastes so good and because of its viscosity and great mouthfeel.

The "magical transformation" referred to can be harnessed in different ways for a dish. It's all about the exchange of flavor at the heart of the infusing process. This is when the aromatics infuse the oil they're heated in, which can then be used in all sorts of ways: a curry leaf oil that is used to make the mayonnaise for OVEN FRIES (see PAGE 89), or for drizzling over MELON AND BUFFALO MOZZARELLA SALAD (see PAGE 80) before serving. Sometimes it's about the look as well as the taste. Our HUMMUS WITH LEMON, FRIED GARLIC, AND CHILE (PAGE 79) is transformed from rather dull to glistening green and red, thanks to the cilantro and chiles that get to bathe in hot olive oil. And texture can also be a factor, when aromatics that have been made crisp through frying can, once they've done their work infusing the oil, be lifted out, set aside, and used later to garnish a dish. Quickly fried curry or makrut lime leaves, strips of ginger and chile, slivers of garlic, sprigs of rosemary or thyme, these all look fantastic sitting on top of WHITE BEAN MASH (see PAGE 76) or a plate of BLACK BEANS (see PAGE 86), and bring an interesting textural contrast when it comes to eating.

Sometimes, of course, it's about all three things: about the exchange of flavor, the look of the aromatics, and the contrast in texture they provide. But not all the recipes do this, of course. With CHILLED AVOCADO SOUP WITH CRUNCHY GARLIC OIL (PAGE 82), the soup element is totally distinct from the garlic and cumin oil that gets drizzled over it. The contrast is part of the point, though, or what makes the dish work well—the chilled, fresh soup jolted out of its summer slumber by a lick of punchy, crunchy oil that has been infused with a mix of garlic, cumin seeds, and coriander seeds.

Part of the crunch in this oil is brought about by finely chopped garlic. Chopping it, rather than crushing it smooth or cooking the cloves whole, makes for these individual pops of garlic throughout the infusion. To disperse the taste of garlic more evenly throughout a dish, the cloves need to be crushed, as happens in the marinade that CUCUMBER SALAD À LA XI'AN IMPRESSION (PAGE 113) sits in. Other times a dish can handle whole slices of garlic, fried until golden brown. As well as infusing the oil that's then used in a dish, the fried slices can be used as garnish and eaten, as in LEEKS WITH MISO AND CHIVE SAUCE (PAGE 257). And then there are all the times in which we confit a whole garlic head by slicing off the top, drizzling it with oil, wrapping it in foil, and cooking it in the oven until soft and mellow and beautifully brown. A whole head of garlic, slow-cooked, in hummus (see PAGE 234), along with all the garlic-infused oil that comes with it? An enthused—and totally infused—"yes, please" from us!

AGING

After a day in the test kitchen, with all the charring and browning and infusing that can go on, Yotam's supper at home tends to be small and simple. More often than not, he'll just have a glass of red wine with a wedge of Parmesan or a square or two of dark chocolate. This isn't much, but it is enough because what wine, Parmesan, and chocolate all have in common is that they've had their flavors dialed up by a process of aging and so it doesn't take much of them to satisfy the taste buds.

Before refrigeration was commonplace, food was aged as a means to preserve it. Covering things in salt or brine or shutting off the air supply to let ingredients ferment meant that the shelf life could be extended beyond the time or season naturally available to them. All means of preservation had one ultimate end: to create an inhospitable environment for the bacteria that cause food to spoil. If all cooking is about transformation—about a certain kind of alchemy—then the process of aging has something particularly magic about it, as the change happens from within. Other cooking processes—including the charring, browning, and infusing we've looked at—require the introduction of heat to the equation for the transformation to take place. Aging, on the other hand, relies only on biology for the organic matter to be transformed from one state to another (more interesting and nutritious) state. As the organic

IF ALL COOKING IS ABOUT TRANSFORMATION—THEN THE PROCESS OF AGING HAS SOMETHING PARTICULARLY MAGIC ABOUT IT.

matter decays and ferments, energy is self-generated and created from within. Whether it's milk to cheese, grapes to wine, rice to sake, barley to beer, cabbage to kimchi, soybeans to miso and soy sauce, these ingredients all come into being, ingeniously, by the fermenter's careful management of rot.

Necessity may be the mother of invention, and this harnessing of the process of decay for edible ends might all be fantastic, but it's not the reason (now that we all have fridges to keep food fresh) these "aged" ingredients have stayed around. For some, these foods are consumed and celebrated primarily for their health-bringing properties. The links between fermented kombucha or kimchi and gut health, for example, are becoming increasingly well known. For us, however, the pull is always—it always has been and always will be—about flavor; about the big, bold, beautiful, and often "funky" flavors that are frequently the by-product of the aging process.

Luckily for anyone who wants to hit the high flavor notes without having to work too hard, the definition of aging in this section refers to the use of ingredients in which the process of aging has already been undertaken by the producer. This is in contrast to recipes that might have started with the instruction to start fermenting or curing or salting or preserving or pickling things in the first place. Doing these things at home is easy, rewarding, delicious, and fun, but it all requires planning and lead time. There are lots of brilliant recipes, people, and books who can teach and inspire you to make your own cultures, starters, and kombuchas. These recipes are about getting big flavors on the table in much less time and with, proportionately, much less work.

So drum roll, please, for the ingredients that do so much of the work here: the mature Parmesan or tangy pecorino; salted anchovies; fermented miso or gochujang chile paste; soy sauce; Chinkiang vinegar or Shaoxing wine.

Starting with the two Italian hard cheeses, it's interesting to look at the differences between them. Parmesan is made from cow's milk, and pecorino from sheep's milk. From the outset, therefore, Parmesan will always be creamier and less "tangy" than pecorino. The difference is also one of age. Parmesan is always mature—either "vecchio," if eaten between twelve and

THESE RECIPES ARE ABOUT GETTING BIG FLAVORS ON THE TABLE IN MUCH LESS TIME AND WITH, PROPORTIONATELY, MUCH LESS WORK.

eighteen months old, or else, if it's aged for more like two years, "stravecchio" or very mature. This very mature Parmesan is wonderfully savory, rich, nutty, and creamy. It punches well above its weight, bringing heft and body to the otherwise light SPRING VEGETABLES IN PARMESAN BROTH (see PAGE 109).

Pecorino, on the other hand, is ready to be eaten at distinctly different stages. Young pecorino—"fresco"—is firm but creamy and moist. Milky and light in flavor, it is delicate enough to be pulled apart by hand and dotted over all sorts of leafy salads. Half-aged or fully aged pecorino ("semi-stagionato" or "stagionato") is more mature: robust, sharper, and more pronounced in flavor. This is the sort of pecorino you want to snack on, with a glass of red wine, but it can also be grated and added to a dish such as ZA'ATAR CACIO E PEPE (PAGE 104).

If the hard cheeses form one group of aged ingredients in this section, then "fermented Asian" ingredients loosely form another. Miso, soy sauce, Shaoxing wine, rice vinegar, gochujang paste; these are all things that start with one ingredient—soybeans, rice, chiles—and then, through the process of fermentation, are broken down and preserved for use in the kitchen in an altogether different way. The process allows these ingredients to be used throughout the year but also enables us to consume much more of them— particularly soybeans—because our digestive system can extract nutrients more efficiently in their broken-down state.

Necessity and digestion notwithstanding, the reason these ingredients play such a large role in our pantry comes back, again—of course!—to flavor.

Play the word-association game with soy sauce and miso and it won't take long to hit upon the apotheosis of savory flavor: umami. *Umami*, roughly translating as "deliciousness" in Japanese, has been recognized as the fully fledged "fifth" taste since the early twentieth century, when a Japanese chemist named Kikunae Ikeda discovered that the white crystals that form on dried kombu contain large amounts of glutamate. Ikeda's discovery was that the savory taste of this molecule was something other than the hitherto recognized tastes of sweet, sour, bitter, and salt. It became the fifth taste. A bit like salt, glutamate draws out—or dials up—the flavor of food but, unlike salt, does not have a distinctive taste of its own. For the home cook, this means that the ability to be able to inject some seriously savory flavor into one's cooking is easily and quickly there.

When using aged ingredients in your everyday cooking, keep in mind the fact that their tastes are big and bold so a small amount goes a long way toward ramping up flavor. Keep in mind, too, that anything so inherently big and bold in savory flavor needs to be balanced with something fresh or zesty, young, or sweet. You'll see this interplay at work in the recipes here: a lemon or lime sauce to bring a smack of citrus to PARMESAN BROTH (see PAGE 109) or POTATO AND GOCHUJANG BRAISED EGGS (PAGE 99). Sweet fresh grapes are needed with SWEET AND SOUR SPROUTS (see PAGE 93) to balance out the soy sauce, and strips of lemon peel are there with GRILLED FIGS (see PAGE 110), once they've been baked with soy sauce, Shaoxing wine, and Chinkiang vinegar. As always, cooking and putting together ingredients is about balance. Aged ingredients are undoubtedly the kind of flavor bombs you want in your larder, but, for us, lemons and limes are still sitting there in a great big bowl, ready to be squeezed and zested.

SERVES FOUR
As a starter or as part
of a spread

CALVIN'S GRILLED PEACHES AND RUNNER BEANS

14 oz/400g runner
  beans, stringy edges
  removed, halved
  crosswise at an angle
3 tbsp olive oil
flaked sea salt
2 ripe (but firm)
  peaches, pitted and cut
  into ¼-inch/½cm-thick
  slices (1½ cups/200g)
¼ cup/5g mint leaves,
  roughly torn
2 tsp lemon juice
black pepper
3 oz/80g young and
  creamy rindless goat
  cheese, roughly broken
  into 1½-inch/4cm pieces
2 tbsp roasted and
  salted almonds,
  roughly chopped
2 tsp honey

Ottolenghi's executive chef, Calvin Von Niebel, first developed this recipe in our test kitchen with beautifully ripe peaches, new-season beans, and honey straight from a London rooftop beehive. It was a memorable moment, thanks to the clarity of the flavors and the quality of the ingredients. It is essential that you also seek the best ingredients you can. This dish in particular relies on them since there is little cooking going on and only a light dressing. Peaches can be substituted with nectarines or apricots, and the runner beans with other green bean varieties.

Serve as a starter, with spicy mushroom lasagne (page 228) as a main, if you like, and with lemon sorbet (see page 289) for dessert.

1. In a large bowl, toss the beans with 2 tbsp of the oil and ½ tsp salt. Place a well-greased grill pan on high heat and ventilate your kitchen. Once the pan is hot, cook the beans for 3–4 minutes on each side, until you get clear grill marks and the beans are almost cooked. Transfer them to a bowl and cover with a plate for 5–10 minutes, depending on how crunchy you like your vegetables; the residual heat will help soften them.

2. Drizzle the remaining 1 tbsp olive oil over the peach slices and grill for 1–2 minutes on each side, until you get visible grill marks.

3. Toss the beans and peaches together with the mint and transfer to a platter (or plate individually). Season with the lemon juice, a good pinch of salt, and a good grind of pepper. Dot the goat cheese and almonds around the platter, and finish by drizzling with the honey. Serve immediately.

ICEBERG WEDGES WITH
SMOKY EGGPLANT CREAM

SMOKY EGGPLANT CREAM
2 medium eggplants, pierced 7 or 8 times all over (1 lb 5 oz/600g)
7½ tsp lemon juice
1 garlic clove, roughly chopped
3 tbsp Greek-style yogurt
2 tsp Dijon mustard
¼ cup/60ml olive oil
½ tsp table salt
black pepper

CRUNCHY BITS
1 tbsp olive oil
½ cup/60g almonds, roughly chopped
3½ oz/100g sourdough bread, crusts removed and then blitzed into coarse crumbs to get ¾ cup/60g
⅓ cup/50g pumpkin seeds (pepitas)
¼ tsp table salt
⅓ tsp Urfa chile flakes (or another variety of chile flake)

1 small head iceberg lettuce (12¼ oz/350g), cut into 12 wedges
¼ cup/60ml olive oil
table salt and black pepper
scant 1 oz/25g Parmesan, finely grated
1½ oz/45g rainbow or breakfast radishes, thinly sliced on a mandoline, if you have one, or by hand
2 small avocados, pitted, peeled, and thinly sliced
¼ oz/5g chives, sliced into ½-inch/1½cm lengths

There are bucketfuls of crisp textures in this salad, and one creamy smoky dressing that brings everything together beautifully. The smokiness is achieved in the tried-and-tested way that is featured in many of our recipes in the past: charring an eggplant over direct heat for a substantial amount of time, until it collapses on itself into a deliciously smoky mess.

This is still our preferred way, but if you wish to avoid all that smoke in your kitchen and hate the sight of a thick layer of charcoal on your grill pan once you're done, here's another method: Preheat the oven to 475°F/230°C, then halve the eggplants lengthwise and cut deep crosshatches into each cut side. Rub with a little oil, place on a parchment-lined baking sheet, cut-side up, and roast until soft and very well browned, 40–45 minutes. Transfer to a large bowl, cover with a large plate, and allow to soften for 20 minutes. Scoop the eggplant flesh out into another bowl, discarding the skin, stems, and water.

This salad is inspired by a dish Yotam enjoyed at Aloette, a splendid restaurant in Toronto, Canada.

1. For the cream: Place a well-greased grill pan on high heat and ventilate your kitchen. Once the pan is smoking, grill the eggplants, turning two or three times, until the outsides have completely charred and the insides have softened, 45–50 minutes. Transfer to a colander set over a bowl and, once cool enough to handle, remove the flesh, discarding the stems and charred skin. Measure out 7 oz/200g of eggplant flesh, reserving any remaining for another use. Transfer to a food processor along with the lemon juice, garlic, yogurt, mustard, olive oil, salt, and a good grind of pepper and blitz until completely smooth. Set aside until needed.

2. For the crunchy bits: Meanwhile, put the olive oil into a large frying pan on medium-high heat, then add the almonds and cook, stirring often, for about 2 minutes. Add the breadcrumbs, pumpkin seeds, and salt and cook for 5 minutes more, stirring continuously, until golden. Add the chile flakes and cook for another 30 seconds. Transfer to a plate and let cool completely.

3. Arrange the iceberg wedges on a large platter. Drizzle with 2 tbsp of the olive oil and a sprinkle of salt and pepper. Spoon in the eggplant cream, followed by the Parmesan, radishes, and avocado. Sprinkle lightly with salt and pepper again and drizzle with the remaining 2 tbsp olive oil. Top with the chives and a generous amount of crunchy topping, serving any additional alongside.

BUTTER BEANS IN SMOKED CASCABEL OIL

SERVES SIX
As an antipasto

SMOKED CASCABEL OIL
4 dried cascabel chiles
(or ancho chiles),
roughly broken in half
5 garlic cloves, skin on,
crushed with the side
of a knife
2 jalapeños, sliced
lengthwise (seeded
for less heat)
1 lime: finely shave the
peel to get 5 strips,
then juice to get 1 tbsp
1 lemon: finely shave the
peel to get 5 strips,
then juice to get 1 tbsp
1½ tsp coriander seeds,
toasted
1 tsp cumin seeds,
toasted
1⅔ cups/400ml olive oil
2 tsp flaked sea salt

1 × 1 lb 9 oz/700g jar
good-quality large
butter beans, drained
(2⅔ cups/500g; Brindisa
Navarrico large butter
beans or cook your own)

Cascabel chiles are, in our modest opinion, the best dried chiles that money can buy. Fruity, nutty, sweet, slightly smoky, and a little bit chocolatey, they check all the right boxes for us when we're trying to inject vegetables with layers of flavor. In our restaurant ROVI, they are used to flavor mussels or new potatoes and to make these beans, sprinkled with additional crushed coriander seeds, which are an antipasto served to customers as they sit down.

Serve the beans as an appetizer or a snack, with some bread and aïoli, or mix them with chopped herbs and arugula to make a salad. They are also a very welcome addition to herb and charred eggplant soup (page 42) and bkeila, potato, and butter bean stew (page 75). They will keep for up to 2 weeks in a jar in the fridge.

The smoked cascabel oil is a wonderful recipe in its own right, and will keep for up to 1 month in a glass jar in the fridge, ready to be spooned over anything from eggs to pasta.

1. For the oil: Place a large, nonstick frying pan on high heat and ventilate your kitchen. Once the pan is smoking, decrease the heat to medium-high. Place the cascabel chiles, garlic, jalapeños, lime peel, and lemon peel in the pan and cook until well blackened in places and very fragrant. This will take about 3 minutes for the citrus peels, 4 minutes for the garlic and cascabel chiles, and 9 minutes for the jalapeños; use metal tongs to remove them individually from the pan.

2. Put all the charred ingredients into a medium saucepan; add the coriander seeds, cumin seeds, lime juice, lemon juice, olive oil, and salt; and place on low heat. Cook gently until the oil begins to bubble a little, about 4 minutes, then remove from the heat. Use a pair of tongs or a potato masher to squeeze or crush all the charred ingredients into the oil to release their flavor.

3. Stir the butter beans into the oil and set aside to cool. Transfer everything to a large jar if refrigerating, or a serving bowl if serving later that day. Allow to infuse for at least 2 hours, or up to overnight, before serving.

HERB AND CHARRED EGGPLANT SOUP

SERVES FOUR

3 medium eggplants, pierced 7 or 8 times all over (1 lb 10 oz/750g)
3 tbsp lemon juice
table salt and black pepper
7 tbsp/105ml olive oil
2 yellow onions, finely chopped (2 cups/300g)
6 garlic cloves, crushed
3 cups/60g cilantro, roughly chopped, plus 2 tbsp whole leaves
3 cups/60g parsley, roughly chopped, plus 2 tbsp whole leaves
2 cups/40g dill, roughly chopped, plus 2 tbsp whole leaves
7 green onions, finely sliced (scant 1 cup/70g)
3 tbsp water, plus 1⅔ cups/400ml
2½ tsp ground cinnamon
2½ tsp ground cumin
1⅛ tsp ground turmeric
9½ cups/400g baby spinach, finely shredded
2 cups/480ml vegetable or chicken stock
1 red chile, thinly sliced into rounds (¼ cup/20g)
2 tsp black mustard seeds

This soup draws on both Middle Eastern and Indian cooking techniques—large amounts of herbs are fried to make the base, eggplants are charred, and the whole thing is finished with an aromatic tempered oil. It's particularly good with our butter beans in smoked cascabel oil (page 41) spooned on top.

Make the soup up to 2 days before but don't mix the eggplants with the lemon juice and herbs, or top with the tempered oil, until you're ready to serve.

1. Place a well-greased grill pan on high heat and ventilate your kitchen. Once the pan is smoking, grill the eggplants, turning two or three times, until the outsides have completely charred and the insides have softened, 45–50 minutes. (Don't worry about over-charring the eggplants; the longer they cook, the better.) Transfer to a colander set over a bowl and allow to drain for about 30 minutes. Peel and discard the stems and skins. Pull the flesh into long ribbons and add to a medium bowl with 1 tbsp of the lemon juice, ¼ tsp salt, and a good grind of pepper. Mix, then set aside until needed.

2. While the eggplants are grilling, put ¼ cup/60ml of the olive oil into a large saucepan on medium-high heat. Add the yellow onions and cook, stirring often, until softened and deeply browned, about 12 minutes. Add the garlic and cook for 30 seconds more, until fragrant, then turn the heat to medium-low and add all the chopped herbs, green onions, and 3 tbsp water. Cook until deeply green and fragrant, about 15 minutes, stirring often so the herbs don't catch and burn. Increase the heat to medium-high; add the cinnamon, cumin, and 1 tsp of the turmeric; and cook for 30 seconds, then stir in the spinach, stock, 1⅔ cups/400ml water, 1¾ tsp salt, and a generous grind of pepper. Bring to a boil, then decrease the heat to medium and let simmer for about 20 minutes.

3. Remove the pan from the heat, add the remaining 2 tbsp lemon juice, and use an immersion blender to roughly blitz the soup (you don't want it to be completely smooth). Alternatively, blitz half the soup in a counter-top blender and return to the pan. Keep warm until ready to serve.

4. Put the chile and remaining 3 tbsp olive oil into a small frying pan on medium heat. Let cook, stirring occasionally, until the chile becomes translucent and glossy, 10–12 minutes. Add the mustard seeds and cook for 1 minute more. Stir in the remaining ⅛ tsp turmeric and immediately pour the mixture into a bowl to stop it from cooking further. Set aside.

5. Divide the soup among four bowls. Stir the herb leaves into the eggplant and add to the soup, finishing with a drizzle of the chile oil before serving.

POINTED CABBAGE WITH NAM PRIK

SERVES SIX
As a side

NAM PRIK
¾ oz/20g fresh galangal
  (or ginger), peeled and
  roughly chopped
1 small garlic clove,
  peeled
1 tbsp fish sauce (or light
  soy sauce)
**1½ tsp Aleppo chile
  flakes or Gochugaru
  Korean hot pepper
  flakes** (or ¾ tsp regular
  chile flakes)
**1 tbsp store-bought
  tamarind paste**
  (or double if you're
  extracting it yourself
  from pulp; see page 20)
1¼ tsp light brown sugar
**1¾ oz/50g cherry
  tomatoes**
1 tsp sunflower oil
4½ tsp lime juice

2 pointed cabbages
  (aka hispi or sweetheart
  cabbage), quartered
  lengthwise (3½ lb/1.6kg)
3 tbsp sunflower oil
½ tsp flaked sea salt
¼ cup/5g cilantro, finely
  chopped
1 lime, cut into wedges

Nam prik (or phrik) is the name of a range of chile sauces that are at the heart of Thai cooking. Their sharp intensity is the perfect counterpoint to anything grilled, as well as to rice and mild vegetable, meat, or fish dishes.

This cabbage is fantastically aromatic. You can serve it as part of a veggie supper with udon noodles with fried tofu and orange nam jim (page 202), or cardamom tofu with lime greens (page 172).

The nam prik can be made up to 1 week ahead and kept in the fridge, but the cabbage should be grilled not long before serving. *Pictured on page 46.*

1. For the nam prik: Put the galangal and garlic into the bowl of a food processor and blitz well. Add the fish sauce, chile flakes, tamarind paste, brown sugar, tomatoes, sunflower oil, and lime juice and pulse until combined and finely chopped but not completely smooth. Transfer to a small bowl and set aside until ready to serve.

2. In a large bowl, toss the cabbage with the sunflower oil and salt. Place on a very hot barbecue or grill pan and grill for 4–5 minutes on each side (12–15 minutes total), until the cabbage softens on the outside, while still retaining a crunch, and you get clear grill marks. Transfer to a platter.

3. Add the cilantro to the nam prik and spoon the mixture evenly over the cabbage pieces. Serve either warm or at room temperature, with the lime wedges alongside.

STEAMED EGGPLANTS WITH CHARRED CHILE SALSA

SERVES FOUR
As a side or as part
of a mezze spread

CHARRED CHILE SALSA
2 large, mild red chiles
  (1 oz/30g)
**5 oz/140g Datterini
  cherry tomatoes** (or
  other ripe, sweet cherry
  tomato), finely chopped
1½ tsp sherry vinegar
¼ tsp flaked sea salt

GARLIC-GINGER OIL
7½ tsp olive oil
2 small garlic cloves,
  very finely chopped
**1 tsp peeled and
  very finely chopped
  fresh ginger**
½ tsp flaked sea salt

2 eggplants (1 lb 8 oz/680g)
flaked sea salt
½ tsp sherry vinegar
1–2 green onions,
  trimmed and julienned
  (¼ cup/15g)
**4½ tsp roasted and
  salted almonds,** roughly
  chopped
1 tbsp cilantro leaves,
  roughly chopped

It takes a bit of coaxing to bring people around to steaming eggplants, as opposed to roasting or frying them. Gitai Fisher, who is a colleague in our test kitchen and a fan of eggplants with a bit of a tan on them, was a particularly hard nut to crack. He was brought around after tasting this dish, where the eggplants are, indeed, pale but they are also fantastically silky and have the ability to soak up the aromas of chile, garlic, and ginger like happy sponges.

The charred chile salsa can be doubled or tripled and kept in a glass jar in the fridge for up to 1 week, ready to be spooned over scrambled eggs, piled onto tortilla chips, or served alongside grilled tofu or fish.

The eggplants should be steamed just before serving, because they tend to discolor if left to sit around. *Pictured on page 47.*

1. For the salsa: Place a frying pan on high heat. Once the pan is very hot, add the chiles and cook for about 10 minutes, turning a few times until well charred on all sides. Transfer to a small bowl, cover with a saucer, and allow to soften for 10 minutes. Remove the seeds from one of the chiles (or both, for less heat) and then finely chop the flesh, along with the skin. Place in a bowl and add the tomatoes, vinegar, and salt; stir together; and set aside.

2. For the oil: In a small pan, combine the olive oil, garlic, ginger, and salt and place on low heat. Cook very gently for about 8 minutes, stirring occasionally, until the garlic and ginger soften when mashed with the back of a spoon. Make sure not to heat the oil too much or the garlic will burn; if the oil does start to bubble, just remove it from the heat until it cools.

3. Cut the eggplants into 3 x ¾ inch/7 x 2cm batons, then toss them with 2 tbsp salt in a large bowl. Transfer to a steaming basket (or colander that can sit over a large saucepan) and set aside.

4. Fill a large saucepan with enough water to come 1½ inches/4cm up the sides. Bring to a boil on high heat, then place the steamer (or colander) in the pan. Cover with a lid (or seal well with aluminum foil) to prevent steam from escaping. Decrease the heat to medium and steam until the eggplants are very soft but still hold their shape, 20–25 minutes. Lift the steamer off the pan and transfer to the sink to drain for 5 minutes.

5. Transfer the drained eggplants to a large platter, drizzle with the vinegar, and season with ¼ tsp salt. Add the green onions and gently mix them through. Top with the salsa, then drizzle with the garlic-ginger oil. Finish with the almonds and cilantro before serving.

SLOW-COOKED CHARRED GREEN BEANS

SERVES FOUR
As a side

1 lb 2 oz/500g green beans, trimmed and halved crosswise

1 lb 2 oz/500g runner beans, stems trimmed, stringy edges removed, and cut on the diagonal into 3–4 pieces

12 garlic cloves, peeled

1 green chile, pierced a few times with a small knife (½ oz/15g)

½ cup/120ml olive oil

2 onions, finely chopped (2 cups/300g)

1 cup/240ml vegetable or chicken stock

table salt and black pepper

2 lemons: finely zest to get 2 tsp, then juice to get 3 tbsp

½ cup/10g tarragon leaves, roughly chopped

½ cup/10g dill fronds, roughly chopped

½ cup/10g parsley leaves, roughly chopped

1¼ oz/35g preserved lemon, insides discarded and skin julienned

While the tendency with green beans is to steam or blanch them, to ensure they remain bright, green, and crunchy, they are also wonderful when cooked longer and a little slower. Given this time, they will soak up the sauce in which they cook, as they do here, while imparting a wonderfully subtle smokiness from the charring.

You can cook the beans the day before, if you want to get ahead, but hold off on adding the lemon zest and juice, and on making the herb mixture, until you're ready to serve.

1. Place a large sauté pan, for which you have a lid, on high heat and ventilate your kitchen. Once the pan is smoking, add one-fourth of the beans (both varieties) and cook for about 5 minutes, tossing the pan occasionally, until the beans are charred in places. Transfer to a large baking sheet and continue in this way with all the beans (do this using two sauté pans if you want to speed up the process). Add the garlic and chile to the pan and cook in the same way, until charred all over, 3–4 minutes, then add to the baking sheet with the beans. Set aside to cool slightly.

2. Add 6 tbsp/90ml of the olive oil to the pan and place on medium-high heat. Once the pan is hot, add the onions and cook, stirring occasionally, until soft and golden brown, about 10 minutes. Add the charred vegetables, stock, 1½ tsp salt, and a good grind of pepper. Bring to a simmer, then decrease the heat to medium-low and cook, covered, until the beans are very soft, about 20 minutes. Stir in the lemon zest and lemon juice.

3. Put all the herbs, the preserved lemon, remaining 2 tbsp olive oil, ¼ tsp salt, and plenty of pepper into a small bowl and mix to combine.

4. Stir the herb mixture into the beans, to just incorporate. Serve warm or at room temperature.

HASSELBACK BEETS WITH LIME LEAF BUTTER

SERVES FOUR
As a side

8–10 medium-large beets, skin on (2½ lb/1.2kg), or 8–10 pre-cooked beets (2 lb 2 oz/1kg)
1 tbsp flaked sea salt

LIME LEAF BUTTER
6 tbsp/90g unsalted butter
7½ tsp olive oil
5 fresh makrut lime leaves, roughly chopped
⅓ oz/10g fresh ginger, peeled and finely chopped
1 garlic clove, crushed
1 tbsp lime juice
1 tsp flaked sea salt

LIME LEAF SAUCE
10 fresh makrut lime leaves, stems removed, blitzed in a spice grinder (or very finely chopped)
½ tsp peeled and very finely chopped fresh ginger
½ garlic clove, crushed
½ green chile, very finely chopped (seeded for less heat)
1 tbsp cilantro leaves, finely chopped
3 tbsp olive oil
¼ tsp flaked sea salt

YOGURT CREAM
⅓ cup/80ml heavy cream
⅓ cup/90g Greek-style yogurt
pinch of flaked sea salt

2 tsp lime juice

Preparing vegetables hasselback involves slicing them thinly but not all the way through, so that the slices remain held together at the base, like a fan. This makes them look great, which is a welcome bonus, but the main reason to add this step is the deliciously crispy edges you get all over the surface.

To offset the extra work involved in hasselbacking, you can easily start with store-bought pre-cooked beets (plain, not in vinegar) and save yourself cooking them. If you do end up using raw beets, try to get bunches, and reserve the stems and leaves. These are delicious tossed in salads, or, better yet, use them to make our tempura stems, leaves, and herbs (page 184), along with the charred peppers and fresh corn polenta (see page 140) that make up part of the ROVI spread on page 303.

If starting from raw, the beets can be cooked, peeled, and sliced up to 3 days before and kept in the fridge.

Double or triple the lime leaf butter if you like—it will keep in a glass jar in the fridge for up to 2 weeks, ready to ramp up all sorts of roasted vegetables, or to melt over grilled fish. *Pictured on pages 52–53.*

1. Preheat the oven to 450°F/220°C fan.

2. Place the raw beets in a baking dish big enough for them to fit in a single layer. Fill the dish with enough water to come ¾ inch/2cm up the sides. Sprinkle with the salt, cover tightly with aluminum foil, and bake for 1 hour and 20 minutes, or until a knife inserted goes through easily (some larger beets may need longer). Discard the water and, when the beets are cool enough to handle, peel off the skin under cold running water (use gloves so as not to stain your hands). Halve any larger beets lengthwise. Decrease the oven temperature to 400°F/190°C.

3. For the butter: While the beets are cooking, put the butter, olive oil, lime leaves, ginger, and garlic into a small saucepan and place on medium-high heat. Cook gently until the butter melts and begins to bubble, about 4 minutes, then remove from the heat and set aside to infuse for 40 minutes. Strain and discard the aromatics, then stir in the lime juice and salt.

4. For the sauce: In a small bowl, stir together the lime leaves, ginger, garlic, chile, cilantro, olive oil, and salt and set aside.

5. For the cream: In a medium bowl, whip the cream, yogurt, and salt until light and fluffy, with medium-stiff peaks, about 3 minutes. Set aside in the refrigerator.

6. Line a small baking sheet with parchment paper. Place one beet at a time in the cup of a wooden spoon, and cut slits in the beets at ⅛-inch/4mm intervals, stopping about ⅜ inch/1cm from the bottom so that the slices stay connected. Place the beets on the prepared baking sheet and fan the slices out as much as possible. Spoon the melted butter mixture evenly over and around the beets and especially between the slices. Roast for 1¼ hours, easing apart the slices and basting very well with the butter on the sheet every 20 minutes or so, until the edges are crisp and caramelized. Set aside to cool for 15 minutes.

7. Spread the yogurt cream on a platter, then arrange the beets on top, spooning any butter mixture from the pan over and around them. Drizzle with the sauce, finish with the remaining 2 tsp lime juice, and serve at once.

WHOLE ROASTED CELERY ROOT, THREE WAYS

———————

1 large celery root,
hairy roots discarded
(no need to peel)
and scrubbed clean
(2 lb/900g)
¼ cup/60ml olive oil
1½ tsp flaked sea salt

This simple way of slow-roasting whole celery root, with nothing but oil and salt, is a method we have explored in the past, serving it simply with a squeeze of lemon or a spoonful of crème fraîche. You can definitely do that with this. Here, though, this process, in which the starches are converted into sugars (see page 29) that seep out in a wonderful celery root–flavored caramel, is harnessed to make three very different celery root–centered dishes. If you don't get a lot of that aforementioned caramel after roasting, just brush the celery root with oil and a little maple syrup or honey once it's been cut.

The celery root is best cooked on the day of serving, but you can roast it the day before if you want to get ahead. You'll need to double the recipe for celery root steaks with Café de Paris sauce (page 60).

1. Preheat the oven to 375°F/170°C fan. Line a baking sheet with parchment paper.

2. Pierce the celery root with a fork all over about forty times and place on the prepared baking sheet. In a small bowl, mix together the olive oil and salt, then rub the celery root generously with the oil mixture. Roast for a minimum of 2¼ hours, or up to 2¾ hours, depending on the size of your celery root, basting with oil every 20 minutes or so, until the celery root is deeply browned, soft all the way through, and oozes a celery root caramel.

3. Let rest for 15 minutes, then cut into either wedges or steaks (depending on the recipe you are going to make; see pages 55, 59, and 60), brushing each cut side with the oil and caramel left on the baking sheet (you may need to add a little more oil if there isn't enough to coat the cut sides).

1. ROASTED AND PICKLED CELERY ROOT WITH SWEET CHILE DRESSING

SERVES TWO
As a main or four as a side

PICKLED CELERY ROOT
1 medium celery root, trimmed, peeled, and cut into thin 2½-inch/6cm-long batons (4 cups/500g)
3 celery stalks, cut into thin 2½-inch/6cm-long batons (1 cup/120g)
2 garlic cloves, skin on, crushed with the side of a knife
3 limes: finely shave the peel to get 6 strips, then juice to get ¼ cup/60ml
½ cup plus 2 tbsp/ 150ml rice vinegar
1½ tsp flaked sea salt

SWEET CHILE DRESSING
½ cup/120ml sunflower oil
5 garlic cloves, very finely sliced
3 red chiles, finely sliced into rounds (⅓ cup/30g)
2 whole star anise
4½ tsp white or black sesame seeds, or a mixture of both, well toasted
7½ tsp maple syrup
1 tbsp rice vinegar
¼ cup/60ml soy sauce
2 tbsp finely chopped chives

1 Whole Roasted Celery Root (facing page), cut into 8 wedges
flaked sea salt
2 green onions, finely sliced at an angle
¼ cup/5g Thai basil leaves

This dish features celery root in two very different guises—slow-roasted and pickled—giving it textural contrast and flavor complexity that enables it to take center stage in a three-course meal (see page 303).

You can make the dressing a day ahead, but don't mix in the fried chile and garlic until you're ready to serve. You'll make more pickle than you need, but it keeps in the fridge for 3 days and is great stuffed into sandwiches or tossed in a salad. If you don't want to pickle a whole celery root, use just halve and roast the other half, instead. *Pictured on page 57.*

1. For the pickled celery root: In a large bowl, combine the celery root batons, celery, garlic, lime peel, lime juice, vinegar, and salt and set aside for 2 hours, stirring now and then.

2. For the dressing: Heat the sunflower oil in a small saucepan on medium-high heat. Once very hot, add the garlic, chiles, and star anise and fry for 2–2½ minutes, stirring to separate the garlic slices, until the garlic is crisp and pale golden (it will continue to color after you take it out of the oil, so don't take it too far). Strain through a sieve set on top of a small heatproof bowl to collect the oil. Set the fried chile and garlic aside. Remove ⅓ cup/80ml of the aromatic oil and reserve for another recipe. Combine 7½ tsp of the remaining aromatic oil with the sesame seeds, maple syrup, vinegar, soy sauce, and chives and stir to mix.

3. Preheat the oven to 425°F/200°C fan. Line a baking sheet with parchment paper.

4. Place the roasted celery root wedges on the prepared baking sheet, cut-side up. Make sure they've been brushed with their cooking oil and caramel (if not, brush with some olive oil and a little maple syrup or honey; see opposite). Roast for 20 minutes, or until golden brown.

5. Arrange the wedges on a large platter and sprinkle with a little salt.

6. Add the reserved fried chile and garlic to the dressing and spoon over and around the celery root. Top with 1⅓ cups/200g of the pickled celery root mixture (avoiding the pickling liquid). Garnish with the green onions and Thai basil and serve immediately.

2. CABBAGE "TACOS" WITH CELERY ROOT AND DATE BARBECUE SAUCE

DATE BARBECUE SAUCE
6 tbsp/90ml olive oil
1 small shallot, finely chopped (¼ cup/30g)
2 garlic cloves, crushed
¼ tsp red chile flakes
¼ cup/60ml balsamic vinegar
¼ tsp smoked paprika
½ tsp ground cumin
½ cup/100g pitted dates, roughly chopped
¼ cup/20g black garlic (about 10 cloves; optional)
½ cup plus 1 tbsp/130ml water
½ tsp table salt

AROMATIC OIL
6 tbsp/90ml olive oil
2 red chiles, finely sliced into rounds
2 garlic cloves, finely chopped (not crushed)
2 tsp coriander seeds, lightly crushed
¼ tsp table salt
2 tsp finely chopped chives

16 whole cabbage leaves, from 1 large cabbage, base trimmed
1 Whole Roasted Celery Root (page 54), cut into 16 wedges
4½ oz/120g soft rindless goat cheese, roughly broken into ¾-inch/2cm pieces
2 limes, cut into wedges

This recipe broke a world record by being the first vegetarian dish ever to be selected for the obviously meat-centric barbecue festival Meatopia. It took a fair bit of pleading to get the organizers to agree to this heretical move, but our celery root went down a storm with the meat lovers.

The cabbage is a great vessel for the celery root, but the combination of the celery root and the very special date barbecue sauce is wonderful in its own right, if you don't want to blanch cabbage leaves.

You'll make more sauce than you need, which is no bad thing. It will keep in the fridge for 3 weeks and can be used in any situation that calls for barbecue sauce.

1. For the barbecue sauce: Put 2 tbsp of the olive oil, the shallot, and crushed garlic into a small saucepan on medium heat. Fry for about 6 minutes, stirring often, until the shallot is soft and golden. Add the chile flakes, vinegar, paprika, cumin, dates, black garlic (if using), water, and salt and stir to combine. Bring to a gentle simmer, then decrease the heat to medium-low and cook for 8 minutes, or until the dates have softened completely. Let cool for 10 minutes, then transfer to a spice grinder or the bowl of a small food processor with the remaining ¼ cup/60ml olive oil and blitz to a smooth sauce.

2. For the aromatic oil: Combine the olive oil, chiles, chopped garlic, coriander seeds, and salt in a small saucepan on medium-low heat and fry gently for 8 minutes, until the garlic is soft and fragrant. You may need to decrease the heat if the garlic is coloring too much. Remove from the heat and stir in the chives.

3. Bring a large pot of salted water to a boil. Add the cabbage leaves and blanch for 30 seconds to 1 minute, until just cooked but still crunchy, then drain very well, transfer to a clean kitchen towel, and carefully pat dry—you don't want the leaves to be at all wet.

4. When you're ready to serve, turn the oven to the highest broil setting. Line a large baking sheet with parchment paper (make sure there is no overhanging parchment that could burn). Place the roasted celery root wedges, spaced apart, on the prepared baking sheet. Make sure they've been brushed with their cooking oil and caramel (if not, brush with some olive oil and a little maple syrup or honey; see page 54). Broil on the top rack of the oven for 6 minutes, until golden brown. Remove from the oven and brush with 6 tbsp/90ml of the barbecue sauce, carefully smothering all sides.

5. Place a celery root wedge on each cabbage leaf. Top with the goat cheese and then drizzle with some of the aromatic oil. Serve hot, with the lime wedges and additional barbecue sauce alongside.

3. CELERY ROOT STEAKS WITH CAFÉ DE PARIS SAUCE

SERVES FOUR
As a main

CAFÉ DE PARIS SAUCE
½ cup/110g unsalted butter, cut into ¾-inch/2cm cubes
1 small shallot, finely chopped (¼ cup/30g)
1 garlic clove, crushed
3 anchovy fillets in olive oil, drained and finely chopped (optional, but adjust seasoning if not using)
1 tbsp mustard powder
½ tsp medium curry powder
¼ tsp cayenne pepper
¼ tsp flaked sea salt
1 tbsp baby capers
2 tbsp finely chopped chives
2 tbsp tarragon leaves, finely chopped
1 tbsp finely chopped parsley
2 tsp thyme leaves
black pepper

2 Whole Roasted Celery Root (page 54), each cut crosswise into 1-inch/2½cm-thick steaks
½ cup/120ml heavy cream
2 tsp lemon juice
flaked sea salt and black pepper

A long time ago, in Paris, Ixta had a steak with Café de Paris sauce and thought she'd died and gone to butter heaven. This single memory, etched in her mind since childhood, formed the basis on which we relied when creating this dish, plus a bunch of conflicting versions published over the years that had a stab at cracking the secret recipe. Whether our version gets us anywhere near the original we will probably never know, but it certainly delivers in turning celery root seriously meaty, only without the meat, and making it the perfect alternative to a Sunday roast (serve it along with iceberg wedges with smoky eggplant cream, page 38, and oven fries with curry leaf mayonnaise, page 89).

Don't worry about the sauce splitting; it's supposed to.

1. For the sauce: In a small saucepan on medium heat, combine the butter, shallot, garlic, anchovies, mustard powder, curry powder, cayenne, and salt. Cook for about 6 minutes, swirling the pan, until the shallot has softened and the butter has melted and become golden and caramelized. Add the capers, all the herbs, and a very generous grind of black pepper and continue to cook for 1 minute, then remove from the heat.

2. Turn the oven to the highest broil setting. Line a large baking sheet with parchment paper (make sure there is no overhanging parchment that could burn). Place the roasted celery root steaks, spaced apart, on the prepared baking sheet in a single layer. Make sure they've been brushed with their cooking oil and caramel (if not, brush with some olive oil and a little maple syrup or honey; see page 54). Broil on the top rack of the oven until they are golden brown on top, 6–8 minutes. Turn off the oven, keeping the baking sheet warm in the oven until you're ready to serve.

3. Return the sauce to medium heat and cook gently for 1 minute, then add the cream and lemon juice. Swirl for another 2 minutes or until warm, but don't mix it too much—you want the sauce to be split, not emulsified.

4. Pour the sauce onto a large platter with a lip and arrange the celery root steaks on top (or plate individually with some sauce poured on top and the rest served alongside). Sprinkle the steaks with a little salt and black pepper and serve.

SERVES FOUR
As a starter

SPICED PLANTAIN WITH COCONUT, APPLE, AND GINGER SALAD

————————

2 very ripe plantains, peeled, sliced in half crosswise and lengthwise (14 oz/400g)

¼ cup/60ml olive oil

2 tsp light brown sugar

½ tsp peeled and finely grated fresh ginger

¾ tsp ground cinnamon

¾ tsp ground cumin

½ tsp cayenne pepper

½ tsp ground nutmeg

½ small coconut, thinly sliced on a mandoline, if you have one, or by hand (3¼ oz/90g)

2 limes: finely zest to get 1 tsp, then juice to get 2 tbsp; cut the remainder into wedges

1 green chile, seeded and julienned

1 Granny Smith apple, skin on, cored and julienned (¾ cup/140g)

table salt

1 tbsp unsalted butter

½ cup/10g cilantro leaves

½ cup/10g mint leaves

Ixta's mother grew up in Brazil and Cuba eating plantains alongside pretty much every savory meal, from feijoadas (the national Brazilian dish) to guisos (Cuban stews). It was a tradition that carried through to Ixta's childhood, where plantains featured at nearly every mealtime.

Plantains are larger, firmer, and slightly less sweet than bananas. For this recipe, you need very ripe plantains: deep yellow, soft, and covered in black spots. You should be able to find them in many markets, and especially in West Indian supermarkets.

This is a special starter, or could be bulked up with some fried tofu or grilled prawns to make a meal. *Pictured on page 64.*

1. Place the plantains in a medium bowl with 3 tbsp of the olive oil, the brown sugar, ¼ tsp of the ginger, ½ tsp of the cinnamon, ½ tsp of the cumin, the cayenne, and nutmeg. Mix to coat, then set aside to marinate for 30 minutes.

2. Meanwhile, place the coconut; lime zest; lime juice; chile; apple; and remaining ¼ tsp ginger, ¼ tsp cinnamon, ¼ tsp cumin, and 1 tbsp olive oil in a medium bowl with a pinch of salt. Mix well and set aside.

3. Preheat the oven to 400°F/180°C fan.

4. Put the butter in a large, ovenproof nonstick frying pan and place on high heat. Once the butter has melted and is hot, add the plantains, spaced apart (if you don't have a big enough pan, you can fry in two batches). Reserve the oil and spices in the bowl in which you marinated the plantains—you need these later for the salad. Decrease the heat to medium-high and fry the plantains for 3 minutes, turning them every so often until all sides are golden brown and crisp. Transfer the pan to the oven and cook for another 3 minutes.

5. Add the cilantro, mint, and the coconut salad to the bowl in which you marinated the plantains. Toss together, making sure to incorporate the oil and spice left in the bowl.

6. Divide the plantains and salad among four plates and serve with the lime wedges alongside.

CURRY-CRUSTED RUTABAGA STEAKS

SERVES FOUR
As a main

FENUGREEK MARINADE
4½ tsp fenugreek seeds
6 small garlic cloves, peeled and roughly chopped (3 tbsp)
1½ tsp cayenne pepper
1½ tsp ground turmeric
2 tsp superfine sugar
2 tbsp lime juice
⅓ cup/80ml olive oil
¾ tsp table salt

2–3 rutabagas (4 lb/ 1.8kg), peeled and cut crosswise into eight 1¼-inch/3cm-thick steaks

SALAD
3–4 ruby grapefruits (1 lb 10 oz/750g)
1–2 shallots, finely sliced on a mandoline, if you have one, or by hand (½ cup/70g)
2 red chiles, finely sliced into rounds
1 cup/20g mint leaves
½ cup/10g cilantro leaves
2 tsp olive oil
1 tbsp lime juice
table salt

½ cup/120g crème fraîche (or coconut yogurt)
2 limes, cut into wedges

This vegetarian main course—easily veganized by using an alternative to the crème fraîche, such as coconut yogurt—celebrates the natural bitterness of rutabaga, complemented by a sweet, sharp, and spicy marinade that permeates the flesh and coats it with a delicious crust. Due to the fenugreek, the general flavor of the dish is like a great Indian curry (in fact, this dish works perfectly as part of the korma feast on page 303). Beware, though, the smell of this wondrous seed will linger in your kitchen for quite a while (we love this, but not everyone does).

The marinade will keep in the fridge in a sealed jar for up to 2 weeks, if you want to get ahead. Make double or triple, if you like, to use as a base for curries or for marinating vegetables or different meats. *Pictured on page 65.*

1. Preheat the oven to 400°F/180°C fan. Line a large baking sheet with parchment paper.

2. For the marinade: In a spice grinder or the bowl of a small food processor, combine the fenugreek seeds, garlic, cayenne, turmeric, sugar, lime juice, olive oil, and salt and blitz to a paste, scraping the sides as you go if necessary. Put 2 tsp of the marinade into a small serving bowl and set aside.

3. Put the remaining marinade into a large bowl with the rutabaga steaks and mix well to coat all sides (this is easiest with gloved hands). Place the steaks, spaced apart, on the prepared baking sheet. Cover tightly with aluminum foil and roast for 1 hour and 20 minutes. Remove the foil, turn the oven to the broil setting, and broil for 3–4 minutes, until the rutabaga is cooked through and the marinade has turned into a golden brown crust.

4. For the salad: When the rutabaga is nearly cooked, cut the grapefruits into thin wedges by removing the skin and the white pith, then release the segments by cutting in between the white membrane, discarding any seeds. Put the wedges into a large bowl, avoiding the juice (which can be kept for another use).

5. When you're ready to serve, add the shallots, chiles, mint, cilantro, olive oil, and lime juice to the bowl with a generous pinch of salt and mix gently together.

6. Arrange the steaks and any marinade left on the baking sheet on a large platter with the salad (or plate individually). Swirl the crème fraîche into the reserved marinade and serve alongside the steaks, and squeeze the lime wedges over the top.

SERVES FOUR
As a side or six as a dip

CURRIED CARROT MASH WITH BROWN BUTTER

1–2 red chiles, finely sliced into rounds (seeded for less heat)
4½ tsp white wine vinegar
½ tsp superfine sugar
table salt
1 lb 12 oz/800g carrots (roughly 8), peeled and roughly chopped into ¾-inch/2cm pieces
2 tbsp unsalted butter or olive oil
¼ oz/5g fresh ginger, peeled and julienned
½ tsp nigella seeds
½ tsp fennel seeds
½ tsp cumin seeds
2 tbsp olive oil
1 tsp medium curry powder
¼ tsp ground cinnamon
1½ tsp lime juice
1 green onion, trimmed and julienned
¼ cup/5g mint leaves, finely shredded

You'll be surprised how much delicious carrotiness you'll get from simply steamed carrots when they are matched with browned butter, sweet spices, and chile heat. You can then count on them to inject a whole meal with deep flavor, and serve them alongside some grilled tofu, haloumi, fish, or chicken, or as part of a selection of vegetable dishes.

The mash and pickled chiles can be made the day before if you want to get ahead, but the butter should be made not long before serving, so the seeds stay crunchy. Use olive oil instead of butter if you want to keep this dairy-free.

1. Put the chiles, vinegar, and sugar into a small bowl with ¼ tsp salt, massage together, and set aside to pickle for 30 minutes.

2. Put the carrots into a steaming basket (or colander that can sit over a large saucepan). Fill a large saucepan with enough water to come 1½ inches/4cm up the sides. Bring to a boil on high heat, then place the steamer (or colander) in the pan. Cover with a lid (or seal well with aluminum foil) to prevent steam from escaping. Steam the carrots for about 25 minutes, or until you can cut through them easily with a knife.

3. While the carrots are steaming, put the butter, ginger, nigella seeds, fennel seeds, cumin seeds, and a generous pinch of salt into a small saucepan on medium heat. Cook gently for 3–5 minutes, stirring occasionally until the butter begins to foam and turns light brown and the seeds become fragrant. Set aside until ready to serve. (You may need to gently melt the butter again, if it has set, when you're plating.)

4. Put the carrots into the bowl of a food processor with the olive oil, curry powder, cinnamon, and 1 tsp salt and blitz for about 1 minute, until you get a semismooth mash (it should still have some texture and not be completely smooth).

5. Spoon the mash onto a large plate, creating dips with the back of the spoon. Drizzle with the butter, ginger, and seeds, followed by the lime juice. Drain the pickled chiles well and scatter them over the mash. Finish with the green onions and mint and serve warm.

BARLEY, TOMATO, AND WATERCRESS STEW

SERVES FOUR
As a main

4 small kohlrabi
(2 lb 2 oz/1kg)

**4 anchovy fillets in olive
oil,** drained and finely
chopped (optional,
but adjust seasoning
if not using)

**½ cup plus 2 tbsp/
150ml olive oil,** plus
more to drizzle

4 garlic cloves, crushed,
plus 1 large head of
garlic, top fifth cut off
to expose the cloves

**table salt and black
pepper**

**10½ oz/300g sweet,
ripe cherry tomatoes**
(such as Datterini)

**1½ cups/300g pearl
barley**

2–3 shallots, finely sliced
(¾ cup/120g)

2 tsp caraway seeds

2 lemons: finely shave the
peel of 1 to get 5 strips,
then juice to get 2 tbsp;
cut the remainder into
wedges

1 red Scotch bonnet chile
(optional)

3 tbsp tomato paste

**½ cup plus 2 tbsp/
150ml dry white wine**

2 cups/480ml water

2¼ cups/100g watercress

**¼ cup/60ml heavy
cream** (optional)

Mostly eaten raw, kohlrabi isn't the first vegetable you would think to roast. We'd love you to try, though, because, in the process, it morphs into a gloriously caramelized, golden brown version of its former self. We use it here to spoon over a rich barley stew, resulting in a one-pot meal that is light enough for a summer's evening but also warming when the temperatures start to drop.

Vegans, vegetarians, and those who don't like too much heat are welcome to make this stew without the anchovies (increase the salt if you do that) or cream, or with less or no chile. There is still plenty going on to keep everyone jolly.

This dish is not at all complicated to make, as long as you are okay cooking three things simultaneously—roasting the vegetables that go on top of the barley, boiling the barley itself, and preparing the aromatics that flavor the stew. They are all super-easy and come together simply at the end. *Pictured on pages 70–71.*

1. Preheat the oven to 400°F/190°C fan. Line a large baking sheet with parchment paper.

2. Trim and peel each kohlrabi, then cut lengthwise into eight wedges. You want the wedges to be about 1 inch/2½cm wide, so if the kohlrabi is particularly large, you may need to cut it into more wedges. Put the wedges into a large bowl and toss with the anchovies (if using), 2 tbsp of the olive oil, half the crushed garlic, ½ tsp salt, and a good grind of pepper. Spread out on the prepared baking sheet. Drizzle the garlic head with 1 tbsp olive oil and sprinkle with a little salt and pepper. Wrap the head tightly in aluminum foil, place in one corner of the baking sheet, and roast for 25 minutes. Turn the kohlrabi wedges, add the tomatoes to the sheet around the kohlrabi, and then return to the oven for another 15–20 minutes, or until the kohlrabi wedges are soft and a deep golden brown and the tomatoes are blistered. Keep warm (or warm up when you serve).

3. When cool enough to handle, remove the foil from the garlic and squeeze the cloves into a small bowl, discarding the papery skin.

4. While the vegetables are in the oven, put the barley into a medium saucepan, cover with plenty of cold water, and place on medium-high heat. Simmer for 20 minutes, until the barley is semicooked but still retains a good bite. Drain and set aside.

5. While the barley is simmering, place a large sauté pan, for which you have a lid, on medium-high heat with 3 tbsp olive oil, the cooked and crushed garlic, shallots, caraway seeds, lemon peel, chile (if using), and 2½ tsp salt. Fry gently for 12 minutes, stirring often, until the shallots are soft and golden brown. Decrease the heat to medium if the shallots are coloring too quickly. Add the tomato paste and continue to cook for 30 seconds before adding the wine, water, and plenty of pepper. Bring to a gentle simmer and cook for 7 minutes, then add the cooked barley and continue to cook for 10 minutes, until the barley has swollen a little and taken on the flavor of the stew. Discard the chile and lemon peel.

6. In a spice grinder or the bowl of a small food processor, blitz half the watercress with the lemon juice, the remaining ¼ cup/60ml olive oil, and ¼ tsp salt to get a smooth sauce.

7. Transfer the stew to a large serving bowl (or serve straight from the pan)— drizzle the watercress sauce and cream (if using) over the barley and gently swirl them in. Top with the remaining watercress, roasted kohlrabi, and roasted tomatoes. Serve with the lemon wedges alongside.

LIME AND COCONUT POTATO GRATIN

SERVES SIX
As a side or as part
of a spread

4–5 shallots, sliced
⅛ inch/3mm thick on
a mandoline, if you
have one, or by hand
(8 oz/220g)
2 garlic cloves, crushed
2 tbsp olive oil
table salt
**3 lb/1.4kg Yukon gold
potatoes** (about
6 medium potatoes;
or other baking potato
that's somewhere
between floury and
waxy), skin on, sliced
⅛ inch/3mm thick on
a mandoline, if you
have one, or by hand
**⅓ cup/100g coconut
cream,** melted
3 limes: finely zest to
get 1½ tsp, then juice
to get ¼ cup/60ml
black pepper
**¾ cup plus 2 tbsp/200ml
vegetable or chicken
stock**

CRISPY AROMATICS
**½ cup plus 2 tbsp/
150ml olive oil**
2 red chiles, finely sliced
into rounds
3 garlic cloves, thinly
sliced
¼ oz/5g fresh ginger,
peeled and julienned
4 green onions, finely
sliced at an angle
(½ cup/40g)
flaked sea salt

This gratin was part of a Christmas feast that we created for the *Guardian* newspaper, which also included a roasted Szechuan lamb shoulder, steamed eggplants, and a cucumber salad. You can easily stick to this spirit, even if you lose the lamb, and serve the gratin as part of a Chinese-ish vegetable feast with our cucumber salad à la Xi'an Impression (page 113), steamed eggplants with charred chile salsa (page 45), and sweet and sour sprouts with chestnuts and grapes (page 93).

Ideally, you want to cut the potatoes thinly using a mandoline or a food processor with the appropriate attachment. Don't worry if you have neither, though—cutting them by hand is also fine; you might just need to cook them a little longer if they are thicker than ⅛ inch/3mm.

You can bake the gratin the day before and reheat it in a very hot oven just before serving if you want to get ahead. Top with the aromatics and zest just as you serve, and not before.

1. Preheat the oven to 400°F/180°C fan. Put the shallots, garlic, olive oil, and ¼ tsp table salt into a 12-inch/30cm ovenproof sauté pan on medium heat. Fry for 8–10 minutes, stirring occasionally, until soft and deeply golden. Transfer to a large bowl and set the pan aside (no need to clean it).

2. Add the potatoes, coconut cream, lime juice, 2 tsp table salt, and plenty of pepper to the bowl with the shallots and very gently mix everything together, taking care not to break the potato slices.

3. Add one-fourth of the mixture to the sauté pan; any smaller or broken slices of potato are best used here, saving the larger, whole slices for the top. Spread out to create an even layer. Use the remaining three-fourths to create a spiral effect on top of this layer, so each slice is at an angle and overlapping the next. Pour in the stock, cover tightly with aluminum foil, and bake for 40 minutes.

4. For the crispy aromatics: Meanwhile, heat the olive oil in a medium pan on medium heat, then add the chiles, garlic, and ginger and fry gently for 5 minutes, stirring occasionally, until the garlic is light golden brown. Use a slotted spoon to transfer the aromatics to a plate. Add the green onions to the oil and fry for 2 minutes, stirring to separate, until crisp. Add to the plate of garlic, spread everything out, and sprinkle with some flaked sea salt. Remove the foil from the potatoes and drizzle ¼ cup/60ml of the aromatic oil evenly over the gratin (reserving any remaining oil for another use), then return it to the oven, uncovered, and bake for another 50 minutes. Increase the heat to 425°F/200°C for the last 5 minutes, until the top is golden brown and crispy.

5. Set the gratin aside to cool for 10 minutes, then top with the crispy aromatics, the lime zest, and a generous pinch of flaked sea salt and serve.

BKEILA, POTATO, AND BUTTER BEAN STEW

SERVES FOUR
As a main

4 cups/80g cilantro, roughly chopped, plus 1 cup/20g

1½ cups/30g parsley

14 cups/600g baby spinach

½ cup/120ml olive oil, plus more to drizzle

1 onion, finely chopped (1 cup/150g)

5 garlic cloves, crushed

2 green chiles, finely chopped (seeded for less heat)

1 tbsp plus 1 tsp ground cumin

1 tbsp ground coriander

¾ tsp ground cinnamon

1½ tsp superfine sugar

2 lemons: juice to get 2 tbsp; cut the remainder into wedges

1 qt/1L vegetable or chicken stock

table salt

1 lb 2 oz/500g waxy potatoes, peeled and cut into 1¼-inch/3cm pieces

1 × 1 lb 9 oz/700g jar good-quality large butter beans, drained (2⅔ cups/500g; Brindisa Navarrico large butter beans or cook your own)

Tunisian Jews make a condiment called bkeila or pkaila, which is extraordinary. It is prepared by cooking plenty of spinach for hours in a generous quantity of oil. The spinach—Swiss chard is often used as well—loses all its water and very slowly fries in the oil, resulting in a small amount of greasy paste as black as crude oil, which is used to flavor all kinds of soups and stews. Our version here is modified and highly simplified but it still imparts an essence-of-spinach flavor in this rustic stew, which makes it rather special; the kind of dish you keep coming back to for sustenance and comfort.

If you have time to make butter beans in smoked cascabel oil (page 41), or indeed if you've cleverly made a stash already, they are a wonderful addition to this stew in place of the plain butter beans.

The stew will keep in the fridge for up to 3 days, or in the freezer for up to 1 month.

1. In batches, put the 4 cups/80g cilantro, parsley, and spinach into a food processor and pulse until finely chopped (or finely chop by hand). Set aside.

2. Put 5 tbsp/75ml of the olive oil into a large, heavy-bottomed pot on medium heat. Add the onion and fry gently for 8 minutes, stirring occasionally, until soft and golden. Add the garlic, chiles, and all the spices and continue to cook for 6 minutes, stirring often.

3. Increase the heat to high and add the chopped herbs and spinach to the pot along with the remaining 3 tbsp olive oil. Cook for 10 minutes, stirring occasionally, until the spinach turns a dark green, almost gray color. You want the spinach to catch a bit at the bottom but not to burn, so decrease the heat if necessary. Stir in the sugar, lemon juice, stock, and 2 tsp salt, scraping the bottom with a spatula as you go. Bring to a rapid simmer, then decrease the heat to medium, add the potatoes, and cook gently until they are soft all the way through, about 25 minutes. Add the butter beans and cook until warmed through, about 5 minutes.

4. Remove the pot from the heat and stir in the remaining 1 cup/20g cilantro. Divide among four bowls, drizzle with some olive oil, and serve with the lemon wedges alongside.

WHITE BEAN MASH WITH GARLIC AÏOLI

SERVES SIX
As a side or as part
of a mezze spread

**1¾ cups/350g cannellini
  beans,** soaked
  overnight in plenty
  of cold water
  and **1 tsp baking soda**
1 onion, peeled and
  cut into 8 wedges
  (1½ cups/150g)
10 garlic cloves, peeled
2 rosemary sprigs
3 thyme sprigs
1 green chile, halved
  lengthwise
**¾ cup plus 2 tbsp/
  200ml olive oil**
1 tbsp Dijon mustard
**2 anchovy fillets in
  olive oil,** drained
  and roughly chopped
  (optional, but adjust
  seasoning if not using)
6 tbsp/90ml lemon juice
  (from about 4 lemons)
**table salt and black
  pepper**
½ cup/10g dill, roughly
  chopped
**½ tsp Aleppo chile flakes
  or Gochugaru Korean
  hot pepper flakes**
  (or ¼ tsp regular chile
  flakes)

Garlic-infused olive oil is used three times here: first to flavor a basic bean mash, then to make a thick aïoli to go on top, and finally to dress a layer of whole cooked beans that add texture. The result is a happy symphony of beans, garlic, and lemon, which can be served as part of a spread with bread and other dips (see pages 79 and 192). It can also be assembled on a heatproof dish and warmed in the oven, ready to double up as a side to a main.

Start a day ahead by soaking the beans in cold water and baking soda to ensure that they cook quickly and evenly. You can also use canned or jarred beans, if you like, in which case you won't need the onion.

All elements of the dish can be made up to 3 days ahead and kept in the fridge, bringing back to room temperature and assembling when you're ready to serve.

1. Drain the soaked beans and put them into a large saucepan with the onion. Add enough water to cover by about 1½ inches/4cm. Place on medium-high heat and bring to a boil, then decrease the heat to medium and cook for about 50 minutes, or until the beans are completely soft and starting to break up; you may need to top with more water as you go. Drain well.

2. While the beans are cooking, put the garlic, rosemary, thyme, green chile, and olive oil into a small saucepan, for which you have a lid. Place on medium-low heat, cover, and cook for 25–30 minutes, or until the garlic has softened and is just beginning to color. Leaving the lid on, remove from the heat and set aside for 10 minutes; the garlic will continue to cook in the heat of the oil. Strain through a sieve set over a bowl, reserving the oil. Pick out the garlic, herbs, and chile and set aside.

3. Put the cooked garlic into a food processor along with a mounded ½ cup/100g of the cooked beans, the mustard, anchovies, 2 tbsp of the lemon juice, 5 tbsp/75ml of the garlic oil, 1 tbsp water, ⅛ tsp salt, and a good grind of pepper. Blitz to a mayonnaise-like consistency and set this aïoli aside.

4. Combine a scant 1 cup/150g of the cooked beans in a small bowl with 4½ tsp lemon juice, 3 tbsp garlic oil, the dill, ¼ tsp salt, and a good grind of pepper. Set aside.

5. Put the remaining cooked beans and onion into the food processor along with the remaining 7½ tsp lemon juice, 3 tbsp garlic oil, ½ tsp salt, and a good grind of pepper. Blitz to a thick, smooth mash, about 1 minute, then transfer to a shallow bowl and spread out to create a shallow well in the center. Fill the well with the aïoli, then top with the dressed beans. Finish with the chile flakes, reserved green chile, rosemary, and thyme. Serve at once.

BASIC COOKED CHICKPEAS

MAKES 3¾ CUPS/ 600G

1⅓ cups/250g dried chickpeas
1½ tsp baking soda
1 tsp table salt

This recipe yields enough for both hummus recipes in the book (see below and page 234).

Start the day before by soaking the chickpeas in plenty of cold water to cover with 1 tsp of the baking soda. Drain and rinse, then put them into a large pot, for which you have a lid, with 7⅔ cups/1.8L of water and the remaining ½ tsp baking soda. Bring to a boil on medium-high heat, then decrease the heat to medium, cover, and cook for 35 minutes. Remove the lid, add the salt, and continue to cook for 15 minutes, or until the chickpeas are very soft when squashed between your fingers (cook longer if you need to). Drain well. These are best used as soon as they're cooked, but will keep, stored in a sealed container, in the refrigerator for up to 3 days.

HUMMUS WITH LEMON, FRIED GARLIC, AND CHILE

SERVES FOUR
As part of a mezze spread

HUMMUS
scant 2 cups/300g Basic Cooked Chickpeas (above recipe), or canned chickpeas
⅓ oz/10g fresh ginger, peeled and finely grated
1 tbsp olive oil
1 tbsp tahini
1 small garlic clove, crushed
2 lemons: finely zest to get 1 tbsp, then juice to get 3 tbsp
2 tbsp ice-cold water
¾ tsp flaked sea salt

FRIED AROMATICS
6 tbsp/90ml olive oil
3 red chiles, seeded and finely sliced
3 large garlic cloves, thinly sliced
½ oz/15g fresh ginger, peeled and julienned
2 cinnamon sticks
½ oz/15g cilantro sprigs, cut into short lengths
flaked sea salt

crusty bread to serve

This is great as part of a mezze spread. It's also lovely warm, with whole cooked chickpeas on top, or some shredded chicken or fried ground lamb.

The hummus can be made the day before and kept refrigerated if you want to get ahead. The aromatics should be fried on the day of serving, to ensure they stay crisp.

1. For the hummus: Put the chickpeas, ginger, olive oil, tahini, garlic, lemon zest, lemon juice, water, and salt into a food processor and blitz until smooth, scraping down the sides as you go if necessary. Set aside.

2. For the aromatics: Heat the olive oil in a large frying pan on medium heat. Once hot, add the chiles, garlic, ginger, and cinnamon and fry for 4–5 minutes, stirring every once in a while to separate the garlic slices, until the garlic is just starting to become golden. Add the cilantro and fry for 1 minute more, until the garlic is a light golden brown and the chiles are aromatic. Transfer the aromatics to a plate with a slotted spoon (reserving the oil) and sprinkle them generously with salt.

3. Spoon the hummus onto a large plate, creating a shallow well in the center with the back of the spoon. Spoon the aromatic oil inside the well. Top with the fried aromatics and serve with bread to mop up the oil.

SERVES FOUR
As a starter or six as part
of a spread

MELON AND BUFFALO MOZZARELLA SALAD WITH KASHA AND CURRY LEAVES

1 large shallot, finely sliced into rounds

2 lemons: finely zest to get ½ tsp, then juice to get 3 tbsp

flaked sea salt

¼ cup/60ml olive oil

30 fresh curry leaves (or 20 fresh basil leaves, patted dry with a paper towel)

1 tsp black mustard seeds

1 small watermelon, rind on or off, halved lengthwise, then cut into ¾-inch/2cm-thick triangles (1 lb 8 oz/680g rind-on weight)

⅔ cantaloupe, rind on or off, seeded and cut into 8 wedges (1 lb 5 oz/ 600g rind-on weight)

2–4 balls buffalo mozzarella, roughly broken into 10 pieces (14 oz/400g)

1 tbsp kasha (toasted buckwheat groats), roughly crushed (optional)

This isn't the first time, and it's definitely not the last, that we combine fresh melons with young white cheeses; and every time, something slightly different happens. On this occasion, it's not the saltiness of feta or the mild muskiness of goat cheese or young pecorino that give the fruit a savory edge, but rich mozzarella that adds a wonderful creaminess. The savory flavors are achieved by a pool of olive oil infused with curry leaves and mustard seeds. A brilliant start to a summer's feast (see page 304).

The salad tastes great once the flavors have had a chance to get to know each other, so dress the melons with the aromatic oil, shallots, and lemon juice up to 1 hour before, if you want to get ahead, but hold off on topping with the lemon zest, mustard seeds, kasha, and crispy curry leaves until you are ready to serve.

We love the look of the melons with their rind on, but you can, of course, remove it if you prefer.

This is a variation on a tomato salad by Peter Gordon. We thank him for the inspiration.

1. In a small bowl, combine the shallot with the lemon juice and a good pinch of salt.

2. Put the olive oil into a small saucepan on medium-high heat. Once hot, add the curry leaves and mustard seeds and fry for 30 seconds to 1 minute, swirling the pan, until crisp and fragrant. Strain through a sieve set over a small bowl, setting the oil and aromatics aside separately.

3. Arrange the watermelon, cantaloupe, and mozzarella on a large platter and sprinkle with ½ tsp salt. Drizzle with the aromatic oil, then sprinkle with the shallot and lemon juice. Let sit for 10 minutes, or up to 1 hour, for the flavors to come together. Finish with the lemon zest, fried mustard seeds, kasha (if using), and crispy curry leaves and serve.

SERVES FOUR

CHILLED AVOCADO SOUP WITH CRUNCHY GARLIC OIL

¼ cup/60ml olive oil

½ tsp cumin seeds, lightly crushed

½ tsp coriander seeds, lightly crushed

2 garlic cloves, finely chopped

table salt

1¼ cups/180g frozen peas, defrosted

2 large very ripe avocados, peeled and pitted (9¼ oz/260g)

½ cucumber (5¾ oz/ 160g), peeled: 4¼ oz/ 120g roughly cut into chunks, 1½ oz/40g finely diced

1 lemon: finely zest to get 1½ tsp, then juice to get 4½ tsp

1⅔ cups/400ml cold water

1 small green chile, seeded and finely chopped

⅓ cup/80g sour cream (optional)

1 tbsp dill fronds, finely chopped

This soup is creamy from the avocado and refreshing from the cucumber all at once, so it's a great way to open a summery meal. It will keep in the fridge for 2 days without losing its bright green color. The garlic oil can also be made ahead of time and will keep for up to 2 days in a sealed jar.

Make more of the aromatic olive oil, if you like. It's delicious drizzled over toast, salads, or pasta.

1. Put 2 tbsp of the olive oil into a small saucepan and add the cumin seeds, coriander seeds, garlic, and a good pinch of salt. Place on low heat and cook gently for 8 minutes, stirring often, until the garlic softens when mashed with the back of a spoon. Make sure not to heat the oil too much or the garlic will burn—if it does start to bubble, just remove it from the heat. Set aside to cool.

2. Put the peas into a blender and add the avocado, cucumber chunks, lemon zest, remaining 2 tbsp olive oil, ¾ tsp salt, and the water. Blitz to form a very smooth soup and put into the fridge to chill.

3. Put the diced cucumber into a small bowl along with the lemon juice, chile, and a pinch of salt and stir to combine.

4. Divide the chilled soup among four bowls and top with a spoonful of the sour cream (if using), a spoonful of the diced cucumber, a generous drizzle of the garlic oil, and the dill and serve.

SERVES FOUR
As a side

½ cup/120ml olive oil
1–2 green chiles, finely
    sliced into rounds
    (¼ cup/15g)
1–2 red chiles, finely sliced
    into rounds (¼ cup/15g)
20 fresh curry leaves
    (optional)
1½ tsp black mustard
    seeds
table salt
1 × 14-oz/400g can whole,
    peeled tomatoes
5 garlic cloves, finely
    chopped (not crushed)
6–8 ripe tomatoes,
    roughly chopped
    (3⅓ cups/600g)
2 bay leaves
½ cup/10g basil leaves,
    roughly torn
1 tsp superfine sugar
black pepper
3½ oz/100g crustless
    sourdough bread, well
    toasted and roughly cut
    into 1½-inch/4cm pieces
1 lime: finely zest to
    get ¼ tsp, then juice
    to get 1 tbsp

PAPPA AL POMODORO WITH LIME AND MUSTARD SEEDS

Pappa al pomodoro is a Tuscan peasant dish, typically prepared with overripe tomatoes that are too soft for a salad and stale bread that's too old for a sandwich. A delicious lesson in repurposing, this dish featured heavily in Ixta's childhood in Italy, most memorably at Podere il Poggiolo, a garden-to-table restaurant down the road from her childhood home, where the owner, Serena, makes the pappa al pomodoro of dreams.

This version has been given a serious Ottolenghi twist with the addition of a mustard seed–chile–curry leaf–infused oil. It's an unlikely combination that really works, but you can also do without the fresh curry leaves if you can't get hold of them; the pappa will still have tons of flavor.

Make the pappa a few hours before, if you like—the flavors will only get better—but hold off on topping with the crispy aromatics, basil, and lime zest until you're ready to serve.

This makes a wonderful starter to an Italian-inspired three-course meal (see page 303).

1. Line a plate with a double layer of paper towel. Heat the olive oil in a large sauté pan on medium-high heat. Once hot, add all the chiles and fry gently for 3 minutes. Add the curry leaves (if using) and fry for 45 seconds, then add the mustard seeds for a final 15 seconds, swirling the pan as you go. Strain the oil through a sieve set over a heatproof bowl. Transfer the chiles, curry leaves, and mustard seeds to the prepared plate and sprinkle generously with salt. Let the oil cool for 5 minutes.

2. In a medium bowl, roughly crush the canned tomatoes with a fork until broken up, along with any liquid from the can.

3. Return 3 tbsp of the reserved oil to the sauté pan and place on medium heat. Add the garlic and ¼ tsp salt and fry gently for 4 minutes, stirring, until soft and fragrant (you don't want the garlic to brown, so decrease the heat if necessary). Add the canned tomatoes, 2¼ cups/400g of the chopped tomatoes, the bay leaves, two-thirds of the basil, the sugar, ½ tsp salt, and a generous grind of pepper, then increase the heat to medium-high and simmer for 8 minutes. Remove from the heat, stir in the bread and the remaining chopped tomatoes, and allow to soak up the sauce for 5 minutes. Discard the bay leaves.

4. Spoon the mixture onto a large, lipped platter and drizzle with the lime juice and 3 tbsp of the remaining aromatic oil (reserve the rest for another use). Let sit for at least 25 minutes, or up to a few hours, for the flavors to come together. Finish with the lime zest, fried aromatics, and remaining basil and serve at room temperature.

SERVES FOUR
As a side

BLACK BEANS WITH COCONUT, CHILE, AND LIME

───────

FRIED AROMATICS
6 tbsp/90ml olive oil
2 garlic cloves, thinly sliced
2 red chiles, thinly sliced into rounds
10 fresh makrut lime leaves
2 tsp black mustard seeds

2 shallots, finely chopped (¾ cup/120g)
2 garlic cloves, crushed
4 fresh makrut lime leaves
1 ancho chile, torn in half
1¼ tsp table salt
1¼ cups/350g black beans, soaked overnight in plenty of cold water with **1 tsp baking soda** (or 4¾ cups/800g cooked beans)
3 cups/700ml water
3 tbsp lime juice
½ small coconut, finely shaved on a mandoline, if you have one, or roughly grated (⅔ cup/50g)

Lime, chile, and garlic are the predominant flavors here, coming through both the infused oil and the crispy sprinkle at the end, and making these beans particularly delicious.

We suggest starting with dried beans, in which case you'll need to soak them a day in advance, but you can also opt for canned or jarred beans; simply skip the stage where they get simmered—just add them to the cooked shallots, along with about ¼ cup/60ml of water, and cook until heated through.

1. For the aromatics: Heat the olive oil in a small saucepan on medium-high heat. Once hot, decrease the heat to medium; add the garlic, chiles, and lime leaves; and fry for 2 minutes, stirring to separate the garlic slices, or until the garlic is beginning to turn golden. Add the mustard seeds and fry for another 30 seconds or so, until the garlic starts to turn a light golden brown. Strain the aromatics through a sieve set over a bowl to collect the oil. Set the aromatics and oil aside separately.

2. Put 3 tbsp of the reserved aromatic oil into a medium saucepan on medium-high heat, then add the shallots, garlic, lime leaves, ancho chile, and salt. Decrease the heat to medium and fry for 6 minutes, stirring often, until the shallots are soft and golden brown. Rinse the beans well, then add them to the pan with the 3 cups/700ml water. Increase the heat to medium-high and bring to a simmer, then decrease the heat to medium and cook for 40 minutes, stirring occasionally, until the beans are cooked through but still hold their shape. Remove from the heat, cover, and let rest for 10 minutes.

3. Transfer the beans to a lipped platter or a large, shallow bowl. Discard the lime leaves and ancho chile. Drizzle with the lime juice and the remaining reserved aromatic oil. Top with the coconut and fried aromatics and serve.

OVEN FRIES WITH CURRY LEAF MAYONNAISE

SERVES FOUR
As a side

CURRY LEAF MAYONNAISE

14 cardamom pods: pods discarded and seeds blitzed in a spice grinder (or crushed in a mortar and pestle)

30 fresh curry leaves: 20 blitzed in a spice grinder (or finely chopped) and 10 left whole

½ cup/120ml sunflower oil

1 egg yolk

½ small garlic clove, crushed

4 limes: finely zest to get 4½ tsp, then juice to get 4 tsp; cut the remainder into wedges

flaked sea salt

2 lb 2 oz/1kg russet potatoes, skin on, cut into ½-inch/ 1cm-thick fries

3 tbsp sunflower oil

¾ tsp table salt

You won't regret putting a little extra effort into your fries' condiments, we promise! Taking our cue from Belgium and Holland, where they realized a long time ago that nothing beats mayonnaise as a dipping sauce, we have injected our mayo with curry and cardamom flavor. The fries themselves are also tossed with lime salt, so you end up with a potato experience that is at once rich, warm, sharp, and creamy.

Double the mayonnaise, if you like. It will keep in the fridge for up to 2 weeks and will transform your sandwich, burger, and wrap repertoire. Or you can do as we do at our restaurant ROVI and serve it alongside freshly grilled prawns. The fries go exceptionally well with celery root steaks with Café de Paris sauce (page 60) or Romano pepper schnitzels (page 146).

1. For the mayonnaise: Put the cardamom and blitzed curry leaves into a small saucepan on high heat for 1 minute, until fragrant. Pour in the sunflower oil and heat for 30 seconds, or until bubbling gently, before adding the whole curry leaves and frying gently until they are crisp, about 30 seconds. Take the pan off the heat, then remove the whole curry leaves with a slotted spoon and set them aside. Let the oil infuse with the rest of the aromatics for 30 minutes, or until completely cool. Set aside 1½ tsp of the oil (with some of the aromatics). Strain the remaining oil into a measuring cup, discarding the remaining aromatics.

2. Put the egg yolk, garlic, 3 tsp of the lime juice, and ⅛ tsp flaked sea salt into the bowl of a small food processor and blitz to combine. With the motor running, add the strained infused oil, very slowly and in a very thin stream, until it thickens to mayonnaise. Transfer to a small bowl and stir in the remaining 1 tsp lime juice to thin the mayonnaise a little. If it splits or gets too thick, whisk in 1 tsp water until it's emulsified. Mix the lime zest with 1½ tsp flaked sea salt, gently crushing it as you go. Set aside.

3. Preheat the oven to 425°F/200°C fan. Line a large baking sheet with parchment paper.

4. Spread the fries out on the prepared baking sheet. Add the sunflower oil and table salt and toss gently to coat the fries. Immediately transfer to the oven and bake for 20 minutes, then turn the fries and bake for another 25 minutes, turning the fries again halfway through, until crisp and golden brown all over.

5. Add the lime salt to the fries and toss to coat. Transfer the fries to a large platter, drizzle the mayonnaise with the reserved infused oil, and top with the crispy curry leaves. Serve at once, with the lime wedges alongside.

MAKES EIGHT
PANCAKES
Serves four

7½ tsp olive oil
12 fresh curry leaves
(or 12 fresh mint leaves,
patted dry with a paper
towel)
**2 tsp peeled and finely
minced fresh ginger**
2 small garlic cloves,
crushed
1 green chile, finely
chopped
2 green onions, finely
chopped
**2¾ cups/250g chickpea
flour**
⅓ cup/50g cornstarch
1 tsp baking powder
**1¼ cups/300ml sparkling
water**
**¼ cup/60ml apple cider
vinegar**
1 tsp ground cumin
1½ tsp garam masala
1 tsp table salt

MANGO PICKLE
YOGURT
**½ cup/150g Greek-style
yogurt**
½ mango, peeled
and finely chopped
(⅓ cup/60g)
2 tbsp hot mango pickle,
roughly chopped
1 tsp lime zest
table salt

¼ cup/60ml sunflower oil
1 lime, cut into wedges

CHICKPEA PANCAKES WITH
MANGO PICKLE YOGURT

These pancakes, flavored with ginger, garlic, and chile, are thick, light, and soft all at once. Soft-boiled eggs are a welcome addition, but feel free to leave out the egg and use a yogurt alternative if you want to keep things vegan.

These are great with a quick salad of green onions, mint, cilantro, and green chile, dressed with lime juice. Or for a more substantial meal, serve with some roasted eggplant (see page 251) or our spicy berbere ratatouille with coconut sauce (page 209) or both! The pancakes tend to lose their puffy texture as they sit, so eat them as soon as they've been fried.

1. Line a plate with a double layer of paper towel. Heat the olive oil in a small saucepan on medium-high heat. Once very hot, add the curry leaves and fry until crisp and bright green, 30 seconds to 1 minute. Use a slotted spoon to transfer the leaves to the prepared plate, leaving the oil in the pan. Take the pan off the heat and let the oil cool for a few minutes, then return it to medium-low heat and add the ginger, garlic, chile, and green onions. Fry gently for 6 minutes, stirring often, until soft and aromatic. Set aside to cool.

2. While the green onion–ginger mixture is cooling, whisk together the chickpea flour, cornstarch, baking powder, sparkling water, vinegar, cumin, garam masala, and salt in a large bowl until smooth. Stir in the cooled green onion mixture and let rest for 15 minutes, for the flavors to come together.

3. For the yogurt: In a small bowl, combine the yogurt, mango, mango pickle, and lime zest with a good pinch of salt; swirl to get streaks; and set aside.

4. Put 7½ tsp of the sunflower oil into a large, nonstick frying pan over medium-high heat and swirl to coat the bottom. Once hot, pour in about 6 tbsp/80g of the pancake batter—you want the pancakes to be about 5 inches/12cm in diameter. Fry for 1–1½ minutes on each side, until puffed and golden brown. Keep the pancakes warm while you continue with the remaining batter, adding more oil as needed.

5. Divide the pancakes among four plates, spoon the yogurt alongside, and top with the crispy curry leaves. Serve at once with the lime wedges on the side.

SWEET AND SOUR SPROUTS WITH CHESTNUTS AND GRAPES

12 small shallots (8½ oz/ 240g), peeled and left whole (8 oz/220g)

5 garlic cloves, peeled and crushed with the side of a knife

1¼ cups/250g pre-cooked and peeled chestnuts

4 bay leaves

1 tbsp maple syrup

9 tbsp/135ml olive oil

6 tbsp/90ml Shaoxing wine (or pale dry sherry)

¼ cup/60ml soy sauce

6⅓ oz/180g red grapes

1¾ lb/800g Brussels sprouts, trimmed and halved lengthwise

table salt

2 green chiles, finely sliced into rounds

2 tbsp rice vinegar

1 tsp superfine sugar

3 tbsp parsley leaves

Something magical happens to the Brussels sprouts, chestnuts, and grapes when they are left to soak with each other in a bath of Shaoxing wine, soy sauce, and their own natural juices. A subtle sharp sweetness, with hints of bitterness, gradually emerges, giving the dish a real festive quality. It's the Shaoxing that makes the greatest impact (see page 20), with its complex sweetness and depth. This Chinese wine, fermented from rice, is available in most Asian supermarkets, but if you can't get hold of it, use pale dry sherry instead.

The Brussels sprouts and chestnuts make this dish an obvious candidate for a holiday feast. Luckily, you can easily get ahead by cooking the shallots, garlic, chestnuts, and grapes the day before and allowing them to sit in the liquids overnight (refrigerated). The Brussels sprouts should be roasted and added to the bath the day you plan to serve the dish. Hold off on adding the pickled chiles and parsley until you serve.

1. Preheat the oven to 350°F/160°C fan.

2. Put the shallots, garlic, chestnuts, bay leaves, and maple syrup into a 9 x 13-inch/23 x 33cm high-sided roasting pan with 7 tbsp/105ml of the olive oil, 5 tbsp/75ml of the Shaoxing wine, and 2 tbsp of the soy sauce. Cover tightly with aluminum foil and cook for 35 minutes, until the shallots are soft but still hold their shape. Stir in the grapes, cover again with foil, and cook for another 10 minutes. Remove the pan from the oven, take off the foil, and set aside.

3. Increase the oven temperature to 450°F/220°C fan. Line two baking sheets with parchment paper. Mix the Brussels sprouts with the remaining 2 tbsp olive oil and ¼ tsp salt, then spread out on the prepared baking sheets. Roast for about 16 minutes, switching the sheets halfway through, until the sprouts are browned, then add to the pan of grapes and chestnuts, gently mix everything together, and let rest, uncovered, at room temperature for 1 hour, if you can, or at least 30 minutes, for the flavors to develop.

4. Meanwhile, in a small bowl mix, the chiles with the rice vinegar, sugar, and ⅛ tsp salt and allow to pickle for 30 minutes.

5. Once the Brussels sprouts have rested, stir in the remaining 1 tbsp Shaoxing wine and remaining 2 tbsp soy sauce. Stir in the parsley and transfer to a large, shallow serving bowl. Top with the pickled chiles and the pickling liquid and serve.

RUTABAGA GNOCCHI WITH MISO BUTTER

SERVES FOUR
As a main

1–2 russet potatoes, skin on (14 oz/400g)
2–3 small rutabagas, peeled and cut into roughly ¾-inch/2cm cubes (2½ cups/600g)
5 tbsp/75ml olive oil
1 egg yolk
table salt
1 cup plus 3 tbsp/150g "00" flour
2 cups/480ml vegetable or chicken stock
7 oz/200g morning glory (or large-leaf spinach), roughly chopped into 3¼-inch/8cm lengths
1 tbsp white or other miso paste
1 lime: finely zest to get 1 tsp, then juice to get 2 tsp
¼ oz/5g fresh ginger, peeled and finely grated
¼ cup/50g unsalted butter, cut into ½-inch/1½cm cubes
3 green onions, thinly sliced (⅓ cup/30g)
1 tsp white sesame seeds, toasted

If you want to use store-bought potato gnocchi instead of making your own, you are more than welcome to—the miso butter will transform them. If, however, you choose to make our rutabaga-potato gnocchi, which have a seductive bitter-sweetness, we can make your life slightly easier. Instead of rolling and cutting the gnocchi, which can be messy, we spoon the mixture into a piping bag (you can use a zip-top plastic bag), snip off a corner, and squeeze the gnocchi directly into simmering water. It's a nice trick that also makes them lighter because you don't need the extra flour to roll them.

Morning glory is an Asian leafy green; its hollow stalks make it the perfect vehicle for the sauce. It's available in most Asian supermarkets, but if you can't get hold of it, large-leaf spinach will also work well.

The gnocchi mixture can be made the day before and stored in a piping bag in the fridge until you are ready to cook. You can also boil the gnocchi the day before and keep them refrigerated, ready to be fried the next day. *Pictured on pages 96–97.*

1. Preheat the oven to 450°F/220°C fan. Line two baking sheets with parchment paper.

2. Wrap the potatoes individually in aluminum foil and bake for 1 hour, or until cooked through. Meanwhile, place the rutabagas on a prepared baking sheet. Toss with 1½ tsp of the olive oil, cover with foil, and bake for 30 minutes, or until cooked through (you can roast the rutabagas at the same time as the potatoes).

3. While the potatoes are still warm, peel and discard the skin and mash them in a bowl using a potato ricer or masher to get about 1 cup/230g of smooth mash. Transfer the rutabagas to a food processor with 2 tbsp olive oil and blitz until smooth with no lumps—you may need to stop and scrape down the sides a few times. You should have about 1¼ cups/320g. Put in the bowl with the mash, add the egg yolk and ¼ tsp salt, and mix well to combine, then fold in the flour until well combined with no lumps. Transfer the dough to a piping bag and refrigerate for 1 hour, or until well chilled.

4. Snip the end off the piping bag to give an opening about ¾ inch/2cm wide. Fill a medium pot with 1½ qt/1½L of water, add 2 tsp salt, and bring to a boil on high heat, then decrease the heat to medium-high so the water is simmering gently. Add the gnocchi in about five batches, so as not to overcrowd the pan, piping 1¼-inch/3cm pieces of gnocchi into the water, using a small sharp knife to cut off each piece of dough. Cook for 2–3 minutes, or until the gnocchi float to the top. Lift out with a slotted spoon and place them on the second prepared baking sheet, spaced apart. Once all the gnocchi are cooked, drizzle them with 2 tsp olive oil and refrigerate for 20 minutes until slightly chilled—this will help them to set and keep their shape when you fry them.

5. Pour the stock into a large sauté pan on medium-high heat and cook for 12–14 minutes, or until reduced to ¾ cup plus 2 tbsp/200ml. Add the morning glory and cook for 2 minutes until tender, then use the slotted spoon to remove from the pan and set aside, leaving most of the liquid in the pan. Return the pan to medium heat and whisk in the miso paste, lime juice, ginger, and butter, then cook for 3 minutes, whisking until the butter melts and the sauce is smooth and slightly thickened. Take care not to let it boil, as it will split. Remove the pan from the heat and set aside.

6. Heat the remaining 4½ tsp olive oil in a large frying pan on medium-high heat. Once very hot, add half the gnocchi and fry for 1–2 minutes on each side, or until nicely browned all over. Transfer to a plate and continue with the other half. Add the cooked gnocchi and morning glory to the sauce, return to medium-high heat, and gently heat through for a minute or two.

7. Divide the gnocchi among four plates; sprinkle with the lime zest, green onions, and sesame seeds; and serve at once.

POTATO AND GOCHUJANG BRAISED EGGS

SERVES FOUR
As breakfast or
a light supper

**2 medium russet
  potatoes,** peeled and
  cut into ¼ × 1½-inch/
  ½ × 4cm batons
  (13⅓ oz/380g)

1 small kohlrabi, peeled
  and cut into ¼ × 1½-inch/
  ½ × 4cm batons
  (5¾ oz/160g)

**1 tbsp gochujang chile
  paste** (adjust according
  to the brand you are
  using; see page 18)

**2 tsp white or other
  miso paste**

2 small garlic cloves,
  crushed

3 tbsp olive oil

table salt

8 eggs

SAUCE

1 tbsp lime juice

**1 tsp gochujang chile
  paste** (adjust according
  to the brand you are
  using; see page 18)

2 tbsp olive oil

**2 tsp finely chopped
  chives**

**2 tsp white or black
  sesame seeds,**
  preferably a mixture of
  both, toasted

1 lime, cut into wedges

Eggs are baked nestled inside a giant rösti with a crispy bottom here, a bit like hash browns and eggs, all in one pan. If you're not a fan of kohlrabi, feel free to use potato only, though we like the complexity that kohlrabi brings with it. Try to stick to ¼-inch/½cm batons for the vegetables and not grate them, because you won't get the crispiness you're after when they're grated. You can achieve this using a sharp knife or, more conveniently, a mandoline or a food processor with the appropriate attachment. Prep the vegetables just before you cook them, so they don't get soggy.

Try to source good-quality gochujang, a Korean fermented chile paste, and not the generic supermarket brands. It makes all the difference.

1. Preheat the oven to 425°F/200°C fan. Lightly grease a round 12-inch/30cm ovenproof baking dish or nonstick sauté pan, for which you have a lid, or a similar-size round ovenproof dish, and transfer it to the oven to heat for 5 minutes.

2. In a large bowl, combine the potatoes, kohlrabi, gochujang, miso paste, garlic, olive oil, and ¼ tsp salt and toss until thoroughly coated (this is easiest with gloved hands). Remove the pan from the oven, tip in the potato mixture, and spread out evenly. Bake for 25 minutes, uncovered, rotating the pan halfway through, until golden brown and crisp on top.

3. Make eight wells in the potato mixture with the back of a spoon. Crack an egg into each hole, then cover the pan with the lid and return to the oven for 8–10 minutes, or until the whites are cooked and the yolks are still runny. Check for doneness after 8 minutes and every minute thereafter—the exact timing will depend on your oven and pan. Use a small spoon to carefully peel away the white film that has formed over the eggs, if you like, to reveal the yolks beneath. Season with a little salt.

4. For the sauce: In a small bowl, combine the lime juice, gochujang, olive oil, chives, and sesame seeds and stir to mix.

5. Drizzle the sauce over the eggs and serve straight from the pan, with the lime wedges to squeeze on top.

THE ULTIMATE ROASTING-PAN RAGÙ

SERVES SIX TO EIGHT
As a main

2 carrots, peeled and chopped into large chunks (7 oz/200g)
1 onion, peeled and chopped into large chunks (8½ oz/240g)
8½ oz/240g oyster mushrooms, roughly chopped
1¼ oz/50g dried porcini mushrooms, roughly blitzed
3 garlic cloves, crushed
2–3 plum tomatoes, chopped into large chunks (9¾ oz/280g)
6 tbsp/90ml olive oil
3 tbsp white or other miso paste
2 tbsp rose harissa (adjust according to the brand you are using; see page 20)
3 tbsp tomato paste
5 tbsp/75ml soy sauce
1½ tsp cumin seeds, crushed
¾ cup/145g dried brown or green lentils
¼ cup plus 2 tbsp/80g pearl barley
3¼ cups/770ml vegetable or chicken stock
7 tbsp/130g coconut cream (not coconut milk!)
⅓ cup/80ml red wine
½ cup/120ml water
table salt and black pepper

In our mission to create the best meatless ragù, enough versions were made to sink a large ship (Ixta nearly lost her will to live, but that has happened once or twice before). There's no denying the list of ingredients is long, but these are all here to give the ragù its fantastic umaminess. The method, however, could not be simpler. If you have a food processor, the first six ingredients can all be pulsed in it until finely chopped, saving you lots of time and effort.

The ragù will keep in the fridge for up to 3 days, or in the freezer for 1 month, ready to be spooned over anything from pasta to polenta (try it with the fresh corn polenta on page 140, minus the peppers and egg), or used as the base for lasagne or shepherd's pie. For the latter two, cook the ragù a bit less, as it will carry on cooking in the oven.

Thank you to Emily Moore and Josh Renaut, who tirelessly took home every single version of this ragù to give their thoughtful feedback as recent converts to veganism.

1. Preheat the oven to 400°F/190°C fan.

2. Working in batches, put the carrots, onion, oyster mushrooms, porcini mushrooms, garlic, and tomatoes into a food processor and pulse until everything is very finely chopped (or very finely chop everything by hand if you don't have a food processor).

3. Put the chopped vegetables into a 9 x 13-inch/23 x 33cm nonstick roasting pan with at least 2½-inch/6cm sides and add the olive oil, miso paste, harissa, tomato paste, soy sauce, and cumin seeds and mix very well. Bake for 40 minutes, stirring halfway through, until browned in places and around the edges.

4. Decrease the oven temperature to 375°F/180°C fan.

5. Add the lentils, barley, stock, coconut cream, wine, water, ¼ tsp salt, and a very generous grind of pepper to the roasting pan. Stir very well, scraping the crispy sides and bottom with a spatula. Cover tightly with aluminum foil and bake for another 40 minutes. Remove the foil and bake for a final 5 minutes. Set aside to rest for 15 minutes, for the sauce to be absorbed a little before serving.

DIPPING SAUCE
3 tbsp light soy sauce
1 tbsp honey
2 tsp sesame seeds,
  toasted
2 tsp rice vinegar
1 garlic clove, crushed
½ red chile, seeded
  and finely chopped

1 cup plus 1 tbsp/135g
  all-purpose flour
½ cup/60g rice flour
  (not Asian glutinous
  rice flour)
table salt
1 egg
1⅓ cups/325ml
  ice-cold water
4½ tsp gochujang chile
  paste (adjust according
  to the brand you are
  using; see page 18)
¼ cup/5g cilantro,
  roughly chopped,
  plus more to serve
½ red chile, seeded
  and finely chopped
5 tbsp/75ml
  sunflower oil
14 oz/400g asparagus,
  woody ends trimmed
  and discarded, spears
  halved lengthwise
  (9¾ oz/280g)
4½ oz/120g green onions
  (6–7), halved crosswise
  and then again
  lengthwise

ASPARAGUS AND GOCHUJANG PANCAKES

These pancakes are springy and less cakey than regular pancakes, which helps preserve the texture of the asparagus. They are only moderately spicy and are wonderful when served at a weekend breakfast or as a light lunch or supper.

When it comes to gochujang, a Korean fermented chile paste, you want to get your hands on the real deal. Korean brands, such as O'Food, have a serious depth to them, compared to the often dull brands sold in supermarkets. If you still end up with a mild gochujang, serve some more alongside the dipping sauce.

Serve the pancakes with an avocado salad and some grilled prawns, if you like.

1. For the dipping sauce: In a small bowl, whisk together the soy sauce, honey, sesame seeds, vinegar, garlic, and chile until well combined. Set aside.

2. Put both flours into a large bowl, add ½ tsp salt, and mix well to combine. In a separate bowl, lightly whisk together the egg, water, gochujang, cilantro, and chile. Make a well in the center of the flour mixture, slowly pour in the wet ingredients, and whisk until just smooth; don't overmix.

3. Add just over 1 tbsp of the sunflower oil to a 7-inch/18cm nonstick pan on medium-high heat. Once hot, add one-fourth of the asparagus, all pointing in the same direction, and a tiny pinch of salt and cook for 1½–2 minutes, turning the asparagus over a few times, or until beginning to soften and color. Add one-fourth of the green onions and cook for 30 seconds more. Pour in about one-fourth of the pancake batter, spreading it to cover the bottom of the pan, and cook for 2½ minutes before flipping and cooking for 2½ minutes more, or until crispy and golden. Transfer to a plate and continue in this way to make four pancakes in total. You may need to adjust the heat and timings a little as you go along.

4. Divide the pancakes among two plates, sprinkle with some chopped cilantro, and serve with the sauce alongside or lightly drizzled on top.

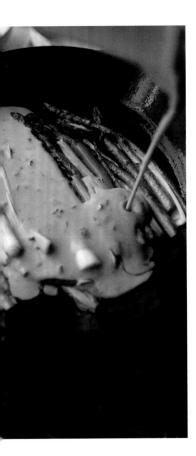

SERVES FOUR
As a main

table salt
14 oz/400g dried bucatini (or other long pasta, cooking time adjusted if necessary)
¼ cup/50g unsalted butter
1 tbsp za'atar, plus 1½ tsp
2 tsp black pepper
4½ oz/130g Parmesan, very finely grated
1 oz/30g pecorino, very finely grated
7½ tsp olive oil
2 tsp whole marjoram leaves (optional)

ZA'ATAR CACIO E PEPE

Messing with an Italian classic is not something that we do lightly, but adding za'atar really doesn't take anything away from the much-admired simplicity of this dish. All it does is add a layer of delicious herbiness that goes hand in hand with the pepper and the cheese.

The technique for getting your cacio e pepe right is not complicated, but it's essential that you follow it to a T if you want to get a rich and smooth sauce, as Ixta would confirm after testing it about a thousand times. Using a wide pan and little water to cook the pasta is essential because it ensures there is a lot of starch in the water, which is the key to getting the sauce to emulsify. Grate the Parmesan and pecorino as finely as possible, and keep them separated to make sure they melt happily into the sauce. Finally, have everything measured out before you begin cooking; it all happens rather quickly after that.

1. Bring 5½ cups/1.3L of water to a boil in a wide pan on medium-high heat, then season with ¾ tsp salt. Add the bucatini and cook for 9 minutes (or per package instructions) until al dente, stirring every now and then so they don't stick together or to the bottom of the pan, and to ensure they are submerged. Drain, reserving all the cooking water (you should have about 2¼ cups/520ml—if not, top up with a little hot water).

2. Melt the butter in a large, high-sided, nonstick sauté pan on high heat until bubbling, then add the 1 tbsp za'atar and pepper and cook for 1 minute, stirring, until fragrant. Add the reserved cooking water, bring to a rapid boil, and cook for 5 minutes, until silky and reduced a little. Add the pasta and stir vigorously into the sauce. Add the Parmesan in two batches, continuing to stir vigorously as you go and waiting until the first half has melted before adding the next. Once the Parmesan has all melted, add the pecorino, continuing to stir until it has also melted and the sauce is smooth and silky.

3. Transfer the pasta to a lipped platter and finish with the olive oil, marjoram (if using), remaining 1½ tsp za'atar, and a small pinch of salt. Serve at once.

SERVES FOUR
As a starter

SPRING VEGETABLES IN PARMESAN BROTH WITH CHARRED LEMON SAUCE

BROTH
2 tbsp olive oil
½ onion, finely chopped
table salt
2 garlic cloves, crushed
⅔ cup/80g Nocellara olives (or other green olive), pitted and finely chopped (⅓ cup/50g)
3½ oz/100g Parmesan, cut into 3 chunks (the rind should be included)
1 tbsp lemon juice
¼ cup/5g parsley stems
¼ cup/5g basil stems
7⅔ cups/1.8L water

CHARRED LEMON SAUCE
1 small lemon, cut into 8 × ¼-inch/½cm-thick slices and seeded (2¼ oz/60g)
⅔ cup/80g Nocellara olives (or other green olive), pitted and finely chopped (⅓ cup/50g)
2 small garlic cloves, finely chopped
½ cup/10g parsley leaves, finely chopped
½ cup/10g basil leaves, finely chopped
5 tbsp/75ml olive oil
¼ tsp table salt

6¼ cups/400g sugar snap peas, halved lengthwise at an angle
1¼ cups/100g snow peas, finely sliced at an angle
⅔ cup/100g fresh or frozen peas (defrosted if frozen)
finely grated Parmesan to finish

You can do as much or as little as you like with the spring's bounty of peas and beans. Here, we go for a maximalist approach, stirring them into a broth loaded with the intensity of lemon, olive, garlic, and Parmesan.

There are three good takeaways from this recipe. First, never throw out your cheese rinds. They keep in the fridge or freezer for months, ready to be added to stocks, stews, and broths for extra flavor. Second, the sautéed onion, garlic, and olive base packs a heavy punch, adding serious depth to the broth. You could double or triple this part alone, blitz it to a paste, and keep it refrigerated to use in soups and stews. Third, the charred lemon sauce is a wonderful recipe in its own right. Double it, if you like, it will keep in a jar in the fridge for 2 days, ready to be spooned over grilled vegetables, fish, or chicken, or to toss in salads.

If you want to get ahead, the broth and sauce can be made the day before and kept refrigerated, but don't cook the vegetables in the broth until you are ready to serve. Bring the broth back up to a simmer and the sauce to room temperature, if making ahead.

1. For the broth: Put the olive oil, onion, and ¾ tsp salt into a large saucepan on medium-high heat. Fry gently for 6 minutes, stirring every now and then, until soft and golden. Add the garlic and olives and continue to fry for 2 minutes until soft and fragrant. Add the Parmesan chunks and fry for 30 seconds, then add the lemon juice, herb stems, water, and 1¼ tsp salt. Bring to a simmer, then decrease the heat to medium and cook for 20 minutes. Strain the broth, then return it to the saucepan to keep warm. Discard the left-behind vegetables and Parmesan.

2. For the sauce: Heat a nonstick frying pan on high heat and, once hot, add half the lemon slices and char for about 3 minutes on each side, or until nicely charred but not completely burnt. Finely chop the charred slices, along with the fresh slices, and put into a small serving bowl. Stir in the olives, garlic, parsley, basil, olive oil, and salt and set aside.

3. Return the strained broth to medium-high heat and bring to a simmer. Decrease the heat to low, stir in all the peas, and cook for 3 minutes, until they are just cooked and still crunchy.

4. Divide the peas and broth among four bowls and top each with 1 tbsp of the sauce. Finish with some grated Parmesan and serve with the remaining sauce alongside.

GRILLED FIGS WITH SHAOXING DRESSING

8 ripe purple figs, halved (11¼ oz/320g)
1 tbsp soy sauce
7½ tsp maple syrup
2 tbsp Shaoxing wine (or pale dry sherry)
2½ tsp Chinkiang vinegar (or half the amount of balsamic vinegar)
¼ cup/60ml olive oil
2 red chiles, finely sliced into rounds (¼ cup/20g)
1 lemon: finely shave the peel to get 5 strips
3 cups/60g arugula
mounded ½ cup/140g ricotta

On paper it may not sound like it would work, but the combination of figs, Chinese rice wine, and ricotta is a truly marvelous one. The dish is a fine balance of sweet and savory, so it's important that your figs are ripe and sweet. If they aren't, increase the amount of maple syrup a little.

The infused oil and cooked figs need time to marinate, so make them a day ahead if you like. The figs, in fact, can be cooked up to 3 days before and kept in the fridge (just bring them back to room temperature before you assemble the salad). You can even leave them in the fridge for up to 3 weeks to ferment (or at least become a little funky); they make a great addition to a cheese board.

1. Preheat the oven to the highest broil setting. Line a baking sheet with parchment paper, make sure there is no overhanging parchment that could burn under the broiler.

2. In a medium bowl, toss the figs with the soy sauce and 4½ tsp of the maple syrup, then arrange, cut-side up and spaced apart, on the prepared baking sheet. Place on the top rack of the oven and roast for 12 minutes, until the figs are soft and caramelized but still holding their shape. Return the figs and cooking juices to the bowl and add the Shaoxing wine, vinegar, and remaining 1 tbsp maple syrup. Mix gently, then set this dressing aside for at least 1 hour (or up to overnight) for the flavors to come together.

3. Meanwhile, heat the olive oil in a small saucepan on medium heat and, once hot, add the chiles and fry for 3 minutes, stirring to separate the slices. Add the lemon peel and fry for 30 seconds until fragrant, then immediately pour into a heatproof bowl and set aside to infuse for at least 30 minutes (or up to overnight).

4. Arrange the arugula on a platter and top with the figs and dressing. Dot with spoonfuls of the ricotta; finish with the infused oil, chiles, and lemon peel; and serve at once.

SERVES FOUR
As a side

CUCUMBER SALAD
À LA XI'AN IMPRESSION

—————

2–3 cucumbers, halved lengthwise, watery centers scraped out, cut into ¾-inch/2cm pieces (4 cups/700g)
2 garlic cloves, crushed
2 tsp rice vinegar
3 tbsp lime juice
flaked sea salt
3 tbsp sunflower oil

TAHINI AND SOY DRESSING
¼ cup/60g tahini (stir very well before using, to combine the solids and fats)
2 tbsp soy sauce
4½ tsp mirin
 (or maple syrup)
4½ tsp rice vinegar
1 tbsp water

1½ tsp black sesame seeds, lightly toasted
2 green onions, finely sliced at an angle

Xi'an Impression and Master Wei are sister restaurants in London serving the food of Xi'an, the capital of Shaanxi Province in central China. These restaurants, which also inspired cabbage with ginger cream and numbing oil (page 196), are tremendously popular with Ottolenghi chefs for their big flavors, based on a brazenly liberal use of chiles, vinegar, soy sauce, and oil. A particular cucumber salad always appears first on the table and it is a loose inspiration for this salad.

The dressing can be made up to 1 week ahead and kept refrigerated—just stir again to loosen it, adding a little water if necessary.

Serve with a few other vegetable dishes to make a meal, such as asparagus and gochujang pancakes (page 102) and fusion caponata with silken tofu (page 135).

1. Put the cucumber into a bowl and add the garlic, vinegar, lime juice, and 1 tbsp salt. Mix to combine, using your hands to lightly crush the cucumber pieces. Gently heat the sunflower oil in a small saucepan over low heat until warm, about 2 minutes, then pour over the cucumber pieces. Set aside to marinate for 30 minutes, or up to 2 hours.

2. For the dressing: Whisk together the tahini, soy sauce, mirin, vinegar, and water until you get a very smooth sauce (it will seize a bit at first, but will then become very smooth).

3. Pour the dressing onto a large plate with a lip, so that it naturally pools into a circle. Drain the cucumbers very well, discarding the liquid, and pile on top of the dressing. Finish with the sesame seeds and green onions and serve at once.

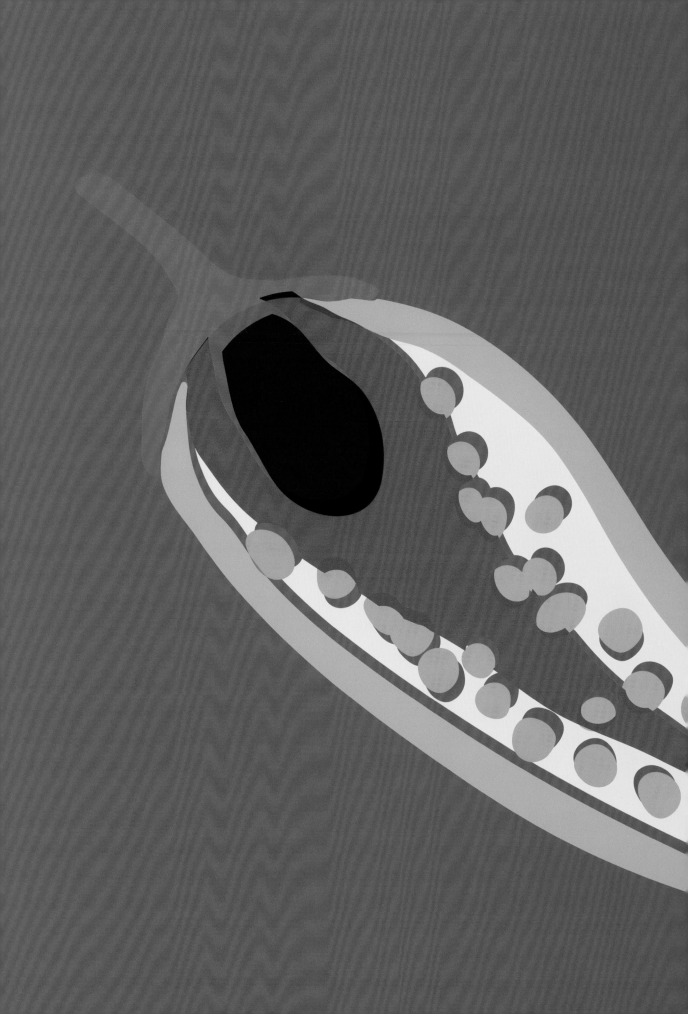

PAIRING

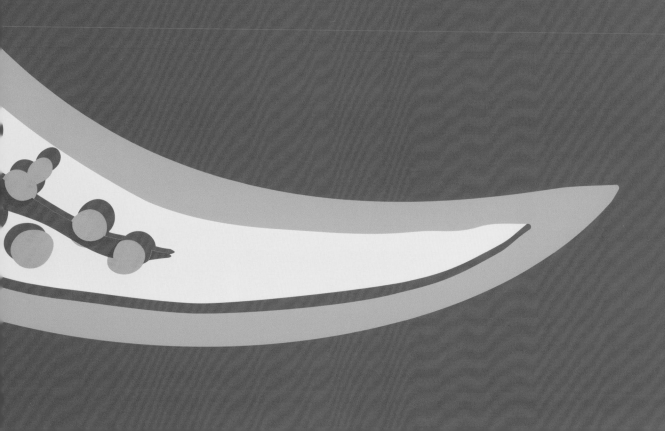

Flavor, as we'll see, can be dialed up by the pairings within a dish. It's not so much what you do to an ingredient ("process") or the ingredient itself ("produce"), but the combination of various ingredients with what we have identified to be the four most important "pairings": sweetness, fat, acidity, and chile heat. These pairings play out, in big and small ways, in so many of the things we all love to eat.

Think of your favorite sandwich. Sandwiches are, arguably, *the* ultimate elevation of the most everyday of ingredients—bread—by virtue of what it's paired with. Spread the bread with butter and you've already hit first base: fat. Ask Ixta what her dream sandwich is and she'll say porchetta and apricot mustard. The combination is not, for obvious reasons, one found in this book but it does demonstrate the principle. The porchetta brings the fat to the equation and then the apricot mustard—which neatly checks all the remaining sweet, acidity, and chile heat boxes—makes this an easy home run. Yotam's sandwich would be a mix of olive oil–roasted vegetables and chiles piled over toasted sourdough with some pecorino shavings or crumbled feta on top. Again: check, check, and check. Not all sandwiches need to hit every note to make perfect sense—think of peanut butter and jelly, or smashed avocado and chile, shrimp salad, or a BLT. You'll see one or two or all of these pairings playing out. Let's look at sweetness, fat, acidity, and chile heat one at a time.

SWEETNESS

When we try to understand how sweetness works in a savory setting, as opposed to the more apparent dessert context (see PAGES 223–225), it is useful to pull back to the title of this book for a minute. *Flavor*—what is it, actually? How does it relate to taste? What are the forces that shape this complex sensory experience of ours?

Taste is what we detect with the taste buds in our mouth. We have five tastes. Sweetness is one of them. The others are sour, bitter, salt, and savory (umami). Flavor, on the other hand, is picked up by the olfactory cells inside our noses. These cells respond to airborne compounds, many of which are released as we chew our food. Flavor is taste plus aroma. The sweet taste of a peach will be happily detected by our little taste buds when we take our first bite. Flavor, though, can't be realized without the additional smell, the aroma, the *fragrance* of that perfectly ripe fruit.

Appreciating the complexity of flavor is essential to shedding light on how sweetness plays its role in a savory dish. Just as flavor is made up of taste and aroma, the different tastes also never work in isolation. In a savory context, something is not simply "sweet," nor is it simply "sour" or "bitter" or "salty." Rather, it is a combination of one or two or all of these things. Take some of

SATISFACTION IS ABOUT THE COMBINATION, THE LAYERING, THE CONTRAST OF TASTES.

our favorite sweet ingredients in the recipes here—white miso or mirin, pink grapefruit, tomatoes, oranges, maple syrup. The experience of eating these is not that they form a neat queue along the taste buds that say "sweetness." Rather, they charge an assault on all the senses!

Not only are all ingredients a combination of more than one "thing"— sweet *and* salty, sweet *and* savory—these tastes all need and rely on each other in order to shine. What would bitter cocoa powder be, after all, without its very opposite, sweet sugar? Satisfaction is about the combination, the layering, the contrast of tastes. With sweetness this is particularly pertinent because without the complexity, you're running the risk of turning your dish into a dessert. Whatever the pairing—whether it's about layering together two of the same tastes or contrasting one against another—it's always about the *balance*. Let's look at some of our recipes to see this playing out.

First, layering, when one sweet ingredient pairs with one or two others. The effect is to bring complexity—another dimension—to a straightforward sweet taste. This is where wedges of sweet pumpkin, for example, are roasted together with a sweet spice, like cinnamon, in our ISRAELI COUSCOUS AND SQUASH IN TOMATO AND STAR ANISE SAUCE (PAGE 137). Or where a tablespoon or two of rich maple syrup and sweet-savory white miso are added to a tray of butternut squash, as we do with ESME'S ROUGH SQUASH MASH (PAGE 136), before the whole thing gets roasted.

All these combinations of sweetness upon sweetness need to be kept in check, though. It's one thing to introduce depth of flavor, but sweetness can tip into cloying. Anyone who has tried the dish that combines sweet potato, sweet cinnamon, marshmallows, and maple syrup, usually served at Thanksgiving,

A WHOLE GENERATION OF KIDS PREFERRING "SWEET" CARROTS TO "BITTER" BRUSSELS SPROUTS IS NOT JUST A GREAT BIG CONSPIRACY AGAINST THEIR PARENTS.

will know what we mean. Roasting a sweet potato alone shows how much long and slow cooking sweetens this starchy vegetable. This is thanks to the action of an enzyme that attacks the starch and breaks it down to maltose, a sugar made up of two glucose molecules that's about a third as sweet as table sugar. And that's all before the marshmallows and maple syrup have been added to the equation. As well as giving us a little lesson in starch conversion, this particular dish is also basically a controlled experiment in the need for a salty slice of ham or piece of bacon at the Thanksgiving table. In the absence of either in *Flavor*, other ingredients do just as well.

Roasting our squash and carrots with a woody spice, like caraway, or a hard herb, like sage, is something we do in our BUTTERNUT, ORANGE, AND SAGE GALETTE (PAGE 132). Doing this keeps the vegetable's sweetness in check (rather than drawing it out, as a sweet spice such as cinnamon would). Sprigs of thyme do this for the CHARRED PEPPERS on PAGE 140. Spreading the base of the galette with a layer of mascarpone also works. At other times, it's a squeeze of lime or lemon juice or the use of a sharp vinegar that does the work to balance the sweetness.

It can, on the other hand, be the addition of something acidic or hot that keeps (or even heightens) the desired sweetness in an ingredient in the first place. Think of a slice of pineapple. Take a bite and the dominant taste is sweet. Sprinkle it with a little salt and chile and try it again. The addition of salt and chile, counterintuitively, serves to actually amplify the fruit's sweetness.

We often talk about the "experience" of tasting sweetness rather than the taste of sweetness being an absolute. This is because everyone's experience of sweetness is different. Furthermore, taste buds change and develop over time. What we experience as bitter or sweet changes as we grow up. A whole generation of kids preferring "sweet" carrots to "bitter" Brussels sprouts is not just a great big conspiracy against their parents. Infants have around 30,000 taste buds, only about a third of which survive into adulthood. Their sensitivity toward extremes of bitter or sweet really *is* heightened.

Separate from what an ingredient is paired with, there can, as well, be a huge range of sweetness within an ingredient itself. Compare an aged balsamic vinegar with a younger version and you'll be reaching for words far beyond simple "sweetness." Ditto premium-grade maple syrup or Shaoxing wine.

Think about those chunks of pumpkin and squash as another example, the many varieties of which could fill a whole book. Pumpkin is just one variety of squash. There are, in addition, all the Asian and African varieties; the cucumbers and gherkins, the melons, watermelons, and gourds. Then there are the North and South American varieties. These are divided into winter squashes (firm and sweet) and summer squashes (soft and only mildly sweet). A deep dive to end on, but it's all to say that discussions about whether we have four or five tastes slightly miss the point; we have about thirty-five different kinds of "sweetness" for squash, for starters! And we haven't even got to dessert! Forget about what to call things, perhaps. Focus instead on the taste, the aroma—the combination of which makes the flavor—of our sweetness-showcasing recipes instead.

FAT

Twice already we've drawn attention to the unscientific nature of our system for understanding flavor through what an ingredient is paired with. It's not that we're *not* interested in the science per se; it's just not the *real* reason we reach for things in the kitchen. When it comes to analyzing our cooking experiences—how they work and what happens if they don't—the option to get technical is absolutely there.

Olive oil and how it works so well as a cooking medium is a good place to start. Olive oil belongs to a large chemical family called lipids, and lipids are chemically unlike water. One of their differences is that they have a much higher boiling point. This allows for a much higher cooking temperature, which, in turn, gives the surface of whatever is being cooked time to dry out and for the texture to become really crispy. With the water removed, the flavor then becomes more concentrated and intense. As we saw when looking at browning in the first chapter, vegetables boiled in water are only ever going to taste like hot versions of themselves. Switch the water for oil, though—oil being a "liquid fat"—and the conditions for the production of intense browning-reaction flavors (the Maillard reaction) are set up. Fat is what makes our KIMCHI AND GRUYÈRE RICE FRITTERS (PAGE 166) crispy when fried. It's what makes our slices of eggplant lightly browned when roasted for CURRY AND COCONUT DAL (see PAGE 152). All the wonderful, intense, interesting flavor and texture is, in short, thanks to the use—or pairing—of fat with the ingredient being cooked.

At the other end of the proceedings, the science can also tell us why fat is such a great way to finish off or complete a dish (rather than to cook with from the start). Take a simple salad—tomato and basil, for example—and it's one thing. It's refreshing and sweet and lovely. That's three things, we know, but you get the picture. Add some slices of mozzarella, or chunks of tangy feta, and it becomes something entirely different. It's no longer just the picture; it's the entire summer vacation. The tangy taste of a sea-salt vacation, to be specific. Add another layer of fat in the form of the requisite olive oil and the dish is complete.

VEGETABLES BOILED IN WATER ARE ONLY EVER GOING TO TASTE LIKE HOT VERSIONS OF THEMSELVES.

The reason the flavor of a good cheese seems to really *fill* the mouth is due to the enzymes from the milk and the rennet and the microbes. These break down the concentrated protein and fat in the cheese into a wide range of flavor compounds. The more diverse the cast of ripening enzymes, the more complex the resulting collection and the richer the flavor will be. The reason barrel-aged feta has a richer and more complex flavor than standard feta is because the enzymes have had longer to ripen (they need six months, rather than the requisite two, to be called "aged") and are, thanks to the beech barrels in which their aging takes place, more diverse.

What the science *doesn't* tell us, though, is the instinctive reason *we*—both in the Ottolenghi test kitchen and in our homes—find ourselves so often reaching for a bottle of olive oil when we are starting or finishing preparation. We reach for it whether we're chopping an onion at the outset or finishing off a dish before serving. We do this for the unashamedly unscientific reason that we just love it. We love the grassy, peppery taste of the oil. We love the green and shiny look of it. To us, a bottle of good-quality olive oil is the Mediterranean sun made liquid.

So, with a little nod to the science and a slightly bigger wink to our appetites, we can have a quick look at the other fats in our recipes and what they are bringing to the dishes they're in.

If olive oil is in the first category of fats—liquid fats—then sunflower oil and butter, once melted and clarified, are part of the same group. You have to match the fat you choose with the dish you are cooking. Butter and olive oil are well suited to rich Italian polenta (see PAGE 163), but when frying fritters (see PAGE 166), on the other hand, you want all the benefits that cooking in oil can bring (a crispy outside, in the case of the fritters) without what's being cooked taking on any of the flavor from the oil. Here, it's oils such as sunflower (or peanut or another mild-flavored variety) that work best.

As well as these "liquid fats," we have used all sorts of dairy products in our recipes, all with a very high fat content. Cheddar cheese has 33 grams of fat per 100 grams, closely followed by Gruyère, Parmesan, feta, and then mozzarella at 17 grams of fat per 100 grams. We hope that putting a figure on the fat does not make anyone balk. Fat is flavor and fat is, in our line of work, good. When reaching for a product that is "fat free" or "low in fat," just remember when something has come out, it needs to be replaced by something else going in. In the case of a lot of low-fat yogurts, for example, this something is often going to be sugar. Give us a spoonful of full-fat, Greek-style plain yogurt any day of the week.

Many is the Ottolenghi recipe, over the years, that has come with the recommendation to serve "with a spoonful of yogurt alongside." In the case of our TOMATO SALAD WITH LIME AND CARDAMOM YOGURT (PAGE 164), up the spoonful to a ladleful so that the yogurt can form the basis of a rich, creamy dressing. Up the ladleful to a whole pot if the dressing is to become an entire sauce, served warm with mafalda pasta (see PAGE 151). Here, the yogurt, with its natural acidity, has the ability to make a pasta sauce that is rich and creamy without any of the "cloying" or "unctuousness" of a cream-based sauce.

Our last category of fats, in these recipes, is vegetable fats such as coconut and avocado. The contribution they bring has to do with both flavor and texture. Cooking the dal for our STUFFED EGGPLANT (see PAGE 152) in coconut milk (with at least 70 percent coconut), again, brings a richness, smoothness, and also sweetness that water alone or a vegetable stock could

TO US, A BOTTLE OF GOOD-QUALITY OLIVE OIL IS THE MEDITERRANEAN SUN MADE LIQUID.

not have done. An avocado is grassy and nutty and rich and buttery to taste, yes, but it also brings an incredible fatty smoothness, like butter, to all with which it is paired. Set it against any or all of the CHEESE TAMALES accompaniments (see PAGE 158)—pickled onions, spicy salsa roja, or chile oil—and the science of pairing fat with sweetness, acidity, and chile heat speaks for itself.

ACIDITY

On the one hand, acidity is really simple. It's a squeeze of lemon, a wedge of lime; it's the vinegar in pickles, the tang of feta. Squeeze that certainty, though, and there's a fair bit of give. Is tanginess quite the same thing as acidity, for example? And while the juice of a lemon is acidic, isn't the zest more floral or citrusy? And might *bitter* be a better word for describing the fruit's pith? Or what about *astringent*? Or *sharp*? Or *sour*? Or *tart*?

We love acidity. We love acidity so much that very few of our recipes *don't* have a pronounced acidic element to them. If Yotam brings lemons to the test-kitchen party, then Ixta walks in with jars full of vinegary quick-pickles under both arms. Noor Murad, our test-kitchen colleague, is also there, blitzing up her favorite dried black Omani limes to flavor tofu (see PAGE 176) or piercing them to add to some BRAISED GREENS WITH YOGURT (PAGE 175). Tomatoes are at the party, too, with their sweet and

ACID HOUSE PARTY, OTTOLENGHI-STYLE!

earthy acidity, bopping along with tamarind pulp, and all the sweet-savory tartness and complexity it brings to the proceedings. Many of the dishes being served at this party would have Greek-style yogurt added to them, and a party is not an Ottolenghi party, as we all know, without sumac and pomegranate molasses. Acid house party, Ottolenghi-style!

So, with our party players assembled, everyone can take a seat and listen to the speeches. First, what actually *is* acidity? Once we've established what it is, we can look at what it *does*. Then we can get back to the party.

Scientifically defined, acids are substances that dissolve in water to release hydrogen ions (i.e., charged atoms). They tend to remove oxygen from other substances and combine it with the hydrogen to form water. If oxygen generally causes food to spoil, then acids act as a preservative. This little controlled experiment will be understood by anyone who's ever made a pot of jam or a jar of ferments or pickles. Any bit of the fruit or vegetable exposed to the air—the top layer of the jam—will develop a layer of mold. Everything below the surface—unexposed to oxygen and preserved by the acetic acid in the vinegar, which inhibits the growth of many microbes—will, meanwhile, be absolutely fine.

Acids are classed as either strong or weak depending on their pH level. The "p" stands for "potential" and the "H" stands for "hydrogen." The pH level depends, therefore, on the quantity of hydrogen ions something can release. Lemon juice is, speaking generally, about 2.1, wine vinegar is about 2.5, ketchup is about 3.9, and yogurt is about 4.0. Milk is about 6.7; distilled water, which is neutral, sits at pH7. Anything above that is alkaline (and would taste soapy to eat).

As ever, our priority is a bit more in-your-face; a bit more "What do we get from this and how does it make our food taste great?" Knowing what acidity is might be all well and good, but what does it *do* for us in the kitchen? The first thing has to do with color, the second with texture, and the third, of course, has to do with flavor.

First: color. As a preservative, adding an acidic substance to certain vegetables and fruit once they're peeled prevents them from losing their color and turning gray. These are the fruit and veg that are prone to oxidation— bananas and apples, artichokes and avocados. Left exposed, they'll discolor. Rub them with a little bit of lemon juice, though, or submerge them in water that has a squeeze of lemon or a capful of vinegar in it, and they'll stay the color you want them to be.

On the other hand, adding acid too soon to certain vegetables will be the precise thing that *causes* them to lose their color and turn gray. Very often, in our recipes, the addition of a dressing to a salad is followed by the slightly unrelaxed instruction to "serve at once." The day won't actually implode if you don't bolt straight to the table and shout at everyone to start eating NOW, but, still, the vibrancy of ASPARAGUS SALAD (see PAGE 171) will diminish fairly quickly once the tamarind and lime dressing is spooned over it. Make the dressing in advance, by all means, and just keep it separate. Everything else can be ready and waiting.

The second great "use" of acidity in the kitchen has to do with texture. The addition of acidic substances to fruit, vegetables, and legumes often causes them to cook much more slowly and, also, to toughen up. The reason we always soak a batch of dried chickpeas in a teaspoon or so of baking soda is the very *opposite*. As baking soda is an alkaline substance, it softens up the chickpeas and so speeds up the cooking time. Adding an acidic substance to one's cooking is totally fine (and often very welcome), but this needs to be done after the onions are softened and sweated down in the pan or after the beans have been cooked.

When you don't cook onions, however, adding something acidic such as vinegar to them will actually start to break down their cell structure rather than harden it. As well as softening onion slices, there is an exchange of flavor the other way—from the onion to the vinegar—which, in turn, can take the harsh edge off the vinegar before it, too, is used in the dish. A mutual mellowing, if you like, as seen in things such as the pickled onions served on top of NOOR'S BLACK LIME TOFU (PAGE 176).

The third—and most exciting—point of acidity in the kitchen has to do with flavor, where the main role it plays is that of balance. Think back to those favorite sandwiches we talked about at the beginning of this chapter. None of these fully makes sense or hits the spot without the acidic element. Together, they offer a great example of how versatile acidity is when it comes to balance, counteracting *fat* (vinegary mustard in Ixta's porchetta sandwich),

TASTING YOUR INGREDIENTS THROUGHOUT THE COOKING PROCESS WILL ALWAYS BE YOUR BEST PARTY TRICK.

sweetness, and *chile heat* (tangy feta in Yotam's roasted vegetable and chile sandwich). This is seen playing out in so many of our recipes: the sumac and lime juice chamoy balancing the sweetness of the maple syrup–roasted carrots in ROASTED CARROT SALAD (see PAGE 187) or the dried black lime or lime juice working to balance the richness of the yogurt in both BRAISED GREENS (see PAGE 175) and CHAAT MASALA POTATOES (see PAGE 193).

The balance works both ways, with the impact of an ingredient's acidity depending very much on what it is paired with. The more maple syrup added to the baking sheet of carrots roasting, for example, the sweeter the dish is going to taste. The pH level of the lime juice or the sumac is not going to change—they will be as inherently acidic as they would be by themselves— but their impact on the dish as a whole will be reduced. It's a balancing act, and you can only set the scales to where you want them to be if you know what you're working with from the outset. It's not just apples and oranges you can't compare when it comes to acidity; you can't really even compare oranges and oranges. Or tomatoes and tomatoes. Or store-bought tamarind paste with making your own from pulp (see PAGE 20). It's why tasting your ingredients throughout the cooking process—before, during, and just prior to serving—will always be your best party trick.

CHILE HEAT

Every time we publish a book, it feels as though the Ottolenghi pantry needs a new shelf. A place to house our latest discoveries and obsessions. For *Flavor*, this new shelf would be full of chiles–fresh chiles, dried chiles, chile flakes, chile pastes, chile oils, chile butters, chile spice mixes, pickled chiles. If Ixta had her way–thanks, Mexico!–we'd have to find a whole new cupboard. We didn't find a cupboard, however, so the kitchen got pretty crowded. It got so crowded because the question of "What's needed?" in a dish was, so often, answered with "chile heat." If we *had* had such a cupboard, though, this is what it might have looked like.

On one shelf we'd have bowls of fresh chiles. These would be the Fresno or serrade varieties–those often sold in supermarkets as just regular "chiles"– in both red and green. The difference between the two is one of ripeness. As with bell peppers (a member of the chile family, albeit one without the "heat"), green chiles are unripe and not as sweet as those that are ripe and red.

The Scoville scale, devised in 1912, assesses how hot a chile is. It counts the number of times that extracts of chile dissolved in alcohol can be diluted with sugar water before the capsaicin (the compound that makes them hot) is no longer discernible to the palate. The more heat units it scores, the more fiery the chile. Sweet peppers (aka bell peppers) score zero. Our "regular" Fresno or

THE QUESTION OF "WHAT'S NEEDED?" IN A DISH WAS, SO OFTEN, ANSWERED WITH "CHILE HEAT."

serrade chiles score between 2,500 and 8,000. There's always quite a range because the amount of capsaicin in individual chiles of the same type can vary dramatically. Between types, the range is obviously dramatically wider; jalapeño and cayenne score around 3,000 on the scale, tabasco chiles around 60,000, and habaneros from 100,000 to 300,000.

As we said previously, chiles are hot because they contain capsaicin. Capsaicin is a flavorless, odorless compound found in the chile flesh. It's concentrated particularly in the white ribs inside the chile where the seeds are (this is why we are asked to seed a chile to moderate its heat; as you shave away the seeds, which aren't actually hot, you also remove the hot white ribs). It's this, the capsaicin, that binds to pain receptors on the tongue and creates a sensation of burning. This increases as the green chiles ripen but then loses its fire the riper, redder, and sweeter they become. If you want the hottest fresh chiles, choose those that are at the turning point from green to red.

The flavor of a fresh chile can be dialed right up through being charred, as we do with the fresh chiles in our SPICY BERBERE RATATOUILLE (see PAGE 209). Charring, as we saw on PAGES 25–27, concentrates flavor. It imparts complexity, bitterness, and sweetness. It's what gives many a sauce or salsa that extra depth of flavor, the thing that takes them to "the next level." Another way of dialing up the flavor of fresh chiles is to pickle them, as we do for SAFFRON TAGLIATELLE WITH RICOTTA AND CRISPY CHIPOTLE SHALLOTS (PAGE 199), where they're spooned over the top as a wake-up garnish before serving. If charring intensifies flavor, then pickling softens the kick, allowing the chiles to bring their "stand to attention" freshness to all the other elements in a dish.

So that's the fresh chile shelf: chiles as they are, chiles heading off to be charred, and fresh chiles in jars, quickly pickled. The next shelf (or three) would be for the dried chiles. This is where we'd have to be disciplined about how much space we'd allow and how much of the globe we'd be allowed to trot over in our search for chiles (a very tiny fraction, it turns out). There

THERE ARE VERY FEW THINGS NOT IMPROVED BY THE ADDITION OF FAT AND HEAT COMBINED.

would be jars full of whole dried chiles, ready to be crumbled or steeped into a slowly cooked dish. Smoky chipotle chiles would be there, the dried and mild version of the jalapeño chile. Round and red cascabels, as well, from central Mexico, which are sweet and nutty and woody. Their name means "little bell" in Spanish, on account of the sound the loose seeds make inside the pod when they're shaken. Mexican ancho chiles would also be in permanent residence. These are the dried and wide ("wide" being what "ancho" means in Spanish) version of the poblano chile. They're fruity and sweet and mild in their heat.

Then we'd have little jars full of dried chiles that have been blitzed up to become chile flakes. We might have to color-code these, just for fun. Bright red bell pepper flakes would be at one end, imparting their vibrant color into infusions. Next to these would be burgundy Aleppo chile flakes. Like the bell pepper flakes, these are as much about the color and sweet aroma they bring to a sauce, such as our BLOOD ORANGE NAM JIM (see PAGE 202), as they are about their heat, which is mild. Next to them would be the chipotle chile flakes and then, alongside and far darker in color, would be the small pots of crimson—almost black—Turkish Urfa chile flakes. If you can't find Urfa chile flakes, you can use an equal amount of crushed ancho or chipotle chile flakes.

It's these top shelves that we'd be reaching for to infuse the numbing oil for our CABBAGE WITH GINGER CREAM (see PAGE 196), or for making chile butter to smear over roasted cauliflower (see PAGE 205). In terms of pairing, in fact, there are very few things not improved by the addition of fat (butter) and heat (chile) combined. Eggs, chicken, tofu, all vegetables, fish, rice; the CHILE BUTTER ON PAGE 205 can sit for two weeks on the shelf (in the fridge, this time), ready to be used as a rub or melted to become a marinade or final garnish.

These top shelves are where we'd also be reaching to make our own chile pastes were it not for the fact that great-quality chile pastes are so easy and available to buy. As such, for the purposes of our imaginary chile-filled cupboard, we'd have shelves given over to all corners of the world. North African rose harissa, bringing its rose-softened kick to our SUPER-SOFT ZUCCHINI (see PAGE 204), along with Korean gochujang fermented chile paste. Argentinian chimichurri, Tripolitan Jewish chraimeh sauce, Louisianan hot sauce, Mexican Luchito smoked chile paste, Thai nam prik, African piri piri, Malaysian sambal, Thai sriracha, Middle Eastern zhoug and shatta; there would be few days and few simple suppers not pepped up with a spoonful or two of one of these.

Any or all of these chiles and pastes and oils and powders are just so useful to have around because, when thinking about food pairing, they can shoot in virtually any direction, even desserts, as in our TANGERINE AND ANCHO CHILE FLAN (PAGE 278). Chiles' great gift, for us, is their ability to somehow marry together a range of flavors—or even to wake up the palate to the existence of these other flavors—and, in so doing, to create a singular harmony. We just need to find a big enough cupboard to keep everything in.

SWEET POTATO IN TOMATO, LIME, AND CARDAMOM SAUCE

SERVES FOUR
As a main

4–5 medium sweet potatoes, skin on, cut crosswise into 1-inch/2½cm-thick rounds (2 lb 2 oz/1kg)
2 tbsp olive oil
4½ tsp maple syrup
½ tsp ground cardamom
½ tsp ground cumin
table salt and black pepper

TOMATO, LIME, AND CARDAMOM SAUCE
5 tbsp/75ml olive oil
6 garlic cloves, finely chopped (not crushed)
2 green chiles, finely chopped (seeded for less heat)
table salt
2 small shallots, finely chopped (¾ cup/100g)
1 × 14-oz/400g can whole, peeled tomatoes, blitzed in a food processor or blender until smooth
1 tbsp tomato paste
1½ tsp superfine sugar
1½ tsp ground cardamom
1 tsp ground cumin
2 limes: finely zest to get 1 tsp, then juice to get 1 tbsp; cut the remainder into wedges
1 cup/240ml water

2 tsp finely chopped dill

This dish has had countless incarnations. It started its life as mackerel kofte in a sauce made with tomato, lime, and cardamom that we fell in love with. It then went through a range of vegan dumplings served in the same sauce. In the end, after an embarrassing number of attempts and every member of the crew giving it a go, we figured that simply roasted sweet potato works best. It is a brilliant combination, but the sauce would also be delicious with chickpeas, tofu, fish, or chicken. In any case, serve rice or couscous alongside.

1. Preheat the oven to 500°F/240°C fan. Line a large baking sheet with parchment paper.

2. In a large bowl, mix the sweet potatoes with the olive oil, maple syrup, cardamom, cumin, ½ tsp salt, and a good grind of pepper. Spread out on the prepared baking sheet, cover tightly with aluminum foil, and bake for 25 minutes. Remove the foil and return to the oven for 10–12 minutes, or until the rounds are cooked through and the undersides are very nicely browned (this might take longer if your sweet potato rounds are particularly large, or indeed less time if they are smaller, so do keep an eye on them).

3. For the sauce: Meanwhile, put the olive oil, garlic, chiles, and ⅛ tsp salt into a large sauté pan, for which you have a lid, and place on medium heat. Fry very gently for 8–10 minutes, stirring every now and then, until the garlic is soft and fragrant (you don't want the garlic to brown or become crisp, so decrease the heat if necessary). Transfer half the oil, chiles, and garlic to a small bowl, leaving the rest in the pan. Add the shallots to the pan and cook for 5 minutes, stirring often, until soft and translucent. Add the blitzed tomatoes, tomato paste, sugar, cardamom, cumin, lime zest, and 1 tsp salt and cook for 5 minutes, stirring a few times. Add the water, bring to a gentle simmer, and then cook for 5 minutes.

4. Transfer the sweet potatoes, browned-side up, to the pan of sauce (not all of them will fit in the sauce, but that's fine, just pile them up haphazardly). Decrease the heat to low, cover, and continue to cook for 10 minutes.

5. Mix the dill and lime juice with the reserved chile and garlic oil and drizzle over the sweet potatoes. Serve from the pan, with the lime wedges alongside.

BUTTERNUT, ORANGE, AND SAGE GALETTE

SERVES FOUR
As a main

PASTRY
¾ cup/100g all-purpose flour, plus more to dust
¼ cup/30g whole-wheat flour
2 tbsp quick-cook polenta
1 tbsp finely chopped sage leaves, (about 6 leaves)
1½ tsp superfine sugar
¾ tsp flaked sea salt
¼ tsp black pepper
4 tsp olive oil
6 tbsp/80g unsalted butter, fridge cold and cut into ½-inch/1½cm cubes
¼ cup/60ml ice-cold water

1 small butternut squash, skin on, seeded and sliced into ½-inch/1cm-thick half-moons (1½ lb/680g)
2 carrots, peeled and cut into ½-inch/1cm rounds (6⅓ oz/180g)
2 tbsp olive oil, plus more to drizzle
2 tbsp finely chopped sage leaves, plus whole leaves to serve
2 tsp caraway seeds, toasted and roughly crushed
table salt and black pepper
1 head of garlic, top fifth cut off to expose the cloves
1 large shallot, skin on, top trimmed to expose the shallot (5¾ oz/160g)
2–3 oranges: finely zest to get 1½ tsp, then juice to get ⅔ cup/160ml
3 tbsp maple syrup
½ cup plus 1 tbsp/125g mascarpone
1 egg, beaten

The hyper-flaky pastry, which is rich from the butter and crunchy from the polenta, is the star here. Double it and keep half in the freezer, ready to use in all sorts of savory bakes.

1. For the pastry: Mix together both flours, the polenta, sage, sugar, salt, pepper, and olive oil in a large bowl. Add the butter and incorporate by lightly squashing each cube between your fingers. Don't over-work; you want chunks throughout the dough. Add the water and use your hands to gather the dough together—it will be quite sticky. Transfer to a well-floured work surface and roll into an 11 x 7-inch/28 x 18cm rectangle, dusting the rolling pin, surface, and pastry as you go. Fold the longer ends toward each other so they meet at the center and roll out once. Fold the shorter ends the same way, roll out once, then fold in half to make a square. Form the dough into a 5½-inch/14cm-wide circle, wrap tightly with plastic wrap, and refrigerate for 30 minutes.

2. Preheat the oven to 450°F/220°C fan. Line two large baking sheets with parchment paper. Toss the squash and carrots with the 2 tbsp olive oil, 1 tbsp of the chopped sage, the caraway seeds, 1 tsp salt, and plenty of pepper. Spread out on the prepared baking sheets. Drizzle the garlic head and shallot with a little oil, wrap individually in aluminum foil, and add to the sheets. Roast the squash and carrots for 25 minutes, or until golden brown, and remove from the oven. Continue to roast the garlic and shallot for 15 minutes more, then set aside. When cool enough to handle, squeeze the garlic and shallot from their papery skins and finely chop.

3. Decrease the oven temperature to 450°F/200°C fan. Line a baking sheet with parchment paper. Transfer the dough to a well-floured surface and roll out to a 12-inch/30cm circle, dusting your rolling pin as you go. Gently lift the dough onto the prepared baking sheet and refrigerate for 30 minutes.

4. Put the orange juice and maple syrup into a small saucepan on medium-high heat and cook for about 10 minutes, or until the liquid reduces to the consistency of a thickened, sticky maple syrup.

5. Put the mascarpone into a bowl with the chopped garlic and shallot, orange zest, and remaining 1 tbsp chopped sage. Season with a pinch of salt and plenty of pepper and stir everything together well.

6. Spread the mascarpone mixture over the dough, leaving a 1½-inch/4cm rim around the edge. Cover with the squash and carrots, then drizzle with the orange syrup. Fold the pastry up and over the vegetables, brush the pastry with the egg, and bake for 30 minutes, until golden brown. Let cool for 20 minutes, then scatter with sage leaves before serving.

FUSION CAPONATA WITH SILKEN TOFU

SERVES FOUR
As a main or six as
a starter

2 medium eggplants, cut into ½-inch/1½cm chunks (6 cups/550g)
½ cup/120ml sunflower oil
table salt
1 small celery stalk, chopped into ¼-inch/½cm cubes (⅔ cup/65g)
3 tbsp pine nuts, very well toasted
3 oz/80g sweet ripe cherry tomatoes, roughly chopped
¾ oz/20g fresh ginger, peeled and julienned
5–6 green onions, finely sliced (¾ cup/60g)
3¾ tsp mixed black and white sesame seeds, toasted
¼ cup/40g raisins
¼ cup/60ml soy sauce
7 tbsp/105ml Shaoxing wine (or pale dry sherry)
3 tbsp rice vinegar
7½ tsp maple syrup
3 large, mild red chiles: 2 left whole, 1 seeded and finely sliced
1 tbsp water
2 × 10½-oz/300g blocks silken tofu, each cut into 8 × ½-inch/1½cm-thick slices
flaked sea salt

The word *fusion* is greeted with suspicion these days. For cooking to be described as fusion is almost to say, without saying, that it is confused and lacks focus. This is odd, really, since ideas travel across the world at the speed it takes to refresh a cell-phone screen, and many chefs and home cooks seem perfectly happy to dabble in plenty of mixing and matching. When done considerately, cross-cultural hybrids can be both eye-opening and delicious. In fact, every kitchen classic was probably considered as fusion at some point in time. Here, caponata (a sweet and sour Sicilian eggplant dish) meets mapo tofu (a spicy and aromatic Szechuan tofu dish) in a union so wrong it's right.

Serve as an elegant starter, or as a main with some sticky rice and sautéed greens. The caponata will keep in a sealed container in the fridge for up to 1 week and the flavor only gets better with time. Try it in a grilled cheese sandwich in place of pickles.

1. Preheat the oven to 450°F/210°C fan. Line a large baking sheet with parchment paper.

2. Toss the eggplants with 5 tbsp/75ml of the sunflower oil and ¼ tsp table salt and spread out on the prepared baking sheet. Roast for 15 minutes, stir well, then add the celery and continue to roast for 15 minutes, until dark golden brown. Set aside to cool, then transfer to a large bowl with the pine nuts, tomatoes, and three-fourths each of the ginger, green onions, and sesame seeds. Set aside.

3. Put the raisins, soy sauce, Shaoxing wine, vinegar, and maple syrup into a small saucepan on medium-high heat and warm until bubbling. Set aside to soak for 10 minutes, then add to the bowl of eggplants.

4. Place a small frying pan on high heat and, once very hot, add the whole chiles and cook for about 9 minutes, turning them a few times until well charred on all sides. Set aside to cool for 5 minutes, then roughly chop them, removing the seeds if you prefer less heat. Add to the bowl of eggplants.

5. Heat the remaining 3 tbsp sunflower oil in a small saucepan until bubbling, then pour over the eggplant mixture. Add the water, gently mix everything together, and let this caponata marinate for at least 2 hours, or up to overnight.

6. Divide the tofu among four to six shallow bowls and sprinkle generously with flaked sea salt. Spoon the caponata next to the tofu, drizzling about 1 tbsp of the liquid over the whole dish. Top with the remaining ginger, green onions, sesame seeds, and sliced chiles and serve at room temperature.

ESME'S ROUGH SQUASH MASH

SERVES FOUR
As a side or six
as a dip

2 small butternut squash, peeled, seeded, and cut into 1½-inch/4cm chunks (8 cups/1.2kg)

5 tbsp/75ml olive oil

4½ tsp maple syrup

2 tbsp white or other miso paste

2 jalapeños, halved lengthwise

½ tsp ground cinnamon

½ tsp ground cumin

4 garlic cloves, peeled and crushed with the side of a knife

2 tbsp water

½ tsp table salt

2 limes: finely zest to get 1½ tsp, then cut into wedges

1 green onion, finely sliced into 1½-inch/4cm-long strips

Esme Howarth, a friend, ex–test kitchen colleague, and chef of great talent, has a particular knack for creating flavor-packed one-pan dishes with minimal effort. This mash is an incredibly easy and delicious case in point. It can double up as a warm side dish and as a dip, at room temperature, served with plenty of bread and olive oil. Other varieties of squash, such as kabocha, would work equally well here.

The mash can be made the day before and reheated gently, or served at room temperature, if you want to get ahead.

1. Preheat the oven to 450°F/220°C fan.

2. In a high-sided baking dish, combine the squash, 3 tbsp of the olive oil, maple syrup, miso, jalapeños, cinnamon, cumin, garlic, water, and salt so that everything fits snugly. Mix well, cover with aluminum foil, and roast for 40 minutes, until beginning to soften. Remove the foil, then continue to roast for 35–40 minutes, or until very soft and browned on top. Remove the jalapeños, finely slice them, and set aside.

3. Roughly mash the squash with a fork or potato masher, then drizzle with the remaining 2 tbsp olive oil and squeeze in the juice from half the lime wedges. Finish with the lime zest, green onion, and jalapeño slices and serve with the remaining lime wedges alongside.

ISRAELI COUSCOUS AND SQUASH IN TOMATO AND STAR ANISE SAUCE

SERVES FOUR
As a main

½ **butternut squash**
(1 lb 10 oz/750g),
skin on, seeded, cut
into ¾-inch/2cm
wedges, and then
halved crosswise
3 tsp **ground cinnamon**
8 **garlic cloves,** crushed
7 tbsp/105ml **olive oil**
table salt and black
pepper
2 **large onions** (12¾ oz/
360g): 1 cut into ½-inch/
1cm-thick rounds,
1 finely chopped
2½ tsp **superfine sugar**
4 whole **star anise**
¼ tsp **chile flakes**
1 lb 10 oz/750g **plum**
tomatoes (6–7),
coarsely grated and
skins discarded
(3⅓ cups/600g)
1 tbsp **tomato paste**
3½ cups/840ml **water**
1⅓ cups/250g **Israeli**
couscous
scant 6 cups/250g **baby**
spinach
¾ cup/15g **cilantro,**
roughly chopped

If you are lucky, you will get a crisp, caramelized layer of couscous at the bottom of the pan. It doesn't happen every time, but it will still be totally delicious without it.

1. Preheat the oven to 475°F/230°C fan. Line two baking sheets with parchment paper. Toss the squash with 1 tsp of the cinnamon, one-fourth of the garlic, 2 tbsp of the olive oil, ¾ tsp salt, and a good grind of pepper. Spread out on one of the prepared baking sheets and bake for 30 minutes, until cooked through and nicely browned.

2. Meanwhile, place the onion rounds, keeping them intact, on the second prepared sheet and drizzle with 1½ tsp olive oil. Sprinkle with ½ tsp of the sugar and a pinch of salt and pepper. Bake for 18 minutes, flipping the rounds halfway through, or until softened and deeply charred. Keep warm.

3. While the vegetables are roasting, put 3 tbsp olive oil into a large sauté pan, for which you have a lid, on medium-high heat. Add the chopped onion and star anise and cook, stirring occasionally, for 8 minutes, or until softened and browned. Add the remaining garlic and remaining 2 tsp cinnamon and cook for 30 seconds more, or until fragrant. Add the chile flakes, tomatoes, tomato paste, remaining 2 tsp sugar, 1½ tsp salt, and a good grind of pepper. Cook for 8 minutes, stirring often, until thickened, then pour in 2 cups/480ml of the water and bring to a boil. Decrease the heat to medium and simmer for 30 minutes, or until the sauce is thick and rich. Measure out 1⅔ cups/400ml of sauce (leaving the star anise in the pan) into a separate saucepan and keep warm.

4. Meanwhile, add the couscous to the sauté pan and mix well to combine. Add the remaining 1½ cups/360ml water and ¼ tsp salt and bring to a boil on medium-hight. Cover, decrease the heat to medium, and let cook for 30 minutes, or until all the liquid is absorbed and the edges of the couscous have crisped up.

5. Put 1 tbsp olive oil into a large frying pan on medium-high heat. Add the spinach, ⅛ tsp salt, and a good grind of pepper and cook until barely wilted, about 2 minutes. Stir in the cilantro and set aside.

6. Top the couscous with the reserved sauce, squash, and spinach, layering as you go, and finish with the onion rounds. Drizzle with the remaining 1½ tsp olive oil and serve warm.

ONE-PAN ORECCHIETTE PUTTANESCA

SERVES FOUR
As a main

5 tbsp/75ml olive oil
6 garlic cloves, crushed
1 × 15-oz/425g can
  chickpeas, drained
  well and patted dry
  (1¾ cups/240g; reserve
  the chickpea water to
  make the coconut ice
  cream on page 286)
2 tsp hot smoked
  paprika
2 tsp ground cumin
2 tsp tomato paste
table salt
2 cups/40g parsley,
  roughly chopped
2 tsp lemon zest
3 tbsp baby capers
¾ cup/125g Nocellara
  olives (or other green
  olive), pitted and
  roughly chopped in
  half (⅔ cup/80g)
9 oz/250g small, sweet
  cherry tomatoes
2 tsp superfine sugar
1½ tsp caraway seeds,
  lightly toasted and
  crushed
9 oz/250g dried
  orecchiette pasta
2 cups/480ml vegetable
  or chicken stock
¾ cup plus 2 tbsp/
  200ml water
black pepper

This is a sweetened version of puttanesca—the famous pasta sauce from Naples "in the style of the prostitute"—minus the anchovies, plus chickpeas and spices. It's quick and super-practical to make because the pasta actually cooks in the sauce. Try it, and you may not feel the need to boil pasta ever again.

1. In a large sauté pan, for which you have a lid, combine 3 tbsp of the olive oil, the garlic, chickpeas, paprika, cumin, tomato paste, and ½ tsp salt and place on medium-high heat. Fry for 12 minutes, uncovered, stirring every now and then, until the chickpeas are slightly crisp—you may need to decrease the heat if they start to color too much. Remove one-third of the chickpeas and set aside.

2. In a small bowl, combine the parsley, lemon zest, capers, and olives. Add two-thirds of the parsley mixture to the sauté pan, along with the cherry tomatoes, sugar, and caraway seeds and cook for 2 minutes on medium-high heat, stirring often. Add the pasta, stock, water, and ¾ tsp salt and bring to a simmer. Decrease the heat to medium, cover, and cook for 12–14 minutes, or until the pasta is al dente.

3. Stir the remaining parsley mixture into the pan, drizzle with the remaining 2 tbsp olive oil, and garnish with the reserved fried chickpeas and a good grind of pepper. Serve at once.

CHARRED PEPPERS AND FRESH CORN POLENTA WITH SOY-CURED YOLK

SERVES FOUR
As a main

5 tbsp/75ml soy sauce
4 good-quality rich-yolk eggs
12 small mixed red, orange, and yellow Romano peppers, stems left on (2 lb 6 oz/1.1kg)
1 head of garlic, top fifth cut off to expose the cloves, plus 2 cloves, skin on, crushed with the side of a knife
table salt and black pepper
1 tbsp maple syrup
1 tsp apple cider vinegar
⅓ oz/10g thyme sprigs
1 lemon: finely zest to get ½ tsp, then finely shave the remaining peel to get 5 strips
¼ cup/60ml olive oil

POLENTA
4–6 small ears fresh corn, kernels shaved off (scant 4 cups/500g), or scant 4 cups/500g frozen corn kernels (defrosted)
3 tbsp unsalted butter
¾ cup/180g Greek-style yogurt
1½ oz/40g Parmesan, finely grated
1¼ tsp table salt
2½ cups/600ml water
⅔ cup/100g quick-cook polenta

olive oil to drizzle
¼ cup/5g basil, finely shredded
table salt and black pepper
Freshly grated Parmesan to serve

Curing egg yolks in soy, as we do here, adds creaminess, complexity, and a hit of umami to this polenta. It's a nifty technique to add to your repertoire, and the process couldn't be simpler. You can use these to top any grain-based dishes, such as pasta or rice, or thick soups. Good-quality eggs, preferably organic with rich yolks, are best here, as they will be eaten raw.

Roast and marinate the peppers up to 3 days before, if you like. The polenta will set quite quickly, so it is best made just before serving.

1. Put the soy sauce into a medium bowl. Separate the eggs, carefully adding the yolks to the bowl of soy sauce. (Reserve the whites for another recipe.) Let the yolks cure for a minimum of 1 hour or up to 2 hours, very gently turning them halfway through with a spoon. Don't cure the yolks for any longer—you want them to be soft and oozy.

2. Preheat the oven to 450°F/220°C fan. Line a large baking sheet with parchment paper.

3. Place the mixed peppers on the prepared baking sheet and spread out as much as possible. Sprinkle the whole garlic head with a little salt and pepper and wrap tightly in aluminum foil. Place on the sheet with the peppers and roast for 20 minutes, then carefully turn the peppers and roast for another 10 minutes, until they are cooked through and blackened in places. (We like the skin, but if you prefer to peel the peppers, do this now.) Place the peppers in a large bowl with the crushed raw garlic, maple syrup, vinegar, thyme, lemon peel, olive oil, ¼ tsp salt, and a good grind of pepper. Once cool enough to handle, unwrap the cooked garlic and squeeze the cloves into the bowl with the peppers, discarding the papery skin. Gently mix the peppers, keeping the stems intact, then cover with a large plate and let marinate for at least 1 hour, or up to overnight.

4. For the polenta: Put the corn kernels into a food processor and blitz to a wet paste. Transfer to a large sauté pan on medium heat and add the butter, yogurt, Parmesan, salt, and water. Cook for 7 minutes, then decrease the heat to low and sprinkle in the polenta, stirring continuously to avoid lumps, for another 5 minutes, until cooked.

5. Divide the polenta among four bowls, then top with three peppers each, drizzling with some of the marinade but avoiding the aromatics. Carefully lift a yolk out of the soy sauce and place on the polenta, next to the peppers. Finish with a good drizzle of olive oil, along with the basil, lemon zest, a sprinkle of salt, a good grind of pepper, and some freshly grated Parmesan.

MAKES EIGHT
OMELETTES
Serves two to four

OMELETTES
2 tbsp sunflower oil
3 garlic cloves, crushed
2 green chiles, finely
    chopped (seeded for
    less heat)
3 shallots, finely chopped
¼ oz/5g fresh ginger,
    peeled and finely
    chopped
table salt
¾ tsp ground turmeric
1 lime: finely zest to
    get 1 tsp, then cut
    into wedges
6 eggs
**1 × 13½-oz/400ml can
    full-fat coconut milk**

GRAPEFRUIT
DIPPING SAUCE
**½ cup/120ml pink
    grapefruit juice,**
    including the bits
    (from 1–2 grapefruits)
2 tbsp rice vinegar
2 tbsp mirin
1 tbsp lime juice
2 red chiles, finely
    chopped (seeded
    for less heat)
⅛ tsp table salt

SALAD
5 green onions, julienned
    (rounded ¾ cup/50g)
¾ cup/15g mint leaves
**¾ cup/15g cilantro
    leaves**
¾ cup/70g bean sprouts
**2½ oz/70g breakfast
    or rainbow radishes,**
    finely sliced

¼ cup/60ml sunflower oil

COCONUT AND TURMERIC OMELETTE FEAST

These are much thinner than your average omelette, more like crêpes, in fact, but without the flour. They are meant to be eaten like bánh xèo (Vietnamese pancakes), stuffing the herb salad into the omelettes and dipping the whole thing into the sauce. It's a messy business, but that's half the fun.

Use a coconut milk with a high percentage of coconut, 70 percent or more, if possible (the ingredient list on the can should specify the percentage).

You can make the batter the day before, if you want to get ahead. The omelettes themselves can be fried up to 2 hours before serving, carefully lay them on a parchment-lined baking sheet as you finish cooking them, ready to be reheated for a few minutes in a very hot oven (450°F/220°C fan) when you're ready to serve.

1. For the omelettes: Put the sunflower oil into a large, nonstick frying pan, for which you have a lid, on medium-high heat. Add the garlic, chiles, shallots, ginger, and ½ tsp salt and fry gently, uncovered, for 8–10 minutes, stirring often, until soft and golden. Set aside to cool for 5 minutes.

2. In a large bowl, whisk the turmeric, lime zest, eggs, coconut milk, and ½ tsp salt until smooth and combined, then stir in the cooled shallot mixture. Transfer to a large liquid measuring cup.

3. For the dipping sauce: In a large bowl, combine the grapefruit juice, vinegar, mirin, lime juice, chiles, and salt and stir to combine. Set aside.

4. For the salad: In a large bowl, combine the green onions, mint, cilantro, bean sprouts, and radishes and toss together.

5. Line a baking sheet with parchment paper. Wipe the frying pan clean and return it to high heat. Once very hot, add 1½ tsp of the sunflower oil. Pour in about ½ cup/100g of the omelette batter and swirl to coat most of the pan. Fry for 1½ minutes, until the bottom is golden brown, then cover with the lid and continue to cook for another 20–30 seconds, or until the top is set. Transfer to the prepared baking sheet and keep warm in a very low oven. Continue with the remaining sunflower oil and batter in the same way until you have eight omelettes.

6. Carefully arrange the omelettes on a large platter, golden-brown-side up. They are very delicate, so they might naturally fold or tear, which is fine. Serve hot, with the salad, dipping sauce, and lime wedges alongside.

ROMANO PEPPER SCHNITZELS

SERVES FOUR
As a starter

MARIE ROSE SAUCE (OPTIONAL)
1 head of garlic, top fifth cut off to expose the cloves
table salt and black pepper
6⅓ oz/180g cherry tomatoes
4 large red chiles
1 tbsp maple syrup
2 tsp Worcestershire sauce
½ tsp chipotle flakes (or 1 whole chipotle chile, minced to yield ½ tsp)
¼ cup/60g mayonnaise

8 red Romano peppers (1 lb 14 oz/850g)
flaked sea salt
¾ cup/100g all-purpose flour
black pepper
4 eggs, beaten
2 cups/100g panko breadcrumbs
6 tbsp/60g white or black sesame seeds, or a mixture of both
16 fresh makrut lime leaves, stems discarded, finely chopped
1 tbsp nori sprinkles (or finely blitz a sheet of nori in a spice grinder and use 1 tbsp)
2½ cups/600ml sunflower oil
2 limes: finely zest to get 2 tsp, then cut into wedges

In 2016, the German minister for agriculture called for a ban on vegetable-based foods being named after their meat-based counterparts, claiming terms such as "vegetarian schnitzel" were unsettling and misleading. Ours aren't vegetarian schnitzels, they are vegetable schnitzels, which is a semantic difference but quite a big one. In any case, we hope that our choice of title does not offend, but if you do have any doubts about whether these can live up to the original, we're confident they'll be dispelled once you try them.

The sauce is a take on the classic Marie Rose but turbocharged, with heavily charred chiles and tomatoes and a whole head of garlic. Double the recipe, if you like; it's great in sandwiches. The fried peppers work perfectly well without the sauce, if you'd rather not make it, and just a squeeze of lime.

Make a decadent meal out of these peppers and serve with oven fries (see page 89) and cucumber, za'atar, and chopped lemon salad (page 191). *Pictured on pages 148–149.*

1. Preheat the oven to 475°F/230°C fan. Line two large baking sheets with parchment paper.

2. For the sauce: Sprinkle the garlic head with some table salt and pepper, then wrap tightly in aluminum foil and place on a prepared baking sheet with the tomatoes and chiles. Roast for 30 minutes, until the tomatoes and chiles begin to blacken and blister. Remove from the oven and, when cool, squeeze the garlic into the bowl of a small food processor, discarding the skins. Add the tomatoes, chiles (seeded for less heat), maple syrup, Worcestershire sauce, chipotle flakes, and ¼ tsp table salt and blitz to a coarse paste. Let cool completely, then mix in the mayonnaise and refrigerate for up to 1 week.

3. Meanwhile, cut a vertical 2-inch/5cm slit in the base of each Romano pepper and place on the second prepared baking sheet (you can roast the peppers at the same time as the garlic and tomatoes, toward the bottom of the oven). Roast for 16 minutes, turning the peppers over halfway through, until cooked and beginning to blacken a little. Transfer to a sieve, cut-side down, to drain any liquid, taking care to keep the stems intact. Once cool enough to handle, carefully peel away as much of the skin as possible without puncturing the flesh, then sprinkle each Romano pepper with a good pinch of flaked sea salt and set aside.

4. Prepare three shallow containers long enough to fit the length of the peppers. Mix the flour with 1 tsp flaked sea salt and plenty of black pepper in the first container. Put the eggs into the second container. In the last container, mix the panko breadcrumbs, sesame seeds, lime leaves, nori, 2 tsp flaked sea salt, and a generous grind of pepper.

5. Set a large metal rack over a baking sheet (on which to place the panko-coated peppers). Prepare a separate sheet lined with plenty of paper towels (on which to place the fried peppers). Dip each Romano pepper into the flour, then into the egg, and finally into the panko mixture, shaking any excess off as you go, and lay it on the prepared rack while you repeat with the rest of the peppers.

6. Pour the sunflower oil into a large, high-sided sauté pan or wok and place on medium-high heat. Once very hot (355°F/180°C if you have a thermometer), carefully lower two peppers into the oil and fry for 1½–2 minutes on each side, until golden brown and crisp. Transfer to the prepared sheet and repeat with the remaining peppers.

7. Serve the peppers right away, with the lime zest and some flaked sea salt sprinkled on top and the lime wedges and sauce alongside.

SERVES TWO
As a main

MAFALDA AND ROASTED BUTTERNUT IN WARM YOGURT SAUCE

QUICK CHILE SAUCE
1 plum tomato, roughly chopped (½ cup/90g)
3 red chiles, seeded and roughly chopped (½ cup/45g)
¼ tsp table salt
4½ tsp cider vinegar
2 tbsp olive oil

1 butternut squash (2 lb 2 oz/1kg), peeled, seeded, and cut into roughly 1-inch/2½cm cubes (8 cups/850g)
1 onion, peeled and cut into 6 wedges
6 tbsp/90ml olive oil
table salt and black pepper
6 garlic cloves, thinly sliced
7 oz/200g short mafalda pasta (or other dried pasta, cooking time adjusted if necessary)
2 cups plus 2 tbsp/500g Greek-style yogurt, at room temperature
1¼ tsp ground cumin
2 egg yolks
1½ tsp cornstarch
¼ cup/5g parsley leaves, roughly chopped, plus more to serve

Yogurt, as opposed to cream, has a natural acidity, so it makes creamy pasta sauces that are rich but not in any way cloying or unctuous. These are found all over the Middle East, but aren't quite as popular elsewhere. Try this version, where a tomato-chile sauce helps cut the fattiness even further. Yogurt can split when heated, so egg yolks and flour are often used to stabilize it, as they do here. Cooking the sauce slowly will give you the smoothest result, so don't try to speed up the process by increasing the heat.

The quick chile sauce is excellent to have on hand. Double or triple the quantities, if you like—it will keep in the fridge for up to 2 weeks, ready to be used as a condiment in sandwiches, or alongside grilled meats, tofu, or fish.

1. For the chile sauce: Put the tomato, chiles, and salt into the bowl of a small food processor and blitz until finely minced, scraping down the sides of the bowl. Add the vinegar and olive oil and pulse for a few seconds more. Transfer to a small bowl and set aside.

2. Preheat the oven to 475°F/230°C fan. Line a baking sheet with parchment paper, and line a plate with a double layer of paper towel.

3. Put the squash, onion, 3 tbsp of the olive oil, ¾ tsp salt, and a good grind of pepper into a medium bowl and mix well to combine. Transfer to the prepared baking sheet and roast for about 30 minutes, stirring once or twice, until softened and charred. Keep warm until ready to use.

4. Meanwhile, put the garlic and 2 tbsp olive oil into a small frying pan and place on medium heat. Cook gently, stirring occasionally, until the garlic becomes deeply golden and crispy, about 12 minutes. Reserving the oil, use a slotted spoon to transfer the garlic to the prepared plate.

5. Cook the pasta in plenty of salted boiling water until almost al dente, about 7 minutes. Reserving ¾ cup plus 2 tbsp/200ml of cooking liquid, drain the pasta well.

6. Put the yogurt, remaining 1 tbsp olive oil, cumin, egg yolks, cornstarch, and ¼ tsp salt into a blender and blitz until smooth, about 1 minute. Pour the mixture into a large sauté pan on medium heat. Cook, stirring continuously, until thickened and just beginning to bubble, about 15 minutes. Add the pasta, reserved pasta water, chopped parsley, and half the squash mixture and cook for another 4 minutes, or until just heated through. Transfer to a large serving platter and top with the remaining squash mixture. Drizzle with one-third of the chile sauce and top with the fried garlic, parsley, and reserved garlic oil. Serve with the remaining chile sauce alongside.

STUFFED EGGPLANT IN CURRY AND COCONUT DAL

SERVES FOUR
As a main

3 large eggplants, stems removed, each eggplant cut lengthwise into 6 × ¼-inch/½cm-thick slices (6 cups/750g)
3 tbsp olive oil
table salt and black pepper

COCONUT DAL
3 tbsp olive oil
5 shallots, peeled and finely chopped (1⅔ cups/250g)
1½ oz/45g fresh ginger, peeled and finely chopped
2 red chiles, finely chopped
30 fresh curry leaves (optional)
1 tsp black mustard seeds
1 tsp ground cumin
1 tsp ground coriander
½ tsp ground turmeric
2 tsp medium curry powder
2 tsp tomato paste
½ cup/100g dried red lentils
1 × 13½-oz/400ml can full-fat coconut milk
2½ cups/600ml water
¾ tsp table salt

8 oz/220g paneer (or extra-firm tofu), roughly grated
2 limes: finely zest to get 1 tsp, then juice to get 2 tbsp
1½ oz/45g hot mango pickle, roughly chopped, plus more to serve
¼ cup/5g cilantro, roughly chopped, plus more to serve
table salt
3½ oz/100g large (not baby) spinach leaves, stems removed (2 cups/60g)
1 tbsp olive oil

Only two ingredients—lemon and milk—are what it takes to make paneer at home. It's an experiment worth trying (it certainly feels like conducting a chemistry experiment), both for a sense of achievement and for unrivaled freshness. Yotam has published a recipe for it in the *Guardian* newspaper, but many others are also available online. If you buy your paneer—which makes the most satisfying filling for the grilled eggplants here, as it soaks up the coconut sauce—try to find a soft variety, which has a texture like compressed ricotta. Other varieties, which are harder and slightly rubbery, are more suitable for making vegetarian tikka kebabs, but they will also do if that's what you've got. For a vegan option, use extra-firm tofu. Try to get a good-quality, chunky Indian mango pickle for this.

Both the eggplant slices and the lentil sauce can be prepared the day before, if you want to get ahead. In fact, you can make the whole dish a day ahead, up until before it goes into the oven, then chill in the fridge and just bring to room temperature before warming up.

The coconut dal is a great recipe in its own right. Double it, if you like, and serve with our curry-crusted rutabaga steaks (page 63) and some rice. *Pictured on pages 154–155.*

1. Preheat the oven to 450°F/220°C fan. Line two baking sheets with parchment paper.

2. In a large bowl, toss the eggplants with the olive oil, ¾ tsp salt, and a good grind of pepper. Spread out on the prepared baking sheets and bake for 25 minutes, flipping halfway through, until softened and lightly browned. Set aside to cool.

3. For the dal: Put the olive oil into a large sauté pan on medium-high heat. Once hot, add the shallots and fry for 8 minutes, until golden. Add the ginger, half the chile, and half the curry leaves (if using) and cook for 2 minutes, then add all the spices, tomato paste, and lentils. Stir for 1 minute, then add the coconut milk, water, and salt. Bring to a boil, then decrease the heat to medium and let simmer for 20 minutes, stirring once in a while, until the lentils are soft and the sauce is thick. Pour into a 7 x 11 inch/28 x 18cm baking dish and set aside.

4. In a small bowl, toss together the paneer, lime zest, 1 tbsp of the lime juice, the mango pickle, cilantro, and ⅛ tsp salt.

5. Place one spinach leaf on top of each slice of eggplant. Put a heaping 1 tsp of the paneer mixture in the middle, then roll up the eggplant, from the thinner end at the top down to the thicker bottom end, so the filling is encased. Put the eggplant roll seam-side down in the lentil sauce and repeat with the remaining eggplant slices, spinach, and paneer. You should end up with about eighteen rolls, all sitting snugly in the sauce. Press the rolls gently into the sauce, but not so far that they are submerged, and bake for 15–20 minutes, until the eggplant is golden brown on top and the sauce is bubbling. Remove from the oven and let rest for 5 minutes.

6. Heat the 1 tbsp olive oil in a small pan on medium-high heat. Add the remaining chile and curry leaves and fry for 1 minute, until the curry leaves are crisp and fragrant. Spoon over the eggplant rolls, drizzle with the remaining 1 tbsp lime juice, and serve with cilantro sprinkled on top.

EGGPLANT DUMPLINGS ALLA PARMIGIANA

1¼ cups/90g fresh breadcrumbs, preferably sourdough (from 2–3 slices)

4 eggplants, roughly cut into 1-inch/2½cm cubes (12 cups/1kg)

½ cup plus 2 tbsp/150ml olive oil

table salt and black pepper

6 tbsp/100g ricotta

2½ oz/75g Parmesan, finely grated, plus more to serve

½ cup/10g parsley, finely chopped

1 egg, plus 1 egg yolk

4½ tsp all-purpose flour

6 garlic cloves, crushed

¾ cup/15g basil leaves, roughly chopped

1½ × 14-oz/400g cans whole peeled tomatoes, blitzed until smooth (2½ cups/600ml)

1½ tsp tomato paste

1½ tsp superfine sugar

¼ tsp chile flakes

¾ tsp paprika

2 tsp fresh oregano leaves, finely chopped

1⅔ cups/400ml water

⅓ cup/45g pitted Kalamata olives, roughly torn in half

If you like melanzane alla parmigiana, these taste like the Italian classic but in dumpling form. The dumplings are gloriously rich and cheesy and yet somehow incredibly light.

Make the sauce ahead and keep it in the fridge for up to 3 days, or in the freezer for 1 month. The dumpling mix can be made up to a few hours in advance and chilled, ready to roll into balls and sear. Serve with spaghetti, rice, or some sautéed greens.

1. Preheat the oven to 350°F/160°C fan. Line a large baking sheet with parchment paper. Spread the breadcrumbs on a second baking sheet and bake for 12 minutes, until lightly browned and dried out. Set aside to cool. Increase the oven temperature to 450°F/220°C fan.

2. On the prepared baking sheet, toss the eggplants with 5 tbsp/75ml of the olive oil, ½ tsp salt, and a good grind of pepper. Spread out as much as possible and bake for 30 minutes, tossing halfway through, until golden brown.

3. Roughly chop the eggplants into a chunky mash, then transfer to a large bowl and refrigerate for 20 minutes, or until cool. Once cool, add the ricotta, Parmesan, parsley, egg, egg yolk, flour, breadcrumbs, one-third of the garlic, ½ cup/10g of the basil, ¼ tsp salt, and a good grind of pepper. Mix well, then with lightly oiled hands, shape the mixture into sixteen golf ball–size dumplings, about 2 oz/55g each, compressing them as you go so they hold together.

4. Put 2 tbsp olive oil into a large nonstick frying pan on medium-high heat. Add half the dumplings and fry for 3–4 minutes, turning them until golden brown all over. Adjust the heat if they're browning too much. Transfer to a plate. Add another 1 tbsp olive oil and fry the remaining dumplings in the same way. Set aside.

5. Preheat the oven to 400°F/180°C fan. Put the remaining 2 tbsp olive oil into a large sauté pan on medium-high heat. Add the remaining garlic and cook for 1 minute until fragrant, then add the blitzed tomatoes, tomato paste, sugar, chile flakes, paprika, oregano, 1 tsp salt, and a good grind of pepper and cook, stirring occasionally, for 8 minutes, or until thickened slightly. Pour in the water, bring to a simmer, then decrease the heat to medium and simmer for another 10 minutes.

6. Pour the sauce into a medium baking dish, top with the dumplings, and bake for 20 minutes, until bubbling. Remove from the oven, then scatter with the olives, remaining basil, and a grating of Parmesan and serve.

Serves six as a starter
or three as a main

CHEESE TAMALES WITH ALL (OR SOME OF) THE FIXIN'S

HIBISCUS PICKLED ONIONS (OPTIONAL)
½ cup/120ml white wine vinegar
2 tsp superfine sugar
2 hibiscus tea bags, or 3 tbsp dried hibiscus flowers
finely shaved peel of 1 lime
1 garlic clove, skin on, roughly crushed with the flat side of a knife
1 red onion, finely sliced on a mandoline, if you have one, or by hand
½ tsp table salt

SALSA ROJA (OPTIONAL)
2 tbsp olive oil
2 garlic cloves, crushed
½ red onion, finely chopped
1½ tsp cumin seeds, toasted and crushed
3 plum tomatoes, quartered
½ tsp dried oregano
1 tbsp red bell pepper flakes (optional)
1 ancho chile, stemmed and seeded (or half, if you prefer less heat)
½ dried habanero chile, stemmed and seeded (optional; leave out if you prefer less heat)
1⅔ cups/400ml water
2 tsp tomato paste
1½ tsp superfine sugar
¾ tsp table salt

These are inspired by the street corners of Mexico City, where Ixta has eaten some of the best meals of her life at rickety food stalls. Business at taco stalls is pretty constant; with no real need to advertise their wares, vendors chat away with customers, who sit on sticky plastic chairs, sipping on warm Coca-Colas. Tamale vendors, on the other hand, are *extremely* vocal, and it's not unusual to hear calls of "TAMAAAAALES" from streets away, which is very handy as you know in which direction to run to get your hands on them.

We would love to be more taco than tamale vendors here and simply play it cool, but we can't possibly do that. Our tamales are so good, we simply won't allow you to just walk by! In fact, we are so uncoolly keen you make them, that we have made all the delicious fixin's completely optional. Simply serve your tamales hot, with some lime wedges alongside, and watch the world go by.

If you do choose to make the accompaniments, or at least some of them, you will not regret it. Each brings an extra personality to the meal, with heat, acidity, richness, and depth. You can also make the accompaniments without the tamales, and pile them on top of warm tortilla chips for a very special nacho experience.

You'll make more salsa roja than you need, but it will keep in the fridge for 3 days, or in the freezer for 1 month, if you want to get ahead. *Pictured on pages 160–161.*

1. For the pickled onions: In a medium bowl, combine the vinegar, sugar, tea bags, lime peel, garlic, red onion, and salt and allow to pickle for at least 2 hours, or up to overnight.

2. For the salsa roja: Put the olive oil, garlic, and red onion into a large saucepan on medium heat and fry gently for 7–9 minutes, until soft. Add the cumin seeds, tomatoes, oregano, pepper flakes (if using), ancho, habanero (if using), water, tomato paste, sugar, and salt and simmer for 25 minutes, or until the tomatoes have softened completely.

3. Discard the habanero, then transfer to a blender or food processor and blitz to a smooth salsa. Keep warm.

4. For the chile oil: Lightly toast the chipotle flakes and bell pepper flakes in a small frying pan on medium-high heat for 1 minute, until very fragrant, then add the sunflower oil and salt. Warm for about 30 seconds, or until the oil bubbles gently, then remove from the heat and set aside.

CHILE OIL (OPTIONAL)

2 tsp chipotle flakes
(or 1 whole chipotle chile, minced to yield 2 tsp)

2 tsp red bell pepper flakes
(or double the quantity of chipotle flakes)

¼ cup/60ml sunflower oil

¼ tsp table salt

TAMALES

4–6 small ears fresh corn, kernels shaved off (scant 4 cups/500g), or scant 4 cups/500g frozen corn kernels (defrosted)

1 tbsp unsalted butter

7 tbsp/105ml heavy cream

2 tsp cumin seeds, toasted and finely crushed

table salt

1 cup/110g masa harina

1½ tsp olive oil

1 tsp baking powder

1 egg, whisked

2¼ oz/60g mature Cheddar, grated

2¼ oz/60g mozzarella, grated

AVOCADO SALAD (OPTIONAL)

2 avocados, pitted, peeled, and thinly sliced

9 green onions, finely sliced at an angle (mounded 1 cup/90g)

1 cup/20g cilantro leaves

4 jalapeños, finely sliced into rounds (seeded for less heat)

6 tbsp/90ml lime juice (from 5 limes)

1 tbsp olive oil

table salt

5. For the tamales: Blitz the corn kernals in a food processor until you get a wet mash. Put a large sauté pan on medium-high heat and melt the butter. Add the corn, cream, 1 tsp of the cumin seeds, and 1 tsp salt. Cook for 3 minutes, stirring a few times, until the corn is cooked through and has the consistency of porridge. Remove from the heat and let cool for 5 minutes, then stir in the masa harina, olive oil, baking powder, and egg until well incorporated—it should have the consistency of play-dough.

6. Cut six rectangles of parchment paper, roughly 10 x 6 inches/25 x 15cm each. With lightly oiled hands, take about 4 oz/110g of the dough and shape into a smooth ball. Place in the middle of one parchment rectangle and flatten to make a 6 x 3½-inch/15 x 9cm rectangle. Combine both cheeses in a small bowl with the remaining 1 tsp cumin and place ¾ oz/20g of the cheese mixture along the center of the dough. Use your hands to shape the dough to enclose the cheese on all sides, pinching and smoothing it with your fingers so there are no cracks, to get a 5 x 2½-inch/12 x 6cm rectangle. Fold the parchment on all sides to enclose the tamale, using the paper to help you shape it, then place the parcel seam-side down on a baking sheet while you make the remaining five tamales.

7. Fill a large saucepan, for which you have a steaming basket and lid, with enough water to come 1½ inches/4cm up the sides. Bring to a boil on high heat. Place the tamales, seam-side down, in the steaming basket (you may have to pile some on top of each other, which is fine). Cover, then decrease the heat to medium and steam for 30 minutes. Let cool for a few minutes before unwrapping.

8. For the salad: Meanwhile, in a large bowl, mix together the avocados, green onions, cilantro, jalapeños, lime juice, and olive oil with a good pinch of salt.

9. Serve the tamales on a large platter, with the chile oil drizzled on top and the salad, hibiscus pickled onions (discard the tea bags), and warm salsa alongside.

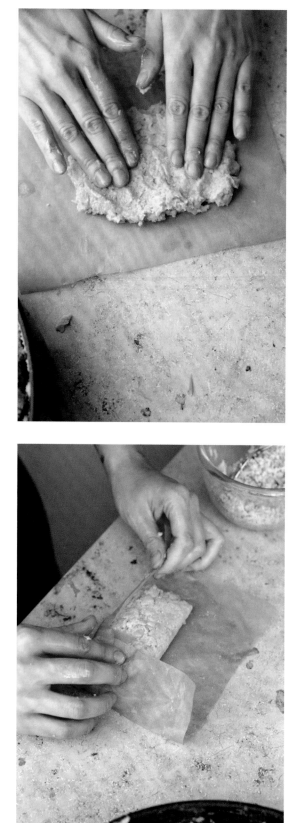

POLENTA WITH FRESH CORN AND BRAISED EGGS

1½ cups/250g fresh or frozen corn kernels (defrosted if frozen)

10 cups/200g baby spinach, roughly shredded

½ cup/10g parsley, roughly chopped

½ cup/10g dill, roughly chopped

1 cup/20g cilantro, roughly chopped, plus 1 tbsp

6 green onions, finely sliced (¾ cup/60g), plus 2 tbsp

4 garlic cloves, crushed

¾ cup plus 3 tbsp/150g coarse polenta (cornmeal; not the quick-cook variety)

1¾ oz/50g Parmesan, finely grated

table salt and black pepper

2¼ cups/520ml whole milk

1¾ cups/450ml vegetable or chicken stock

3 tbsp unsalted butter, cut into ¾-inch/2cm cubes

5¼ oz/150g feta, roughly crumbled

8 eggs

2 tbsp olive oil

½ tsp chile flakes

For Yotam's father, who was born in Italy, there was only one way to cook polenta. He would put everything into a pot and then stand by it watchfully for a good hour, continuously stirring the polenta with great patience, making sure it turned out perfectly and didn't stick to the bottom of the pan. For a *New York Times* column in which we turned classical dishes on their heads and cooked them in the oven in one single pan, our test-kitchen colleague Noor Murad didn't only bust Yotam's childhood myth about the best way to cook polenta, she also did away with the sauce it was normally served with and simply added whole eggs to braise inside the cornmeal. The result is a rather bumpy type of polenta, full of textures and surprises. It's still marvelously delicious, and means you can read a few pages of your favorite book while the polenta essentially cooks itself.

Try to find coarse cornmeal polenta here rather than the quick-cooking kind, which simply won't yield the result you're looking for. This is a great brunch dish, but will work equally well for lunch or a light dinner with a crunchy green salad. The polenta hardens as it sits, so eat this soon after it comes out of the oven.

1. Preheat the oven to 400°F/180°C fan.

2. Put the corn into a food processor and pulse once or twice, until just roughly chopped, then transfer to a large bowl. Add the spinach, parsley, dill, 1 cup/20g cilantro, ¾ cup/60g green onions, garlic, coarse polenta, Parmesan, 1½ tsp salt, and a good grind of pepper, stirring to combine. Put this mixture into a large, high-sided ovenproof sauté pan, then add the milk, stock, and butter, stirring to mix through. Bake for 20 minutes, then remove from the oven and give everything a good whisk before returning it to the oven for another 20 minutes, or until the cornmeal is cooked through and the mixture has thickened. Give the polenta a good whisk—it should be smooth and not completely set—then stir in half the feta. Increase the oven temperature to 425°F/200°C fan.

3. Make eight wells in the polenta, crack an egg into each, and sprinkle lightly with salt and pepper. Sprinkle with the remaining feta and return to the oven for 12–14 minutes, or until the egg whites are cooked and the yolks are still runny.

4. Meanwhile, in a bowl, combine the 1 tbsp cilantro and 2 tbsp green onions with the olive oil. Spoon this mixture all over the polenta, followed by a sprinkling of the chile flakes. Serve at once.

TOMATO SALAD WITH LIME AND CARDAMOM YOGURT

¼ cup/70g Greek-style
   yogurt
1¾ oz/50g soft, rindless
   goat cheese
½ small garlic clove,
   crushed
table salt
1–2 limes: finely zest to
   get 1 tsp, then juice
   to get 4½ tsp
15 cardamom pods,
   pods discarded and
   seeds finely crushed
   (¾ tsp)
1 large green chile, finely
   chopped (seeded for
   less heat)
1 lb 2 oz/500g ripe,
   sweet cherry
   tomatoes (or any other
   great sweet tomato you
   can get), halved
1 large shallot, finely
   sliced (⅓ cup/60g)
¼ cup/60ml olive oil
½ cup/10g mint leaves,
   roughly torn

This recipe has some useful takeaways. First, the timeless combination of tomatoes and shallots, which is the base for an infinite number of summery salads; the simplest of which involves only a drizzle of oil and a splash of vinegar. Then there's the dressing made by mixing together yogurt, soft goat cheese, and garlic; it's great for a potato or cucumber salad (just add some lemon juice and olive oil). Finally, the tomato, lime, and cardamom might not be a familiar combination but we absolutely adore it, either in a salad like this one or when cooked together, as in sweet potato in tomato, lime, and cardamom sauce (page 131). We urge you to try it. Serve with bread to soak up the tomato juices.

1. In a large bowl, combine the yogurt, goat cheese, garlic, and a pinch of salt until smooth. Add half the lime zest, half the crushed cardamom, and half the chile and stir to mix.

2. In a separate bowl, mix together the tomatoes, shallot, lime juice, 2 tbsp of the olive oil, and ½ tsp salt with the remaining lime zest, cardamom, and chile, then add the yogurt mixture and mint. Gently mix everything together but not completely; you want to see the red of the tomatoes and the green of the mint in places. Transfer to a platter, drizzle with the remaining 2 tbsp olive oil, and serve.

KIMCHI AND GRUYÈRE RICE FRITTERS

**MAKES TWELVE
FRITTERS**
Serves four

3 tbsp olive oil
½ onion, finely chopped
table salt
3 garlic cloves, crushed
**¾ cup plus 2 tbsp/200ml
whole milk**
**1 × 9-oz/250g package
cooked brown basmati
and wild rice mix**
(or any combination
of cooked rice)
2 eggs, separated
**1 lb 2 oz/500g good-
quality kimchi**
(we like Cultured
Collective brand)
½ cup/80g green beans,
trimmed and finely
chopped
**4½ tsp finely chopped
cilantro**
3 oz/80g Gruyère (or
other mature cheese),
cut into ½-inch/1½cm
cubes
**2 tbsp mixed black and
white sesame seeds,**
toasted, plus 1½ tsp
**¾ cup/90g all-purpose
flour**
**3⅓ cups/800ml
sunflower oil**
2 lemons: juice to
get 2 tbsp; cut the
remainder into wedges
flaked sea salt

These fritters were conceived to make use of leftover rice, an open jar of kimchi, and some scraps of cheese we had knocking about in the test-kitchen fridge. While the contents of your fridge are likely to be different, we're pretty positive you will sometimes find leftover rice there as well as cheese. For such (happy) occasions, these fritters are perfect.

If you don't happen to have leftover rice, though, you can easily make the fritters with pre-cooked rice or by cooking rice from scratch and letting it cool. (Most rice will triple in volume and weight when cooked, so start with about ½ cup/100g uncooked.) Any combination of white, brown, or mixed rice will work, although we like the nuttiness of brown and wild.

The kimchi we use tends to have a lot of liquid, which we repurpose into a dipping sauce with the addition of lemon juice. Don't worry if your kimchi doesn't yield much liquid with which to make a sauce; the fritters are still absolutely delicious with just a simple squeeze of lemon, or hot sauce, if you have some on hand.

The fritters, which are great as a snack but also good as part of a meal, can be fried up to 3 hours ahead. Simply reheat in a 400°F/180°C fan oven for about 5 minutes, or until warmed through. *Pictured on pages 168–169.*

1. Put the olive oil, onion, and ¾ tsp salt into a medium saucepan on medium-high heat and fry gently for 6 minutes, stirring every now and then, until soft and golden. Add the garlic and continue to fry, stirring, for 30 seconds to 1 minute, until fragrant. Add the milk, decrease the heat to medium, and simmer gently for 5 minutes, until thickened and reduced a little. Remove from the heat and let cool for 5 minutes, then stir in the rice, egg yolks, and ⅛ tsp salt. Refrigerate for 30 minutes, or until completely cool.

2. Meanwhile, set 5¾ oz/160g of the kimchi aside. Squeeze the rest of the kimchi through a sieve, collecting 3 tbsp of the liquid in a small serving bowl (set aside), and transferring the drained kimchi to a chopping board (you should have about 9 oz/250g). Roughly chop the kimchi and add to the pan with the cooled rice mixture, along with the green beans, cilantro, Gruyère, 2 tbsp sesame seeds, and flour. Stir until fully combined.

3. Whip the egg whites with a small pinch of salt, either by hand or with a handheld mixer, until you get medium-stiff peaks. Gently fold the egg whites through the rice mixture until combined, taking care not to overmix.

4. Line a baking sheet with a double layer of paper towel. Heat the sunflower oil in a large, high-sided saucepan on medium-high heat until it reaches about 355°F/180°C. Test if the oil is hot enough by dropping in a tiny bit of batter; it should sizzle but not turn golden brown straight away. Using a large serving spoon, carefully drop around 3¼ oz/90g of batter per fritter into the oil (in batches of three) and fry for 4–5 minutes, turning a few times until crisp and golden brown all over. You may need to decrease the heat if the fritters are browning too quickly. Transfer the fritters to the prepared baking sheet and continue in the same way with the remaining batter.

5. Stir the lemon juice into the bowl of kimchi liquid. Transfer the fritters to a large platter, sprinkling with the 1½ tsp sesame seeds and some flaked sea salt. Serve hot with the kimchi sauce, lemon wedges, and reserved kimchi alongside.

SERVES FOUR
As a side

ASPARAGUS SALAD WITH TAMARIND AND LIME

TAMARIND AND LIME DRESSING
1¾ cups/35g mint leaves
¾ cup/15g parsley, roughly chopped
1 tbsp white wine vinegar
1 tbsp honey
2 tsp store-bought tamarind paste (or double if you're extracting it yourself from pulp; see page 20)
1 anchovy fillet in olive oil, drained (optional, adjust seasoning if not using)
½ tsp ground cardamom
½ tsp ground black lime (see page 18; optional)
2 green chiles, seeded and finely chopped
1 small garlic clove, crushed
1 tsp Dijon mustard
1 tsp lime zest
2 tbsp olive oil
2 tbsp water
¼ tsp table salt

14 oz/400g thick-stemmed asparagus, woody ends trimmed
4½ tsp olive oil
1 tbsp lime juice
¾ cup/15g mint leaves, roughly shredded
3 tbsp pistachios, very lightly toasted and roughly chopped
table salt

We surprised ourselves twice with this salad. First, by how good raw asparagus can taste and feel in the mouth when sliced super-thin; and, second, by how well the asparagus holds its own and actually benefits when being matched with intensely sharp ingredients such as tamarind and lime. Try it the next time you get your hands on a bunch of extra-fresh but not too thin (these will be hard to slice) asparagus spears.

You'll make more dressing than you need here, but it can be tossed with salads or drizzled on roasted vegetables. It will discolor a little, but will still be fine to eat.

Slice the asparagus and mix the salad just before serving, to keep the thin asparagus slices as crunchy as possible.

Serve with fried tofu or roast chicken, or alongside potato and gochujang braised eggs (page 99) for a light lunch or dinner.

1. For the dressing: In a food processor or a spice grinder (for a smoother sauce), blitz together the mint, parsley, vinegar, honey, tamarind paste, anchovy (if using), cardamom, black lime (if using), chiles, garlic, mustard, lime zest, olive oil, water, and salt until you have a thick paste. Spoon into a clean jar and refrigerate for up to 3 days.

2. Using a vegetable peeler, or a mandoline if you have one, finely slice the asparagus into long strips and mix with half of the olive oil, half the lime juice, half the mint, half the pistachios, and ⅛ tsp salt. Transfer to a serving platter or bowl and set aside.

3. In a small bowl, stir together 2 tbsp of the dressing with the remaining olive oil, remaining lime juice, and ⅛ tsp salt. Spoon the dressing over the asparagus, finish with the remaining mint and pistachios, and serve at once.

SERVES FOUR
As a main

CARDAMOM TOFU WITH LIME GREENS

¾ cup/100g all-purpose
   flour
1 cup/100g cornstarch
4½ tsp ground
   cardamom
table salt and black
   pepper
3¾ cups/900ml
   sunflower oil,
   plus 7½ tsp
1 lb 8 oz/680g firm
   silken tofu, cut into
   1-inch/2½cm squares
6 garlic cloves, thinly
   sliced
2 red chiles, finely sliced
   into rounds
1 lb 5 oz/600g choy
   sum, base trimmed
   and leaves and stalks
   separated and cut into
   2-inch/5cm lengths
   (1 lb 2 oz/500g)
2 tbsp sriracha
3 tbsp soy sauce
2 limes: juice to get 2 tsp;
   cut the remainder into
   wedges
1 tbsp water

Aptly named, silken tofu genuinely delivers on the promise of super-smooth, light, and creamy texture. Frying it, as we do here, creates a crisp crust that highlights this texture even more and, as frying does, makes it irresistible. It's definitely the one you want to serve your tofu-skeptic friends if you need them to "see the light," as we heard from our recipe tester, Claudine Boulstridge.

This dish is great on its own for a light supper but you can also bulk it up with some rice and additional soy sauce. Morning glory or large-leaf spinach will also work well here if you can't get hold of choy sum. In the method, you can use one pan by transferring the oil to a heatproof container to be discarded once it has cooled (or you can use a second large sauté pan or wok). If using the same pan, wipe it clean after frying the tofu, then dry well.

1. Place the flour, cornstarch, cardamom, 2½ tsp salt, and plenty of pepper in a medium bowl. Mix together and set aside.

2. Line a plate with a double layer of paper towel. Put the 3¾ cups/900ml sunflower oil into a large, high-sided sauté pan or wok on medium heat. Once hot (just under 355°F/180°C if you have a thermometer), toss the tofu with the flour mixture. In batches, carefully lower the cubes of tofu into the hot oil and fry for 3–4 minutes, turning halfway through, until crisp and golden brown. Use a slotted spoon to transfer the tofu to the prepared plate. Keep warm.

3. Put the 7½ tsp sunflower oil into a large sauté pan or wok on high heat. Once hot, add the garlic and chiles and fry for 1–2 minutes, until the garlic is a light golden brown. Add the choy sum stalks and stir-fry for 4 minutes, then add the leaves and fry, continuing to stir, until they are wilted, about 2 minutes. Add the sriracha, soy sauce, lime juice, and water and stir through for 1 minute, until the liquid is bubbling.

4. Add the tofu to the pan, warm through, and serve with the lime wedges to be squeezed on top.

BRAISED GREENS WITH YOGURT

SERVES FOUR
As a side or as part
of a spread

1 dried black lime (see
page 18), pierced a
few times with a small
sharp knife
**½ cup plus 2 tbsp/150ml
boiling water**
¼ cup/60ml olive oil
1 onion, thinly sliced
(1 cup/150g)
3 garlic cloves, crushed
1 tsp ground cinnamon
1¼ cups/35g dill, roughly
chopped
1¼ cups/35g cilantro,
roughly chopped
1¼ cups/35g parsley,
roughly chopped
6 green onions, thinly
sliced (¾ cup/60g)
**10½ oz/300g cavolo
nero,** woody stems
discarded and leaves
roughly shredded
(2⅔ cups/180g)
**table salt and black
pepper**
**1¼ cups/300g Greek-
style yogurt**
1 tsp dried mint

Mixing extraordinary quantities of chopped herbs with lime or lemon to create soups, stews, or braises is such a genius way of using them, it's hard to want to do anything else. This is the base for many popular dishes in Iran and across the Gulf countries, and it is one we adopt whenever we can (see herb and charred eggplant soup, page 42). We use black lime here for an intense hit of earthy acidity. If you can't get your hands on dried limes, black or otherwise, substitute half a regular fresh lime (no need to soak), seeds removed and flesh and rind finely chopped, adding ½ cup/120ml water when the reserved soaking liquid is called for.

Make the greens up to a few hours in advance, if you want to get ahead, and warm up to serve.

These greens are best served with saffron (or plain, if you prefer) rice.

1. Place the black lime in a small bowl with the boiling water and top with a smaller plate or saucer to fully submerge. Let soak for 20 minutes to soften slightly. Remove the lime, setting it aside, and reserve the water.

2. Put 3 tbsp of the olive oil into a large sauté pan on medium heat. Once hot, add the onion and lime and cook, stirring occasionally, until the onion is softened and lightly caramelized, about 20 minutes. Add the garlic and cinnamon and cook for 2 minutes more, then remove the lime and set aside. Add 1½ cups/30g each of the herbs and all the green onions and cook for 15 minutes, stirring often, until fragrant and deeply green (you may need to decrease the heat if they start to catch).

3. Meanwhile, finely chop the black lime and return it to the pan as the herbs cook. Stir in the cavolo nero, reserved black lime water, 1 tsp salt, and a good grind of pepper, then increase the heat to medium-high and cook for 10 minutes more, until the liquid has been absorbed and the cavolo nero has softened. Remove from the heat and stir in the remaining herbs. Keep warm.

4. Put the yogurt, mint, and ¼ tsp salt into a bowl and mix well to combine. Spread the yogurt over the base of a serving platter, creating a slight well in the center. Spoon the greens into the well and drizzle with the remaining 1 tbsp olive oil before serving.

SERVES FOUR
As a main

1 tbsp apple cider
    vinegar
2 tsp superfine sugar
1 small red onion, thinly
    sliced into rounds on
    a mandoline, if you
    have one, or by hand
    (½ cup/60g)
table salt
2½ cups/600ml
    sunflower oil
2 blocks extra-firm
    tofu (1 lb 4 oz/560g),
    patted dry and cut into
    ¾-inch/2cm cubes
2 tbsp cornstarch
2 yellow onions (10½ oz/
    300g), roughly chopped
6 garlic cloves, roughly
    chopped
¼ cup/60ml olive oil
2 tsp cumin seeds,
    roughly crushed in a
    mortar and pestle
2–3 dried black limes
    (see page 18), blitzed
    in a spice grinder to
    get 2 tbsp (use a food
    processor if you don't
    have a grinder, and
    pass through a sieve),
    or 1 tbsp regular fresh
    lime zest and 1 tbsp
    lime juice
2 tbsp tomato paste
1⅔ cups/400ml water
black pepper
1 cup/20g parsley,
    roughly chopped
scant 6 cups/250g baby
    spinach

NOOR'S BLACK LIME TOFU

Dried limes have been a constant in the Ottolenghi pantry for years. Recently, though, we have been using them with extra vigor thanks to Noor Murad, our test-kitchen colleague who grew up in Bahrain, where they consume dried limes intravenously (well, not literally). The limes go by different names and come in different colors. Go for the black variety, if you can, though for this recipe, regular fresh limes are also fine.

We like to serve this dish with steamed rice or warm flatbreads.

1. Put the vinegar, 1 tsp of the sugar, the red onion, and ⅛ tsp salt into a small bowl and mix well to combine. Set aside to pickle.

2. Line a plate with a double layer of paper towel. Heat the sunflower oil in a medium, high-sided sauté pan on medium-high heat. Once hot, toss the tofu in a bowl with the cornstarch until well coated. In two batches, fry the tofu until crispy and lightly browned, about 6 minutes per batch, then transfer to the prepared plate and set aside.

3. While the tofu is frying, put the yellow onions and garlic into a food processor and pulse a few times until very finely minced but not puréed. Put the olive oil into a large sauté pan on medium-high heat. Add the onion mixture and cook, stirring occasionally, until softened and lightly browned, about 10 minutes. Add the cumin seeds, black limes or fresh lime zest and juice, and tomato paste and cook for 1 minute more. Add the water, remaining 1 tsp sugar, 1¼ tsp salt, and a generous grind of pepper. Bring to a simmer and cook for 6 minutes, stirring occasionally, until thick and rich. Add the crispy tofu, parsley, and another grind of pepper and stir to coat. Add the spinach in increments, stirring until just wilted, about 3 minutes.

4. Transfer the mixture to a shallow serving platter and top with the pickled red onion; or serve straight from the pan.

STICKY RICE BALLS IN TAMARIND RASAM BROTH

SERVES FOUR
As a main

TAMARIND RASAM
1¾-oz/50g block tamarind pulp
1 oz/30g fresh ginger, skin on, thinly sliced
½ oz/15g fresh turmeric, skin on, thinly sliced (or ⅔ tsp ground turmeric)
1 large green chile, roughly sliced (¼ cup/20g)
5 cups/1.2L water
table salt
9 oz/250g cherry tomatoes
7½ tsp sunflower oil
½ lemon, halved again lengthwise, then cut into ⅛-inch/3mm-thick half-moons (seeded)
1½ tsp cumin seeds, finely crushed
1 tsp black mustard seeds
2 whole dried red chiles
20 fresh curry leaves (optional)
3 garlic cloves, crushed
3–4 plum tomatoes (10½ oz/300g), coarsely grated and skins discarded
2 tsp superfine sugar

RICE BALLS
1 cup/200g Thai sticky rice, soaked for 1 hour in cold water, then drained
¾ cup plus 3 tbsp/ 220ml water
¼ tsp table salt
2 tbsp sunflower oil
1 onion, finely chopped (1 cup/150g)
2 garlic cloves, crushed
½ oz/15g fresh ginger, peeled and finely grated
½ cup/10g cilantro, roughly chopped, plus whole leaves to garnish
3 green onions, thinly sliced (⅓ cup/30g)

Our version of rasam, a South Indian broth, is sharp, complex, and rich from the spices and the charring of tomatoes and lemons. We urge you to try it, despite the longish ingredient list, if only to discover a whole range of new flavors.

Use tamarind pulp (see page 20), not paste. The pulp, available in any Indian supermarket, is more complex in flavor and provides the sweet-acid kick that you're after here.

You'll need to soak the rice in water for an hour. The balls can be formed a day ahead and kept refrigerated. Just bring them back to room temperature before pouring in the hot broth.

1. For the rasam: Put the tamarind pulp, ginger, turmeric, green chile, water, and 1 tsp salt into a medium saucepan on medium-high heat. Bring to a boil, then decrease the heat to medium and simmer gently for 20 minutes, stirring to break apart the pulp. Strain through a sieve into a bowl, pushing down with a spoon to extract as much flavor as possible. Discard the aromatics.

2. Toss the tomatoes in 1½ tsp of the sunflower oil. Place a large sauté pan on high heat. Once smoking, add the tomatoes and cook, tossing occasionally, until charred and blistered, about 4 minutes. Set aside. Add the lemon to the pan and cook until charred, 30–50 seconds per side, then set aside. Decrease the heat to medium-high; add the remaining 2 tbsp sunflower oil, the cumin seeds, mustard seeds, dried chiles, curry leaves (if using), and garlic; and cook for 90 seconds, until fragrant. Add the grated tomatoes and cook for 5 minutes more, then add the sugar, tamarind liquid, charred tomatoes, and ½ tsp salt. Bring back to a boil and simmer for 8 minutes. Set aside.

3. For the rice balls: Put the drained rice into a medium saucepan, for which you have a lid, and add the water and salt. Bring to a boil on medium-high heat, then decrease the heat to medium-low and cover loosely with the lid, leaving a small gap for some steam to escape. Cook for 20 minutes, then remove from the heat and let sit, uncovered, until cool.

4. Put the sunflower oil into a sauté pan on medium-high heat. Add the onion and cook for 7 minutes, until softened and browned. Add the garlic and ginger and cook for 90 seconds. Remove from the heat and transfer to a bowl. Add the cooked rice, chopped cilantro, and green onions and mix well. With lightly oiled hands, form into twelve balls, weighing 1 oz/30g each.

5. Return the pan of rasam to medium-high heat to heat through, then add the charred lemon slices and sticky rice balls. Top with cilantro leaves and serve at once.

SERVES FOUR
As a side

RAINBOW CHARD WITH TOMATOES AND GREEN OLIVES

---

14 oz/400g rainbow chard, bases trimmed, leaves and stalks separated and each cut into 2½-inch/6cm lengths

1 tsp olive oil, plus ½ cup/120ml

5 garlic cloves, finely sliced

1 small onion, finely chopped (¾ cup/110g)

1 lemon: finely shave the peel to get 2 strips, then juice to get 1 tbsp

2–3 oregano sprigs (⅓ oz/10g)

2–3 ripe plum tomatoes, cut into ½-inch/1cm dice (1⅔ cups/300g)

table salt and black pepper

¾ cup/120g Nocellara olives (or other green olive), pitted and halved or quartered if large (⅔ cup/70g)

¼ cup/5g basil leaves, roughly torn

This summery side dish will really benefit from using the best-quality, ripe tomatoes. Rainbow chard looks beautiful but, for flavor, Swiss chard will do an equally good job here. Swiss chard stalks tend to be wider, though, so you may need to cut them three times lengthwise, as well as crosswise.

This dish is great served warm soon after it's made, but the flavors actually get better with time. Make it a few hours ahead, if you like, or even the day before, and serve it at room temperature, or gently warmed through. There's quite a lot of aromatic oil, so grab some crusty bread to mop it up with.

Serve alongside za'atar cacio e pepe (page 104) for a midweek dinner.

1. Cut any wider chard stalks in half lengthwise (or into thirds if they are particularly wide). Place a large sauté pan on medium-high heat and add the 1 tsp olive oil. Add the chard stalks and sauté for 4 minutes, then add the leaves and sauté for another 3 minutes, until the leaves are just cooked. Transfer to a large bowl, cover with a plate, and let soften in the residual heat for another 3 minutes, then remove the plate.

2. Wipe the pan clean and return to medium heat. Add 6 tbsp/90ml olive oil, the garlic, onion, lemon peel, and oregano and fry gently for 12 minutes, stirring often, until the onion is soft and golden. Add the tomatoes, ½ tsp salt, and a good grind of pepper and continue to cook until the tomatoes are just beginning to soften (about 2 minutes if they are ripe, or a couple of minutes longer if they are not). Stir in the cooked chard and the olives, then remove from the heat and let sit for 5 minutes, for the flavors to come together.

3. Discard the oregano sprigs and lemon strips and transfer to a lipped platter. Drizzle with the lemon juice and remaining 2 tbsp olive oil. Finish with the basil leaves and a good grind of pepper and serve.

TEMPURA STEMS, LEAVES, AND HERBS

SERVES SIX
As a snack or a starter

TANGERINE DIPPING SAUCE
3 tbsp tangerine juice, with bits (from 2–3 tangerines)
3 tbsp lime juice
1½ tsp maple syrup
½ small garlic clove, finely chopped
4 fresh makrut lime leaves, stems discarded, finely chopped
½ red chile, seeded and finely chopped
⅛ tsp flaked sea salt

BATTER
⅔ cup/80g all-purpose flour
1 tsp baking powder
¾ cup/80g cornstarch
¾ cup plus 2 tbsp/210ml ice-cold sparkling water (small bits of ice are welcome)
4½ tsp black sesame seeds
1 tsp flaked sea salt

3 cups/700ml sunflower oil
2½ oz/70g beet stems and leaves, stems cut into 3¼-inch/8cm lengths, washed and patted dry
1 cup/20g dill, patted dry and separated into 3¼-inch/8cm fronds
½ cup/10g mint leaves, patted dry
⅓ cup/50g cornstarch
1½ tsp Szechuan peppercorns, crushed in a mortar and pestle
flaked sea salt

Huge quantities of beets are roasted across the Ottolenghi restaurants, so we're always on the lookout for clever ways of using the stems and leaves. At ROVI in particular, where an imposing Spanish grill is both the restaurant's pièce de resistance and the place where many a root go to get cooked and receive a smoky bouquet, we end up with big piles of tops and trimmings.

This dish might be the "solution" to ROVI's highly popular hasselback beets (see page 50), but it's totally brilliant in its own right (the two go very well together as part of the ROVI spread; see page 303), with a super-crisp crust and a sweet-and-sour dipping sauce to counteract the oil. If you don't have beet stems and leaves, though, fear not—many different combinations of herbs, stems, and leaves will work here. Try it with basil, parsley, sage, or chard. Just make sure the leaves are not limp and wet or, conversely, hard and dry. The batter will be enough for 3½ oz/100g of leaves and herbs of your choosing.

Organization is key whenever you're frying, and especially with tempura. Make sure your prep is complete well before the oil gets too hot, and that you have a slotted spoon and a rack lined with paper towels at the ready. Tempura doesn't sit too well, so try to eat it as soon as it's all been fried.

1. For the sauce: In a small serving bowl, stir together the tangerine juice, lime juice, maple syrup, garlic, lime leaves, chile, and salt and set aside.

2. For the batter: Put the flour, baking powder, cornstarch, sparkling water, black sesame seeds, and salt into a large bowl and whisk gently, not vigorously, until the mixture just comes together.

3. Line a wire rack with a double layer of paper towel. Pour the sunflower oil into a medium, high-sided sauté pan and place on high heat. Once very hot (just under 355°F/180°C if you have a thermometer), decrease the heat to medium and test by dropping in a little batter; it should sizzle but not brown straight away. In batches, toss the beet stems and leaves, dill, and mint in the cornstarch; shake to remove any excess; and then dip in the batter. Lift, shake excess batter over the bowl, and then place as many pieces as can comfortably fit without touching in the oil. Fry for 30–60 seconds on each side, until crisp and pale golden, then transfer to the prepared rack, using a slotted spoon. Continue in the same way with the rest, then sprinkle the lot with the Szechuan pepper and a generous amount of salt. Transfer to a platter and serve hot, with the dipping sauce alongside.

BROCCOLI TWO WAYS WITH CHILE AND CUMIN

1 lb 8 oz/680g broccoli (about 2 heads), cut into bite-size florets, stems reserved
table salt
3 tbsp apple cider vinegar
½ red chile, thinly sliced into rounds (1 tbsp)
2 tbsp light soy sauce
2 tsp superfine sugar
2 cups/480ml sunflower oil
¼ cup/5g basil leaves, roughly torn
¼ tsp cumin seeds, toasted and roughly crushed in a mortar and pestle

Broccoli, unlike its cousins cauliflower and cabbage, isn't very comfortable being cooked for a long while. All our past attempts at being clever and creating equivalents of cauliflower cheese, for example, only with broccoli at the center, were total fiascos. The creamy sauce simply couldn't hold its own against the dominant broccoli, which went gray and soggy and miserable-looking. To keep things bright green and the broccoli generally happy, we recommend high-impact cooking, like frying, as we do here, broiling (see broccoli with mushroom ketchup and nori, page 227), or charring.

The fried broccoli florets, tossed in sweetened soy, may remind you of similar Chinese dishes you've had out of take-out boxes. Here, they are combined with broccoli stems that have been quickly pickled, so the richness is balanced by light acidity. Double the recipe to turn it into a main course, and serve with some sticky rice alongside.

Get ahead by pickling the broccoli stems up to 3 hours before, if you like, but not for any longer, or they'll lose their crunch. *Pictured on page 188.*

1. Trim each broccoli stem into a rough rectangle (they don't need to be perfectly rectangular). Use a mandoline to shave each stem lengthwise into thin strips, or finely slice by hand. Stacking a few pieces on top of each other at a time, slice them into fine julienne strips. Place in a bowl along with ½ tsp salt and toss well to combine. Let sit for 1 hour, then use your hands to gently squeeze out some of the salty liquid. Place in a clean bowl along with 2 tbsp of the vinegar and the chile and mix well to combine. Set aside to pickle, for up to 3 hours.

2. Put the soy sauce, sugar, and remaining 1 tbsp vinegar into a small saucepan on medium-high heat. Bring to a boil, simmer for 2 minutes, then remove from the heat and set aside to cool. It will thicken as it sits.

3. Line a baking sheet with a double layer of paper towel. Put the sunflower oil into a medium, high-sided saucepan on high heat. Once very hot (the broccoli should sizzle and begin to color as soon as it touches the oil), fry the florets, a handful at a time, until softened and golden in places, about 45 seconds per batch (about six batches in total). You want the oil to be quite hot, so allow it to come back up to temperature if it cools down too much. Transfer to the prepared baking sheet and continue with the rest. In a large bowl, toss the fried broccoli with the soy sauce mixture until well coated.

4. Spread half the pickled broccoli mixture on a round plate, followed by the fried broccoli. Top with the remaining pickled broccoli mixture, the basil, and crushed cumin. Serve at once.

ROASTED CARROT SALAD WITH CHAMOY

2 lb 2 oz/1kg carrots, peeled and cut at an angle into 3¼ × ½-inch/ 8 × 1cm batons
3 tbsp olive oil
4½ tsp maple syrup
table salt and black pepper

CHAMOY
⅓ cup/40g dried apricots
1 tsp maple syrup
2 tsp sumac
3 tbsp lime juice
1½ tsp Aleppo chile flakes or Gochugaru Korean hot pepper flakes (or ¾ tsp regular chile flakes)
1 small garlic clove
2 tbsp olive oil
¼ tsp table salt

½ cup/10g mint leaves
¼ cup/5g dill, roughly chopped
8 dried apricots, finely sliced
¼ cup/30g roasted and salted almonds, roughly chopped
4½ tsp olive oil
2 tsp lime juice

If you need to capture Ixta in a single foodstuff, look no further than chamoy. It's made of pickled fruit (check, for pickle), lime juice (check), and chile (check) and it hails from Mexico (one big massive check). It is sweet, salty, sour, and spicy—all at once—and it has a dramatic effect on any ingredient you pair it with: meat, fish, vegetables, and even fresh fruit. Traditional versions can range from liquid to a paste-like consistency. Our (very) untraditional take on chamoy uses sumac and Aleppo chile, and dried instead of pickled apricots. It's a combination that works well, but feel free to experiment with other dried or fresh chiles.

Double the chamoy recipe, if you like, and keep half in the fridge for up to 1 week, ready to use as a marinade or condiment for roasted vegetables, chicken, or pork. The carrots can be roasted and dressed the day before, if you want to get ahead, and then finished with the herbs, additional apricots, and nuts when you're ready to serve.

This is great as part of a vegetarian spread (see page 304), and also alongside fatty cuts of meat, such as pork belly or duck breast. *Pictured on page 189.*

1. Preheat the oven to 500°F/240°C fan. Line two large baking sheets with parchment paper.

2. In a large bowl, mix together the carrots, olive oil, maple syrup, 1¼ tsp salt, and a good grind of pepper. Spread them out as much as possible on the prepared baking sheets and roast for 18 minutes, tossing the carrots and swapping the sheets halfway through, until the carrots are nicely browned but still retain a bite.

3. For the chamoy: While the carrots are roasting, in a spice grinder (or the bowl of a small food processor), blitz together the apricots, maple syrup, sumac, lime juice, chile flakes, garlic, olive oil, and salt to get a smooth paste.

4. As soon as the carrots are cooked, transfer them to a large bowl with the chamoy, mix well, and set aside for 20 minutes for the flavors to come together.

5. Mix the carrots with the herbs and sliced apricots and transfer to a serving platter. Finish with the almonds, olive oil, and lime juice and serve.

SERVES FOUR
As a side

CUCUMBER, ZA'ATAR, AND CHOPPED LEMON SALAD

3 lemons
¼ cup/60ml olive oil
1¼ tsp dried mint
1½ tsp za'atar
1 shallot, halved
    lengthwise and finely
    sliced (¼ cup/40g)
1½ green chiles, finely
    sliced into strips
    (seeded for less heat)
1 large cucumber, halved
    lengthwise, watery
    center scooped out,
    cut at an angle into
    ¼-inch/½cm-thick
    slices (2½ cups/450g)
1 tsp table salt
1½ cups/60g lamb's
    lettuce
½ cup/10g dill, roughly
    chopped
½ cup/10g basil leaves
¼ cup/5g mint leaves

This salad makes a seriously crisp and refreshing impact, thanks to all the lemon that goes into it—juice, flesh, and skin. It will sit happily alongside virtually any dish in the book. The za'atar gives it a little extra edge, but leave it out if there's already a lot going on in any other dishes you're making.

Squeeze 1–2 of the lemons into a large serving bowl to get 7½ tsp juice. Cut seven thin slices from the remaining lemon, saving any remaining for another recipe. Discard any seeds, then pile the slices on top of each other. Remove and discard half the rind, then finely chop the slices, including the remaining rind, and add to the bowl along with the olive oil, dried mint, za'atar, shallot, green chiles, cucumber, and salt. Mix well, then add the lamb's lettuce and all the herbs, toss gently, and serve at once.

SERVES FOUR
As a side or six as a dip

MASHED SWEET POTATOES WITH YOGURT AND LIME

2–3 purple (or regular orange) sweet potatoes, peeled and cut into ¾-inch/2cm pieces (2⅓ cups/550g)
table salt
boiling water as needed
3 tbsp olive oil
2 limes: finely zest to get 1½ tsp, then cut into wedges
⅔ cup/200g Greek-style yogurt
½ small garlic clove, crushed
1½ tsp pomegranate molasses
2 tsp cilantro leaves, finely sliced
½ large red chile, seeded and finely chopped
1½ tsp sesame seeds, toasted

If you, or your taste buds, are feeling a bit sleepy, this mash will definitely shake things up for you. It's got a built-in tension between deep sweetness and extreme sharpness and it will sit amazingly well in the middle of a jolly mezze selection.

The mash can be made with purple sweet potatoes or with the more familiar orange or golden varieties. The purple potatoes are slightly more savory, with a complex flavor that is smoky, almost bacon-like. They also look striking (be ready for an electric-violet psychedelic surprise in your cooking water).

Purple sweet potatoes tend to be drier than their orange cousins, so if you're using them, be sure to keep the cooking water once they've been boiled—you may need to use it to help loosen the mash.

The mash can be prepared the day before and kept refrigerated if you want to get ahead; assemble when you're ready to serve.

Serve as part of a dip spread (see page 304), along with some grilled flatbreads.

1. Put the sweet potato and ¾ tsp salt into a small saucepan. Pour in enough boiling water so that it rises just above the potatoes, put on medium-high heat, and cook for 10–12 minutes, until soft enough to mash. Drain the potatoes well (reserving the cooking water—you may need some to help loosen the mash) and put in a bowl. Add 2 tbsp of the olive oil, then mash until smooth. Allow to cool slightly, then stir in half the lime zest and 2 tbsp of the yogurt until combined. Spoon onto a serving plate, creating dips with the back of the spoon.

2. Combine the remaining yogurt with the garlic and spoon evenly over the mash. Drizzle with the pomegranate molasses and remaining 1 tbsp olive oil, followed by the cilantro, chile, sesame seeds, and remaining lime zest. Season with a pinch of salt and serve with the lime wedges alongside.

CHAAT MASALA POTATOES WITH YOGURT AND TAMARIND

SERVES FOUR
As a side

1 lb 10 oz/750g baby
   new potatoes, cut
   lengthwise into ½-inch/
   1cm-thick slices
table salt
2 tbsp olive oil
1 tsp chaat masala
½ tsp ground turmeric
black pepper

CILANTRO CHUTNEY
1½ cups/30g cilantro
1 green chile, seeded
   and roughly chopped
   (2 tbsp)
1 tbsp lime juice
¼ cup/60ml olive oil
¼ tsp table salt

SWEET TAMARIND
DRESSING
4½ tsp store-bought
   tamarind paste
   (or double if you're
   extracting it yourself
   from pulp; see page 20)
1½ tsp superfine sugar
¼ tsp chaat masala
1½ tsp water

1 cup/250g Greek-style
   yogurt
½ small red onion, peeled
   and thinly sliced into
   rounds on a mandoline,
   if you have one, or by
   hand (½ cup/60g)
1 green chile, thinly sliced
   into rounds (2 tbsp)
1½ tsp coriander seeds,
   toasted
1½ tsp nigella seeds,
   toasted

This dish is inspired by aloo chaat, an Indian street-food that has many regional variations, all of which are not for the fainthearted because they are loaded with sweet and sour and a fair bit of crunch. This is a slightly tamer version, though still pretty "noisy," both in flavor and looks. It's absolutely perfect for a weekend lunch, alongside other vegetables, such as eggplant with herbs and crispy garlic (page 251) or radish and cucumber salad with chipotle peanuts (page 263). You can also serve it as a side with roasted lamb or chicken.

Chaat masala is the slightly tangy spice mix that gives this dish its distinctive flavor. It gets its sharpness from amchoor, dried mango powder, which is used widely in Indian cooking as a souring agent. You'd recognize the flavor from samosas and pakoras, where it is often used.

Both the cilantro chutney and the tamarind dressing are great condiments to have on hand to brighten up sandwiches and wraps, to spoon over eggs, or to serve alongside tofu or fish. Double or triple them, if you like—the chutney will keep in the fridge for up to 1 week and the tamarind dressing for up to 2 weeks. *Pictured on pages 194–195.*

1. Preheat the oven to 450°F/220°C fan. Line a large baking sheet with parchment paper.

2. Put the potatoes and 2 tsp salt into a medium saucepan and top with enough cold water to cover by about 1½ inches/4cm. Place on medium-high heat, bring to a boil, then simmer for 6 minutes, or until the potatoes are almost cooked through but still retain a bite. Drain through a sieve and pat dry, then transfer to the prepared baking sheet and toss with the olive oil, chaat masala, turmeric, ¼ tsp salt, and a good grind of pepper. Roast, stirring once or twice, for 35 minutes, or until deeply golden.

3. For the chutney: Meanwhile, in the bowl of a small food processor, combine the cilantro, chopped chile, lime juice, olive oil, and salt and blitz until smooth. Set aside.

4. For the dressing: In a small bowl, whisk together the tamarind paste, sugar, chaat masala, and water and set aside.

5. Spread the yogurt on a large round serving platter. Top with the chutney, swirling it through without completely incorporating. Drizzle with half the dressing and top with the potatoes, onion, and sliced chile. Drizzle with the remaining dressing, then sprinkle with the coriander seeds and nigella seeds and serve at once.

CABBAGE WITH GINGER CREAM AND NUMBING OIL

_____

NUMBING OIL
½ cup plus 2 tbsp/150ml sunflower oil
1 shallot, finely chopped (⅓ cup/60g)
2 garlic cloves, finely chopped
⅓ oz/10g fresh ginger, peeled and finely grated
½ red chile, finely chopped
1 whole star anise
1 tbsp red bell pepper flakes (or 1½ tsp Aleppo chile flakes or Gochugaru Korean hot pepper flakes)
1 tsp chile flakes
1½ tsp Szechuan peppercorns, roughly crushed
¼ tsp table salt
1½ tsp tomato paste
1 tsp black sesame seeds
1 tsp white sesame seeds

GINGER CREAM
1¾ oz/50g fresh ginger, peeled and finely grated
8 oz/220g cream cheese
¼ garlic clove, crushed
1 tbsp lime juice
table salt

1 pointed cabbage, (aka hispi or sweetheart cabbage) ends trimmed, halved lengthwise and leaves separated (1 lb 13 oz/820g)
4½ tsp soy sauce

Yotam and Ixta share a love for the unassuming (but downright brilliant) Xi'an Impression restaurant in north London. Highlights there include cold noodles, cold poached chicken, and smacked cucumbers (which inspired our cucumber salad à la Xi'an Impression, page 113). These are all unique, but they are also unified by a wondrous aromatic oil that they are absolutely swimming in. Since we couldn't figure out how to make their oil, we came up with our own version.

Serve this cabbage with fried tofu (see cardamom tofu with lime greens, page 172), soy-roasted chicken, or fried fish. Alternatively, have it with a host of aromatic dishes, such as kohlrabi "noodle" salad (page 260), tomato and plum salad with nori and sesame (page 267), and, the cucumber salad we mentioned, along with a big bowl of rice.

You'll make more oil than you need, but you can store it in the fridge for up to 2 weeks, ready to serve alongside fried tofu, meat, or fish, or to spoon over rice or noodles.

1. For the numbing oil: Heat 2 tbsp of the sunflower oil in a small saucepan on medium-high heat. Add the shallot, garlic, ginger, chile, star anise, bell pepper flakes, chile flakes, peppercorns, and salt; decrease the heat to medium; and fry very gently for 5 minutes, stirring often, until the shallot is soft. Add the tomato paste and all the sesame seeds and cook for another 2 minutes. Stir in the remaining ½ cup/120ml sunflower oil, then decrease the heat to low and simmer very gently for 10 minutes. If the oil starts to bubble at all, just take it off the heat for a minute. Let cool and infuse for 1 hour.

2. For the cream: Meanwhile, press the 1¾ oz/50g grated ginger through a fine-mesh sieve into a medium bowl to get 2 tbsp juice. Discard the pulp. Add the cream cheese, garlic, lime juice, and a good pinch of salt and whisk until smooth. Set aside.

3. Bring a large pot of well-salted water to a boil. Add the cabbage leaves and blanch for 2 minutes, until just cooked. Drain through a sieve, then pat the leaves dry with paper towels—they shouldn't be wet. Let cool.

4. In a small bowl, combine the soy sauce with 3 tbsp of the numbing oil and 1 tbsp of the aromatics at the bottom of the oil. Spread the ginger cream on a platter, pile the cabbage leaves on top, then drizzle the oil-soy mixture evenly over everything and serve at once.

MAKES 14 OZ/400G
Serves four

¼ **tsp saffron threads,**
   soaked in 7½ tsp boiling
   water for 20 minutes
1¼ **cups plus 1 tbsp/**
   225g "00" flour, plus
   more to dust
7 **tbsp/70g fine semolina**
2 **whole eggs,** plus
   2 egg yolks
favorite pasta sauce
   to serve

SAFFRON TAGLIATELLE

This pasta first came about because of the saffron tagliatelle with ricotta and crispy chipotle shallots recipe (facing page). It is also delicious with our ultimate roasting-pan ragù (page 101), the mushroom ragù from spicy mushroom lasagne (see page 228), or just with a plain tomato sauce, Parmesan, and some olive oil. You will need a pasta machine to roll out the pasta. *Pictured on page 200.*

1. Place the saffron, saffron soaking water, flour, semolina, eggs, and egg yolks in the bowl of a food processor and pulse for around 30 seconds to get the texture of sticky breadcrumbs. Tip the dough onto a lightly floured surface and knead vigorously for 7 minutes, until the dough becomes smooth and pliable. Shape it into a circle, wrap with plastic wrap, and let rest at room temperature for 30 minutes.

2. Secure the pasta machine to your work surface. Dust a baking sheet with a little flour. Divide the dough into four pieces and keep them well covered. Removing one dough piece at a time, shape it into a rectangle, then roll it through the widest setting of the machine twice, dusting with a little flour as you go. Fold the ragged sides to meet in the middle like a French door, then turn the sheet and roll it back through the machine twice, dusting as you go, so all sides are straight. Click the machine to the next setting and roll the pasta through twice, dusting as you go. Continue in the same way, rolling the pasta through each setting twice until you get to the fifth setting (or the one before the last; you don't want the pasta to be too thin).

3. Fold the long pasta sheet four times along its length, sprinkling flour between the layers so they don't stick together. Use a sharp knife to cut the pasta at ¾-inch/2cm intervals, to make wide tagliatelle. Hang the strands on the back of a chair to dry while you continue with the rest. Arrange the tagliatelle into nests, flouring as you go, and place them on the prepared baking sheet.

4. If you are not making the recipe opposite, cook the tagliatelle by bringing a very large pot of salted water to a boil (the pot needs to be large so the pasta doesn't clump). Add the tagliatelle and cook for 1 minute, stirring with a fork to separate the strands. Drain, toss with your chosen sauce, and serve.

SAFFRON TAGLIATELLE WITH RICOTTA AND CRISPY CHIPOTLE SHALLOTS

CRISPY CHIPOTLE SHALLOTS
2 tbsp olive oil
3–4 shallots, thinly sliced on a mandoline, if you have one, or by hand, and rings pulled apart (1 cup/150g)
2 tbsp maple syrup
¾ tsp coriander seeds
¾ tsp cumin seeds
½ tsp chipotle flakes (or 1 whole chipotle chile, minced to yield ½ tsp)
¼ tsp table salt

PICKLED GREEN CHILES
2 large green chiles, finely sliced into rounds (⅓ cup/30g)
2 tbsp rice vinegar
½ tsp superfine sugar
¼ tsp table salt

3 tbsp olive oil
3 garlic cloves, crushed
table salt
1 × recipe fresh Saffron Tagliatelle (facing page; or 14 oz/400g store-bought fresh tagliatelle)
¼ tsp saffron threads, soaked in 7½ tsp boiling water for 20 minutes (double the saffron if using store-bought pasta)
½ cup/10g parsley, finely chopped, plus 1 tbsp
black pepper
2¼ oz/60g Parmesan, finely grated
½ cup/120g ricotta

You can use store-bought fresh or dried pasta here, or make your own tagliatelle (facing page). Either way, there is so much going on—from the Parmesan sauce to the pickled chiles to the crispy shallots—that you are sure to both surprise and delight the lucky recipients of this dish.

If you're making fresh tagliatelle, have all your prep done before you boil the pasta because it only takes a minute or so to cook. *Pictured on page 201.*

1. For the shallots: Line a plate with paper towels. Heat the olive oil in a large, nonstick frying pan on high heat. Once hot, add the shallots, maple syrup, coriander seeds, cumin seeds, chipotle flakes, and salt. Fry for 7 minutes, using a spatula to separate the shallots and stop them from clumping so they will crisp up evenly. Decrease the heat to medium-low and continue to cook for 6 minutes, until the shallots are caramelized and deep golden brown. Transfer to the prepared plate and use two forks to spread the shallots out—they will be sticky but will crisp up a little as they cool.

2. For the chiles: Put the green chiles into a small bowl with the vinegar, sugar, and salt; stir to mix; and set aside.

3. Put the 3 tbsp olive oil, garlic, and ¼ tsp salt into a large sauté pan on medium-high heat. Fry gently for 2 minutes, then set aside.

4. Bring a very large pot of salted water to a boil (the pot needs to be large so the pasta doesn't clump). Add the tagliatelle and cook for 1 minute, stirring with a fork to separate the strands. (If using store-bought, cook per package instructions, until al dente.) Drain, reserving ½ cup plus 1 tbsp/140ml of the cooking water.

5. Add the pasta to the sauté pan and return to medium-high heat. Add the pasta water, saffron and its soaking water, ½ cup/10g parsley, and a generous amount of pepper and toss everything together. Add the Parmesan slowly, tossing the pasta as you go and continuing to add more Parmesan as it melts into the sauce; this should take 2–3 minutes.

6. Transfer the pasta to a platter with a lip and dot the ricotta haphazardly over the pasta. Top with the crispy shallots, pickled chiles along with 1½ tsp pickling liquid, remaining 1 tbsp parsley, and a good grind of pepper. Serve at once.

UDON NOODLES WITH FRIED TOFU AND ORANGE NAM JIM

SERVES FOUR
As a main

FRIED TOFU
1 small garlic clove, crushed
2 tbsp soy sauce
1 tbsp maple syrup
1 tbsp sunflower oil,
  plus 4½ tsp
¼ tsp table salt
12¼ oz/350g firm tofu,
  pressed to remove any
  water, very well patted dry,
  and cut into 1¼ × ½-inch/
  3 × 1½cm rectangles

**BLOOD ORANGE
NAM JIM**
1½ tsp basmati rice
**2 tsp Aleppo chile flakes
  or Gochugaru Korean
  hot pepper flakes** (or
  ¼ tsp regular chile flakes)
**4–5 blood (or regular)
  oranges:** juice to get
  ⅔ cup/160ml; cut the
  remainder into wedges
**¾ oz/20g store-bought
  tamarind paste** (double
  if you're extracting it
  yourself from pulp; see
  page 20)
7½ tsp fish sauce
  (or light soy sauce)
2 tbsp maple syrup
2 tbsp soy sauce
½ small shallot, finely
  diced (¼ cup/40g)
¼ cup/5g cilantro, finely
  chopped

**1 lb 5 oz/600g pre-cooked
  udon noodles**
½ cup/10g Thai basil leaves
3 green onions, julienned
  (mounded ¾ cup/50g)
½ cup/10g cilantro leaves,
  finely sliced
2 red chiles, julienned
  (⅓ cup/40g)
**1 tbsp white or black
  sesame seeds,** or a
  mixture of both, toasted

In our take on Thai nam jim sauce—which wonderfully combines sweet, sour, spicy, and salty—we use blood oranges to give a particular kind of sweet acidity. Their season is short, though, so use regular oranges instead if you need to, with a touch of lime juice for extra acidity.

To save time, we use pre-cooked noodles that you can just add to the pan. If you're starting with dried noodles, cook them as instructed on the package and drain well before tossing them with the sauce. The noodles are good hot but they are best served at room temperature, having sat in, and soaked up, the sauce. The accompanying tofu is best hot and freshly fried.

Double the nam jim, if you like—it will keep in a jar in the fridge for up to 1 week and is great with anything from salads, noodles, and rice to grilled meats and fish.

1. For the tofu: Combine the garlic, soy sauce, maple syrup, 1 tbsp sunflower oil, and salt in a container big enough to fit the tofu in a single layer. Add the tofu, toss gently to coat each piece, and let marinate for 30 minutes to 1 hour, turning the pieces halfway through.

2. For the nam jim. Meanwhile, put the rice into a small saucepan on medium-high heat and toast for 2½ minutes, then add the chile flakes and toast for another 30 seconds, until both are fragrant. Transfer to a spice grinder or a mortar and pestle and blitz or pound to a coarse powder. Transfer the ground rice and chile to a medium bowl and add the orange juice, tamarind, fish sauce, maple syrup, soy sauce, shallot, and chopped cilantro. Mix well, then pour into a large sauté pan on medium-high heat and cook gently for 2 minutes, until warm.

3. Add the noodles to the pan and cook for another 3 minutes, stirring to separate the strands. Remove from the pan and set aside until cooled to room temperature.

4. Heat the remaining 4½ tsp sunflower oil in a large nonstick pan on medium-high heat until very hot, then add half the tofu to the pan, spaced apart. Fry for 1½–2 minutes on each side until crisp and golden brown, taking care as it may spit. Set the cooked tofu aside while you fry the remaining tofu (add a bit more oil if necessary and decrease the heat if the tofu is coloring too quickly). Stir any remaining tofu marinade into the noodles.

5. Toss the basil, green onions, cilantro leaves, and chilies with the noodles, then transfer to a serving platter with a lip. Finish with the sesame seeds and hot tofu and serve with the orange wedges alongside.

SERVES FOUR

As a side or as part
of a mezze spread

⅓ cup/80ml olive oil
6 garlic cloves, finely
  sliced
1 tbsp rose harissa
  (adjust according to the
  brand you are using; see
  page 20)
1 red chile, finely chopped
½ preserved lemon, finely
  chopped, discarding any
  seeds (1 tbsp)
4½ tsp lemon juice
2 lb 2 oz/1kg zucchini,
  finely sliced
table salt
½ cup/10g basil leaves,
  roughly torn

SUPER-SOFT ZUCCHINI WITH HARISSA AND LEMON

————

Zucchini, strictly speaking, aren't controversial, but they do tend to get a pretty lukewarm reaction from many, including, regrettably, two of our test-kitchen colleagues. The reason for this is probably zucchini's high water content, which tends to make them, well, watery. There are plenty of ways to combat this—frying and grilling are two examples—but we actually use it to our advantage here, cooking the zucchini slowly in their own juices, making them fantastically soft and enhancing their flavor by a long soak with fried garlic. (And in the process, we also managed to win over our two zucchini-iffy colleagues, we're happy to announce.)

The zucchini are very good hot, but are better after 15 minutes or so, or even at room temperature, once the flavors have had a chance to get to know each other. Make them a day in advance, if you want to get ahead; just hold off on adding the basil until you're ready to serve. *Pictured on page 206.*

1. Place a large, nonstick sauté pan on medium-high heat and add the olive oil and garlic. Fry gently for 4 minutes, stirring often, until soft, golden, and aromatic. You don't want the garlic to become at all browned or crispy, so decrease the heat if necessary. Remove 3 tbsp oil, along with half the garlic, and transfer to a small bowl. Add the harissa, chile, preserved lemon, and lemon juice to the bowl; stir together; and set aside.

2. Return the pan to high heat and add the zucchini and 1¼ tsp salt. Cook for about 18 minutes, stirring often, until the zucchini are very soft but still mostly holding their shape (you don't want the zucchini to brown, so decrease the heat if necessary). Stir in half the basil and transfer to a platter. Spoon the harissa mixture over the zucchini. Let sit for 15 minutes, then sprinkle with a pinch of salt and finish with the remaining basil before serving.

CAULIFLOWER ROASTED IN CHILE BUTTER

SERVES FOUR
As a main

2 large whole cauliflowers, with leaves (4¼ lb/1.9kg)

CHILE BUTTER
8 tbsp/110g unsalted butter, melted (or ½ cup/120ml olive oil, if you want to keep it vegan)
7 tbsp/105ml olive oil
2 tbsp red bell pepper flakes (or 1 tbsp Aleppo chile flakes or Gochugaru Korean hot pepper flakes)
2½ tsp tomato paste
½ cup/90g rose harissa (adjust according to the brand you are using; see page 20)
1¼ tsp Urfa chile flakes (or the same amount of crushed ancho or chipotle chiles)
½ tsp regular chile flakes
3 garlic cloves, crushed
1½ tsp superfine sugar
1 tsp table salt

2 onions, peeled and cut into eighths
8 red chiles, whole, with a vertical slit cut into them
1 lemon, cut into wedges

Normally, when we give a vegetable center stage on the dinner table, in the same way that meat or large fish are often served, our tendency is not to do much to it and let it bask in its own simplicity. In this book, though, we often do the opposite and actually amp up the flavor for our whole vegetables (see celery root steaks with Café de Paris sauce, page 60, and curry-crusted rutabaga steaks, page 63). Through the combination of grilled chiles and onions, lots of browned butter, and a long cooking process, the cauliflower here turns ridiculously rich in flavor, almost meaty.

The chile butter can be made up to 2 weeks before and kept in the fridge in a sealed container, if you want to get ahead. We urge you to make double, in fact; it's seriously special and wonderful melted over eggs, or used as a marinade for vegetables or a killer roast chicken.

Serve as a main, with some bread and a couple of simple salads, or as part of a festive spread (see page 304). *Pictured on page 207.*

1. Trim the leaves at the top of each cauliflower, so that about 2 inches/5cm of the actual cauliflower is exposed. Cut both cauliflowers into quarters lengthwise, making sure the leaves remain attached at the base.

2. Fill a very large pot (large enough to fit all the cauliflower quarters) with well-salted water and bring to a boil. Once boiling, add the cauliflower quarters and blanch for 2 minutes, weighting them down with a lid a little smaller than the pan to ensure they stay submerged. Transfer to a colander to drain well. Preheat the oven to 400°F/180°C fan. Line a large baking sheet with parchment paper.

3. For the chile butter: In a small bowl, combine the butter, olive oil, bell pepper flakes, tomato paste, harissa, Urfa chile flakes, regular chile flakes, garlic, sugar, and salt and stir to mix.

4. Place the cauliflower quarters, onions, and chiles on the prepared baking sheet and pour the chile butter over the top. Mix carefully to make sure everything is very well coated (gloved hands are best for this). Arrange the cauliflower quarters so they are spaced apart as much as possible; one of the cut sides of each quarter should be facedown, so the leaves are exposed. Roast for 30 minutes, baste well, then decrease the temperature to 375°F/170°C fan and continue to roast for another 35–40 minutes, basting twice, until the cauliflower is very well browned and the leaves are crispy.

5. Transfer everything to a platter, spooning in all the remaining chile butter and browned aromatics from the baking sheet. Serve at once, with the lemon wedges alongside.

SPICY BERBERE RATATOUILLE WITH COCONUT SAUCE

SERVES FOUR

RATATOUILLE

4 medium eggplants, cut into 1-inch/2½cm squares (12 cups/1.1kg)

4 mixed red and yellow Romano peppers, seeded and cut into 1¼-inch/3cm pieces (3 cups/420g)

2 kohlrabi, peeled and cut into ½-inch/1½cm squares (4½ cups/460g)

2 tbsp berbere spice mix (we use Bart's brand)

¾ cup plus 2 tbsp/ 200ml olive oil

¾ tsp table salt

⅓ oz/10g fresh ginger, peeled and finely chopped

3 small garlic cloves, crushed

3 tbsp soy sauce

7½ tsp maple syrup

10½ oz/300g sweet, ripe cherry tomatoes, roughly chopped

2 tsp nigella seeds

3 mild or medium-hot chiles, red, green, or a mix

COCONUT AND CUCUMBER SAUCE

1 cucumber, coarsely grated (2 cups/300g)

¼ cup/15g cilantro, finely chopped

scant 1 oz/25g fresh ginger, peeled and finely chopped

⅔ cup/200g coconut cream (not coconut milk!)

2 tbsp lime juice

¼ tsp table salt

If you can get hold of injera (a fermented flatbread used in Ethiopia and Eritrea to scoop up food), do serve it alongside the ratatouille. Alternatively, serve the dish with any other store-bought or homemade flatbread, like our olive oil flatbreads with three-garlic butter (page 246), or even with rice or couscous.

The ratatouille can be made a few days in advance and kept refrigerated; the flavors will improve with time. The sauce, which really helps balance the spiciness of the dish, should be made within a few hours of serving, as it tends to split if left to sit for too long.

The coconut cream you use here should be thick, not liquid. You can test the consistency by shaking the can; if it's thick enough, you shouldn't be able to hear it sloshing around inside.

1. Preheat the oven to 450°F/210°C fan. Line two large baking sheets with parchment paper.

2. For the ratatouille: In a large bowl, combine the eggplants, mixed peppers, kohlrabi, spice mix, olive oil, and salt and spread out on the prepared baking sheets. Roast for 40 minutes, stirring the vegetables and swapping the sheets halfway through, until the vegetables are cooked and a deep golden brown. Place in a large bowl with the ginger, garlic, soy sauce, maple syrup, cherry tomatoes, and nigella seeds.

3. Place a frying pan on high heat and, once very hot, add the chiles and cook for 12 minutes, turning them a few times until well charred all over. Finely chop the chiles (seeding them if you prefer less heat) and stir into the bowl with the vegetables. Set aside for 30 minutes for the flavors to come together. This can be made up to 3 days ahead and gently warmed through before serving.

4. For the sauce: Place the cucumber in a clean kitchen towel and squeeze to get rid of as much water as possible. You should be left with 6⅓ oz/180g of drained cucumber. Place in a large bowl and stir in the cilantro, ginger, coconut cream, lime juice, and salt.

5. Serve the ratatouille with the coconut sauce alongside.

SERVES FOUR
As a main

PORTOBELLO STEAKS AND BUTTER BEAN MASH

PORTOBELLO STEAKS
8 medium to large portobello mushrooms (about 1 lb 7 oz/650g), stems removed
10 garlic cloves, peeled
1 onion, peeled and cut into 6 wedges (1 cup/150g)
4½ tsp chipotle flakes (or 1–2 whole chipotle chile, minced to yield 4½ tsp)
1 red chile
4 tsp cumin seeds, roughly crushed in a mortar and pestle
1 tbsp coriander seeds, roughly crushed in a mortar and pestle
2 tbsp tomato paste
1⅔ cups/400ml olive oil
1 tbsp flaked sea salt

BUTTER BEAN MASH
1 × 1 lb 9 oz/700g jar good-quality large butter beans, drained (2⅔ cups/500g; Brindisa Navarrico large butter beans or cook your own)
4½ tsp lemon juice
1 tbsp olive oil
2 tbsp water
½ tsp flaked sea salt

We're not mad about calling vegetables a "steak" or "burger" or "schnitzel," because it feels as if you are trying to pass them off as something else, something superior. Vegetables are great simply as they are. In fact, they are the best! Sometimes, though, using a meaty name helps you understand what's going on and how delicious it is. Our portobellos aren't trying to be a steak, they are simply as good as any steak (with mash), if not better; in just the same way as our Romano pepper schnitzels (page 146) are as delectable as any other schnitzel. What gives the mushrooms their verve is the chiles and spices and all the flavored oil that coats them.

You'll make more oil than you need here; keep it refrigerated in a sealed container for up to 2 weeks, to spoon over grilled vegetables, noodles, meat, or fish. Serve this with some sautéed greens, if you like.

1. For the steaks: Preheat the oven to 350°F/150°C fan.

2. In a large ovenproof saucepan, for which you have a lid, combine the mushrooms, garlic, onion, chile flakes, red chile, cumin seeds, coriander seeds, tomato paste, olive oil, and salt and stir to mix. Arrange the mushrooms so they are domed-side up, then top with a piece of parchment paper, pushing it down to cover all the ingredients. Cover with the lid, then transfer to the oven for 1 hour. Turn the mushrooms over, replacing the paper and lid, and return to the oven for 20 minutes more, or until the mushrooms are very tender but not falling apart. Use a pair of tongs to transfer the mushrooms to a chopping board, then cut them in half and set aside.

3. Reserving the oil, use a spoon to transfer the onion, garlic, and chile (discarding the stem; don't worry if you scoop up some of the spices and oil) into the bowl of a small food processor and blitz until smooth. Return the blitzed onion mixture to the saucepan, along with the mushroom halves, and place on medium-high heat. Cook for about 5 minutes, for all the flavors to come together.

4. For the mash: While the mushrooms are cooking, put the beans into a food processor along with the lemon juice, olive oil, water, and salt. Blitz until completely smooth. Transfer to a medium saucepan and cook on medium-high heat for about 3 minutes, stirring, until warmed through.

5. Divide the mash among four plates. Top with four mushroom halves per plate and spoon in a generous amount of the reserved oil and its accompanying aromatics (you won't need all of it, though as noted above). Serve at once.

PRODUCE

What you do to a vegetable and what you pair it with are two of the ways in which you amplify its flavor. In some cases, though, there's so much going on *within* the ingredient itself that it can pretty much do all the work on its own. Sure, it may still need baking or toasting or frying or roasting to tease out its deliciousness, but this will more often be a case of releasing what's inherent within the ingredient rather than having to rely on pairing it with something else or somehow transforming its character through process.

There are all sorts of ingredients that do this; ingredients that have the capacity to carry a dish through their sheer "oomph" and depth of flavor, or the interesting textural contrast they bring. These are often intensely savory foods, all rich in the fifth sense, umami. After the first four senses—sweet, sour, salty, and bitter—*umami* roughly translates from the Japanese as something like "deliciousness" or "savoriness." Umami is the result of flavor compounds called glutamates. Unlike monosodium glutamate (which gets a bad rep from being chemically manufactured and liberally sprinkled over many a take-out meal to make it taste generically "good"), there are many natural sources of glutamates—Parmesan or anchovies, tomatoes or fermented pickles, soy sauce, seaweed, Marmite, ketchup. And mushrooms, the first of our four ingredients that we celebrate here.

MUSHROOMS

Play the word-association game with mushrooms and, chances are, the next word to come along will be something like "earthy" or "woody." There's a good reason for this. Unlike plants, which grow above the ground, thereby harnessing energy from the sun, mushrooms—which are fungi—do all their growing underground. As mushrooms don't have the chlorophyll they'd need to get their energy from the sun, they go in search of nourishment elsewhere. Different mushrooms do this in different ways. Some live off plants, others live off plant remains and decay. They feed off whatever they can find. We don't see this network of fibers pushing through the soil to gain the nutrients they need to grow, and neither is this the part of the mushroom that we pick, cook, or eat. It is, nevertheless, the reason mushrooms taste so earthy.

It's also the reason why the flavor of one mushroom can differ so wildly and wonderfully from the flavor of another. What they live off affects how they taste. Mushrooms growing under chestnut trees will taste of chestnut and soil. Mushrooms growing under pine trees will taste of pine and soil. Yotam will never lose the memory of foraging for mushrooms with his grandmother when he was growing up in Jerusalem. They found the fungi under the pine trees in the hills surrounding the city. It was early autumn, after the first rains, and felt to Yotam a bit like magic, filling up sacks with mushrooms that appeared from nowhere to everywhere in one day. What he didn't know at the time, of course, was how much of the work was being done out of sight, as the mushrooms' network of fibers reached out underground, gathering energy and filling up with water. Returning home, it was always a shock, therefore, to witness just how much the booty in the sack shrank once cooked. The reward, on the other hand, was a concentrated essence of pine and soil, autumn and home.

As well as the location of the soil, the flavor, texture, and color of a mushroom are also affected by how long it's left in that soil. Pick a mushroom when it's young and it will be squeaky clean and relatively bland to taste. These are the little white closed-cup button mushrooms that make their way, very happily, into so many quick stir-fries and omelettes. Leave that same mushroom in the soil for a few more days or weeks, and it becomes bigger, browner, with a flavor that's

YOTAM WILL NEVER LOSE THE MEMORY OF FORAGING FOR MUSHROOMS WITH HIS GRANDMOTHER.

more complex and earthy. These are the nutty brown button mushrooms that we love to use in our cooking: grilled and marinated and sitting on top of a bowl of warm hummus (see PAGE 234) or bringing depth and body to the veritable mushroom party that is our SPICY MUSHROOM LASAGNE (PAGE 228). Here, mushrooms fill every conceivable party role: host and guest, DJ and dancer. Leave them a few days longer and they become even browner, earthier, and more robust, as they open to display their inky gills. These are portobello mushrooms, perennially happy to be sat on a baking sheet, gill-side up, dotted with cheese that will melt under the broiler, before being placed inside a brioche bun. Veggie burger sorted, since time immemorial.

Squeaky white buttons, nutty brown buttons, wide-capped portobellos; these are all common field mushrooms, also known as "agaric" mushrooms. Mushrooms in this group can be identified by looking under their caps; if they have fine gills radiating outward from the top of their stem, you are in the right field. It's the gill tissues that generate so much of the aroma of fresh common mushrooms. Those with immature, unopened caps—the baby white buttons, for example—won't have nearly as much flavor as the umbrella-wide

THE WORLD IS NOT ONLY GOING TO BE YOUR OYSTER BUT ALSO YOUR PORCINI AND YOUR SHIITAKE AND YOUR WILDEST OF ALL FLAVOR-BOMB DREAMS.

portobellos, which have been allowed to develop and mature more. Agaric mushrooms feed on plant remains and decay (rather than needing a living tree to grow under), so they can, as a result, be widely cultivated. The reason we have so many little white button mushrooms on our supermarket shelves is that they're really easy to produce.

The other category of mushrooms—the "boletes"—do need the soil beneath a tree as a home. These are the porcini, the carotene-orange chanterelles, and the pearly white oysters. Rather than having a firm stem, separate cap, and distinct gills, these mushrooms are more a spongy mass of gills. Boletes form a symbiosis with living trees, in which both partners benefit. The mushrooms gather soil minerals and share them with tree roots, which in turn share the tree's sugars with the mushrooms. The fact that these mushrooms need living trees—their intensive production requires a forest—and that they're still largely gathered from the wild is the reason they are still relatively rare and expensive. It's because of this, as well, that their taste is so wonderfully transporting, rich, and earthy.

For our purposes in *Flavor*, we've kept things relatively simple, using only six different types of mushrooms: three fresh and three dried. Given that the water content of mushrooms is high—80–90 percent—the difference in potential for the fresh versus dried mushroom to soak up flavors is going to be fairly great. Sure, fresh mushrooms love to be thrown into a pan with some oil and garlic and hard herbs, thirstily taking on the flavors they are paired with, but, first, they'll have to release much of their liquid before they can do this. Thankfully, this transference is pretty rapid because mushrooms, with their thin outer cuticle, can shed liquid as quickly as they can let it in. Just make sure you are not overcrowding the pan—they need space so that the liquid released can evaporate rather than form a soggy puddle—and you'll be five minutes away from a simple, tasty meal.

Start with dehydrated mushrooms, though, and you're going to have a veritable sponge on your hands once they're submerged in a liquid. Dial up the flavor of that liquid with soy sauce, sugar, and apple cider vinegar and the world is not only going to be your oyster but also your porcini and your shiitake and your wildest of all flavor-bomb dreams. When rehydrating mushrooms, always keep the liquid they've been soaking in, after they've been drained. Just as the mushrooms have taken on all the flavors in the stock, so the stock will take on the earthy flavor of the mushrooms. Combining the two in the making of our MUSHROOM KETCHUP (see PAGE 227) will take your appreciation of ketchup as the definitive umami-rich sauce to a whole new level.

Another approach with dried mushrooms, rather than rehydrating them and taking it from there, is to blitz them while still dry to form a mushroom powder. It's when armed with a jar of this, all set to sprinkle on our BROWN RICE AND SHIITAKE CONGEE (PAGE 237), for example, that the case against manufactured MSG can really be made, largely on the grounds of irrelevance. With a pot of dried, blitzed, and now powdered shiitake mushrooms, ready to spread their umami depth throughout the porridge-like congee, you won't need anything more to help boost the flavor. Magical mushroom dust indeed.

ALLIUMS

Behind so many delicious dishes, there's often an onion or two at work. Chopped and added to the pan with some oil, the smell of an onion—or its relatives, shallot or leek—being cooked is one of expectation and promise: a meal is underway! If this all sounds a bit much, it wouldn't be the first time we've been accused of onion-shaped hyperbole. Yotam once wrote in the *Guardian* newspaper that "every time we chop an onion and sweat it in oil, it changes from being something that makes us cry to something that makes us smile with joy." A reader responded. "Every time?" wrote Brian Smith from Berlin. "Don't be daft!" We couldn't help but giggle. Brian clearly had a point— it's a lot to put on a little onion—but we *do* stand by our strength of feeling. The transformation of onions from raw to cooked—from harsh and sulfurous to meltingly soft and sweet—does feel, to us, just a little bit like alchemy.

Peek behind the curtains of the magic show, though, and there's a fair amount of solid science and practical process at play. Unlike other vegetables, the onion family accumulates energy stores not in starch but in chains of fructose sugars, which long, slow cooking breaks down to produce a marked sweetness. The longer and slower the cooking of the onions, either in the oven

BEHIND SO MANY DELICIOUS DISHES, THERE'S OFTEN AN ONION OR TWO AT WORK.

or in a pan on the stove, the sweeter and the more caramelized these sugars become. This gives rise to glutamic acid. And it's this acid that gives rise to the big, yummy umami taste we're so often in search of in *Flavor*.

So much of this work—providing the sweet, caramelized base to many dishes—is what's going on when onions are behind the scenes, playing a background role. They're always there in the sofrito or mirepoix base: the diced onions, celery, and carrots or peppers that are so often sweated down as the first step to a stew or soup. But this everyday way of using onions isn't why they get a section all to themselves here. What we find so thrilling are all the instances in which *onioniness* becomes the "thing" a dish is all about. These are the thick FRIED ONION RINGS WITH BUTTERMILK AND TURMERIC (PAGE 255) or the charred red milder Tropea onions bulking out a summery GREEN GAZPACHO starter (see PAGE 242). They're the SWEET AND SOUR ONION PETALS (PAGE 245) stealing the show of anything they're plated up with, or the yellow onions, simply peeled and halved, baked with miso and butter until melting (see PAGE 258). If anything, we're thinking we need to be laying on a bit *more* hyperbole, Brian—not less!—to do justice to the onion.

The same is true of garlic. A caramelized garlic tart from *Plenty* was probably our first dish to be so clearly and unapologetically all about the garlic. More followed, often using a head or two of garlic in a single dish, cooked in different ways. Our freedom to use such lavish quantities relies totally on a breathtaking transformation of flavor that happens in the cooking; from something harsh, almost metallic, to something utterly sweet and mellow. One raw crushed garlic clove might be enough to make a salad dressing sing; *three whole garlic heads*, cloves separated and peeled, went into that garlic tart, making it the absolute sweetest of all savory tarts.

Again—as with onions—it's the impact of long, slow cooking on the chains of fructose sugars in the garlic that is being seen here. The harsh notes—those that can linger on the breath when garlic is eaten raw—are the result of sulfurous compounds contained within each clove. The more a garlic clove is crushed and minced when raw, the more the cell membranes are broken down and the more activated and released these compounds are. This is why one raw garlic clove, finely minced or crushed, goes a long way in a dressing. Gently crush that same clove, though, with the flat side of a big knife, or roast it whole, and no such activation takes place. Anyone in need of further convincing of the benign qualities of huge quantities of garlic needs to try the THREE-GARLIC BUTTER on PAGE 246, which sees ½ cup/100g of butter being able to handle one whole head of roasted garlic, one small raw garlic clove, and four black garlic cloves mashed in. Do a taste check, followed by a breath check, and *then* cast your vote.

The black garlic in this butter is something that anyone in search of deep umami flavor will adore. Rather than having to enact the transformation yourself in the kitchen, through the application of heat, black garlic is an ingredient where the work has already been done for you. Starting off as regular white cloves, the effects of time, heat treatment, and fermentation change them so that they become the licorice-black, wine-gum-soft-and-squishy cloves that they are. Thinly sliced, the cloves can be added to all sorts of rice dishes—any risotto, for example, or our DIRTY RICE on PAGE 252—or we like to blitz them up in a yogurt-based sauce.

It's not just black garlic cloves that can be thinly sliced to great effect. Several of the other dishes in this chapter—like the gently cooked leeks (see PAGE 257) or the platter of "meaty" chunks of roasted eggplant (see PAGE 251)—showcase the way in which a sliver of fried pale golden garlic can bring with it a welcome crunch and pop of un-fiery flavor that adds yet another layer of allium-ness. When garlic is thinly or "cleanly" sliced (as opposed to being minced or mashed when crushed), the process of activating the sulfurous compounds is relatively contained. As such, the garlic can turn

WHISTLING, WEARING GOGGLES: YOU CHOOSE. US? WE JUST THINK OF THE JOY AS WE CHOP.

crisp and crunchy and golden—thanks to its natural sugars—without being troubled by the acid enzyme. It's these same sugars that can, at the same time, see slices of garlic pass from being warm and sweet to burned and bitter in a matter of seconds, though, so keep a close eye on them in the pan and transfer them from the oil to a plate lined with paper towels just seconds before you think they're ready. As always, with alliums, it's a fine balance you need to strike to tease all the sweetness out of those bulbs. It takes some attention, applying judgment, and keeping an open eye—all small efforts for the sake of those magical flavors.

Of course, the opposite of the joy that alliums can bring—whether they are chopped or sliced—is the tears they can produce. These tears are the result of volatile compounds within the onion or garlic that are only released when they're cut. The best way of minimizing the release of these compounds is to start with a really sharp knife. This will lead to as "clean" and "neat" a break in the cell wall as possible, thereby reducing the level of volatile compound activation. Other recommendations abound. Some swear by putting onions into the freezer for 10 minutes before chopping, and/or sticking a piece of bread between your teeth as you work. Whistling, wearing goggles: you choose. Us? We just think of the joy as we chop—the expectation! the promise!—and smile, daftly, on.

NUTS AND SEEDS

If mushrooms, onions, and garlic are all about body and depth, nuts and seeds can all too easily be seen as sprinkle, surface, and light. And with their crunchy texture and nutty aroma, this can, clearly, be the case. As with our other categories of produce, though, nuts and seeds can also be about body and depth. They perform both roles—substance and surface—fantastically well.

First, though, some nuts and bolts. Strictly speaking, nuts—alongside grains (wheat, barley, rice, etc.) and legumes (beans and peas)—fall under the umbrella term "seeds." This broad definition, however, doesn't capture the way we use the words "nuts" and "seeds" as ingredients in the kitchen. For cooks, the definition relies on a couple of factors. One is that, when dry, they're ready to eat as they are. Unlike a dried pulse, for example, you can snack on a nut without any soaking or cooking or any other sort of -ing. Toasting them teases

OUR LIST OF THE WAYS IN WHICH TAHINI CAN BE ADDED TO A DISH . . . COULD BE VERY LONG INDEED.

out the flavor, sure, but it's not a necessary part of making them edible or digestible. They taste, well, nutty, and are full of rich and fatty oils. This makes them not only edible but, also, super-satisfying and very delicious.

It's useful to spell out what makes a nut *a nut* because it's these factors—their "being ready to be eaten as they are," their "nuttiness," and their "fattiness"— that, precisely, make them so good at bringing body and depth to a dish. Nut pastes, of which tahini is our favorite, are a marvelous manifestation of these three factors. To state what might seem like an obvious point, nut pastes are simply pastes made from blitzing nuts or seeds together. There is nothing else in tahini apart from sesame seeds! All the nutty flavor, rich oil, and fatty smoothness is sitting right there in the seeds, waiting to be released once the hulls are blitzed together. Our list of the ways in which tahini can be added to a dish to bring it substance could be very long indeed. From the obvious

HUMMUS (see PAGE 234) at one end to ROAST POTATOES (see PAGE 276) to the less obvious CUCUMBER (see PAGE 113) at the other, a dribble or drizzle or spoon of tahini can turn unassuming vegetables, such as chickpeas, potatoes, and cucumbers, into something rich and substantial.

As well as being rich and substantial, tahini also has the ability to be nutty and light. It's this that we really love about it. Tahini is happy to be thinned down as much as a dish requires. This allows the sauce to work well with vegetables without their flavor being subsumed. This dilution can happen with all sorts of things—again, depending on what the dish requires. Lemon juice and water work really well, as do tamarind or soy sauce by themselves, or soy sauce mixed with honey.

If dilution is one approach to lightening up the nuttiness, mixing the nut paste with another fat altogether is a very different approach. An Italian pesto is a familiar example, in which pine nuts, olive oil, and Parmesan are mixed to a paste (along with basil leaves and garlic). The nuttiness is broken down and, at the same time, complemented by other rich and fatty flavors, giving us a brilliantly complex experience. This same dynamic can be seen in our pumpkin seed and butter paste, into which our CORN RIBS (PAGE 264) are dipped. The butter both moderates the pumpkin seed flavor and, at the same time, enriches it. It also, rather wonderfully, melts nicely into the grooves between the corn kernels to give them a good coating.

In both these examples—the pesto and the pumpkin seed butter—we've mixed crushed nuts or seeds with dairy. We love to do this—it's a win-win!—but the dairy factor is not always necessary. Indeed, and thankfully—for vegans who want to experience the milky sensation without eating dairy—the crossover between nuts and seeds on the one hand and milk and eggs on the other is fairly direct. Take a small handful of seeds and nuts and see this for yourself; take your time chewing them and you'll get a genuinely milky sensation in your mouth.

Even if you're not vegan or don't think of nut pastes as alternatives to milk or eggs, we have found a natural tendency, in *Flavor*, to use them in places where, otherwise, a dollop of sour cream or a spoonful of mayonnaise would have made an appearance (see our CUCUMBER SALAD, PAGE 113, and our ROAST POTATOES, PAGE 276, respectively). More often than not, though, vegans use the natural creaminess of nuts consciously to make rich sauces that are normally impossible to achieve without eggs or dairy.

Coconuts are famously popular and very effective in giving depth, body, and smoothness to vegan soups and stews. We use coconut cream to achieve this in our STUFFED EGGPLANT (see PAGE 152), and there's also COCONUT ICE CREAM (see PAGE 286) that has a similar dairy-free creaminess. With a little more effort, a comparable texture and body can be achieved with other nuts too. Soaking or boiling almonds or cashews in water, then blitzing them smooth, is the basis for the frothy nut milks some like to pour into their cappuccinos. It's also a great way to get a splendidly creamy and rich sauce in which you can submerge your favorite roasted vegetable or our TOFU MEATBALLS (see PAGE 268).

As well as having an uncanny talent for disguising themselves as milk, nuts are also naturally "meaty," thanks to the high levels of fat and protein they contain. This quality has, however, led to what we think of as an unfortunate consequence called the Nut Loaf. Though we hear that there are versions of nut loafs out there that people swear by and love, we are yet to be convinced. From our experience, they are never as good as a good meatloaf (which is what they are modeled on), nor are they a great showcase for nuts, being soggy and often bland. As a vegetarian or vegan stand-in for the star turkey at the holiday table, we'd far rather have a whole roasted cauliflower, or our CELERY ROOT STEAKS WITH CAFÉ DE PARIS SAUCE (PAGE 60), with protein coming from side dishes with lentils, chickpeas, or soybeans.

AS WELL AS HAVING AN UNCANNY TALENT FOR DISGUISING THEMSELVES AS MILK, NUTS ARE ALSO NATURALLY "MEATY."

However, for anyone still craving nuts as the main star at the holiday table, we have our TURNIP CAKE (PAGE 270). Steamed, fried, then sprinkled with clusters of shiitake mushrooms, nuts, and seeds that are flavored with soy sauce, garlic, and maple syrup, this vegan take on a dish from a Chinese dim sum spread is a glorious centerpiece in both looks and complex flavor.

Our turnip cake is also an example of a dish that showcases the second role nuts and seeds can play in a dish. If we've looked at all the ways these can bring body and depth, the last-minute smattering of nuts here shows how effective their "surface and light" role can be as well. This is the case as much for an involved dish such as the turnip cake as it is for dishes that are simply and quickly assembled—our TOMATO AND PLUM SALAD WITH NORI AND SESAME (PAGE 267) or KOHLRABI "NOODLE" SALAD (PAGE 260).

There are all sorts of ways to achieve this sprinkle and crunch. The simplest is to take one kind of nut, roughly chop it up, and go from there. The impact of the almonds in our POTATO SALAD WITH THAI BASIL SAUCE (PAGE 275) is a case in point. The fact that you can easily buy already smoked, roasted, and salted almonds makes this almost a cheat's way of disseminating a cluster of little flavor bombs throughout a dish.

Starting with plain shelled nuts (sometimes also called "raw" nuts), then adding layers of flavor oneself, is also an easy win. The unsalted blanched peanuts in our RADISH AND CUCUMBER SALAD (see PAGE 263) confidently steal the show once they've been coated in a mix of chile, golden syrup (or maple syrup), salt, lime, and olive oil. At this point they're also, incidentally, the bar snack of all bar snacks.

Putting together a combination of seeds and nuts—rather than just starting with almonds or peanuts—is also a simple option that can yield disproportionate results. Individually, a tablespoon or two of sesame seeds or half a teaspoon of chile flakes might not seem too exciting. Combine them, though, with a bit of flaked sea salt and half a sheet of blitzed, umami-rich nori seaweed, as we do in our TOMATO AND PLUM SALAD, and you suddenly have something that punches well above the little sesame seeds' weight.

A couple of practical notes to end on. The first is to always taste your seeds and nuts before you use them. The same oils that make nuts so appealing also make them go rancid quite easily. Walnuts, cashews, and peanuts are particularly prone to spoilage. Have a nibble and if they taste rancid or floury, get yourself some more. Unfortunately, no amount of toasting or blitzing is able to *undo* rancid or floury! Second, even if a recipe does not call for nuts or seeds to be toasted, we tend to always give them a little bit of time spread out on a baking sheet in a 350°F/160°C fan oven. Doing this draws out the oil in the nut or seed and just makes them taste a bit "nuttier" and "seedier." You can toast them in a pan on the stove, instead, if you prefer; just be sure to stir very frequently and keep a close eye on them. Also, remove them from the pan a little bit before they are done—they keep on browning off the heat. Don't get distracted, or you'll be cursing your half-raw, half-burned pine nuts before the fun has even started.

SUGAR—FRUIT AND BOOZE

When we say that particular types of ingredients—mushrooms, onions, nuts, and sugar being the four we have identified—have a unique ability to carry a whole dish by themselves and give it its particular edge, sugar is probably the simplest example. How the natural umaminess in mushrooms is key to making a vegetarian lasagne taste meaty is not an intuition we all have. The fact that desserts need sweetness in them, in one form or another, is a natural truth everyone understands.

For this reason, it is tempting to look at umami, sitting at the opposite end of the flavor spectrum to sweet, as being interesting, complex, and nuanced in a way a dessert could never be, while dismissing sweetness as being one-dimensional. Sweetness equals sugar and sugar equals sweetness; the two get conflated in the mind. Sugar comes in a package saying either "granulated," "confectioners," "light brown," or "dark brown," and we all know that we shouldn't eat too much of it. That's all there is to it, right?

But what about all the other ways sugar can be introduced into our cooking and baking—all the different places and produce it can be harnessed from or teamed with for its complexity of flavor? What about all the amazing varieties of honey we can use for our TAPIOCA FRITTERS (see PAGE 280), for example? What about the natural sweetness of vanilla and star anise, or the smoky sweetness that happens when sugar is mixed with ancho chile to make a flan (see PAGE 278)? Or the perfumed sweetness of the orange blossom water used for POACHED APRICOTS (see PAGE 282)? The sugar we get from a package might be one thing, but there are so many more shades of sweetness. Rather than looking at sugar per se, it's in these sugary shades and shadows that our interest lies. In our constant pursuit of flavor—big, nuanced, dialed-up flavor—it's here that we want to head.

If it's shades and shadows we're interested in, one of the best places to look is under a sun-dappled tree. A fruit-growing tree, specifically, which is our first stop at the sweet shop. Using fruit as a means to create all kinds of intricate and complex layers of sweetness is our absolute favorite way of getting sugar into our cooking, particularly when making dessert. All but one of our desserts, in fact, have fruit in them, in one form or another. Watermelons and strawberries bring the sweetness of summer to our WATERMELON AND STRAWBERRY SORBET (PAGE 283), and bananas, coconuts, lychees, and passion fruit bring the taste of the tropics to our CRÊPES WITH ROASTED BANANAS AND BARBADOS CREAM (PAGE 290) and our COCONUT ICE CREAM (see PAGE 286). Our favorite lemons, limes, oranges, and tangerines are so often there, ensuring that sweetness comes also with a citrus tang. In

THE SUGAR WE GET FROM A PACKAGE MIGHT BE ONE THING, BUT THERE ARE SO MANY MORE SHADES OF SWEETNESS.

some desserts this is happening in a big, look-at-me way: MAX AND FLYNN'S LEMON SORBET (PAGE 289), for example, is served inside a hollowed-out lemon, no less! But citrus fruit can be equally as important when playing a background role, serving mainly to pull back the sweetness from becoming too cloying.

Chopping, pulping, juicing, zesting—these are some ways to get fresh, fruity sweetness into a dessert. Dig in and dig down, though, and you see the fruit at work in different ways, often with altogether different ingredients. Take our POACHED APRICOTS WITH PISTACHIO AND AMARETTI MASCARPONE (PAGE 282). The fresh apricots are there, of course, halved and pitted and ready to be poached. But then apricot pits have also been used to make the amaretto liqueur, which, in turn, is used in the making of amaretti cookies, which are then crushed into the mascarpone. Look further into that mascarpone and, again, you see citrus juice at work. Although lemon juice might not be listed as an ingredient in the recipe for poached apricots, it's what's added to whole milk in the first place, to activate the coagulation that needs to take place in the making of mascarpone. Fruit is playing every role here: out front in the foreground, in the middle with the pack, as well as in the background, offstage but still important.

The relationship between sweetness and ripeness in fruit is clear; the riper the fruit, the sweeter, softer, and juicier it will be. What might be less obvious is the difference between climacteric and non-climacteric fruit. Climacteric fruit such as bananas, apricots, tomatoes, and melons store their sugar in the form of starch. Once picked, this starch is converted back into sweetness. This makes them forgiving and versatile to the home cook, who can either ripen them at home or enhance their sweetness through cooking. Non-climacteric

IF WE HAD OUR WAY, EVERY DESSERT WOULD BE DRENCHED IN SOME SORT OF SWEET WINE.

fruit, on the other hand, is not so malleable. This category includes things such as peaches, strawberries, grapes, and citrus fruit. Their sweetness will not develop beyond the point at which they're picked. So, when we state the need for 3 cups/300g of *ripe* strawberries for our watermelon and strawberry sorbet, then ripe-and-ready they need to be. Making a sorbet with unripe strawberries is never going to capture the essence of summer.

Second only to fresh fruit as our favorite means of bringing sugar to the dessert table in an interesting way, is fermented fruit in the form of sweet wine. If we had our way, every dessert would be drenched in some sort of sweet wine, with a boozy trifle being the definition of perfection. Sauternes, the sweet French wine, has a wonderfully concentrated, honeyed, crisp, exotic, raisin-like taste. This is due to the "noble rot"—or good fungus—that attacks the three grapes from which the wine is made, adding flavor to and intensifying their natural sweetness. The fermentation we trumpeted so passionately in a savory context in the Aging section is also a massive flavor-enhancing factor here.

It's not just sweet fruit that can be boozy and bottled as wine. Rum, for example, used in our BARBADOS CREAM (see PAGE 290), is made from the fermenting and distilling of sugarcane molasses. Amaretto, the sweet Italian liqueur, is made from brown sugar, vodka (itself made from sweet corn), almond extract, and vanilla extract. The number of different and various sweet notes contained within just these three tipples—honeyed, raisiny Sauternes; grassy, toasted, spiced rum; and bitter almond amaretto—points to quite how many very sweet directions in which recipes that use them can be taken. The idea that sweetness is one-dimensional becomes, after a few sips, very hard—quite literally—to sustain.

SERVES FOUR
As a starter or as a side

BROCCOLI WITH MUSHROOM KETCHUP AND NORI

MUSHROOM KETCHUP
¾ oz/20g dried porcini mushrooms, soaked in 1⅔ cups/400ml hot water for 20 minutes
7½ tsp superfine sugar
3 tbsp light soy sauce
7 oz/200g shiitake mushrooms, stems discarded and caps roughly chopped
2 tbsp apple cider vinegar
2 tbsp olive oil
1½ tsp flaked sea salt
black pepper

1 lb 5 oz/600g Broccolini, trimmed and leaves removed
2 garlic cloves, crushed
3 tbsp olive oil
flaked sea salt and black pepper

NORI TOPPING
1 tbsp sesame seeds, toasted
2 tsp nori sprinkles (or finely blitz ½ sheet of nori in a spice grinder and use 2 tsp)
4½ tsp crispy shallots, roughly crumbled
3 tbsp roasted and salted peanuts, finely chopped
1 tsp Aleppo chile flakes or Gochugaru Korean hot pepper flakes (or ½ tsp regular chile flakes)
1½ tsp flaked sea salt

We suggest using Broccolini to make this dish. Normal broccoli is fine as well, but you'll need to blanch the florets for 2–3 minutes, then drain and dry them before you roast them in the oven. The mushroom ketchup is full of complexity and flavor. It's good spread on toast, or in any situation that calls for ketchup, so feel free to double the recipe. It will keep in a sealed jar in the fridge for up to 1 week.

1. Preheat the oven to 500°F/240°C fan. Line a baking sheet with parchment paper.

2. For the ketchup: Drain the porcini mushrooms, reserving their liquid, and roughly chop them.

3. Put the sugar into a medium saucepan and place on medium heat. Let cook, resisting the urge to stir, for about 12 minutes, or until the sugar is a light caramel color. Carefully add the soy sauce and 3 tbsp reserved porcini liquid and stir to combine; it will bubble and sizzle vigorously (don't worry if it seizes up a little, it will melt back down). Increase the heat to medium-high, add the shiitakes, and cook for 4 minutes, or until they have released their liquid and are well coated in the caramel. Add the rehydrated porcini and 1 cup/240ml of their soaking liquid, then bring to a boil and cook for 8 minutes, or until the sauce has reduced by half. Transfer the mixture to a food processor and blitz until quite smooth, about 1 minute. With the machine still running, add the vinegar, olive oil, salt, and a good grind of pepper and blitz for another 2 minutes, until completely smooth, then set aside to cool (you want it at room temperature).

4. In a large bowl, toss together the Broccolini, garlic, olive oil, 1 tsp salt, and a good grind of pepper. Transfer to the prepared baking sheet and roast for 8 minutes, or until cooked through and lightly charred.

5. For the topping: While the Broccolini is in the oven, in a small bowl, combine the sesame seeds, nori sprinkles, crispy shallots, peanuts, chile flakes, and salt. Stir to mix.

6. Spread the mushroom ketchup on a platter, then top with the Broccolini and a few spoonfuls of the nori topping, serving any additional alongside.

SPICY MUSHROOM LASAGNE

SERVES SIX
As a main

1 lb 10 oz/750g brown button mushrooms, halved
1 lb 2 oz/500g oyster mushrooms
9 tbsp/135ml olive oil
table salt
2¼ oz/60g dried porcini mushrooms
1 oz/30g dried wild mushrooms
2 dried red chiles, roughly chopped (seeded for less heat)
2 cups plus 2 tbsp/500ml hot vegetable stock
1 onion, peeled and quartered
5 garlic cloves, roughly chopped
1 carrot, peeled and quartered (3¼ oz/90g)
2–3 plum tomatoes, quartered (7 oz/200g)
⅓ cup/75g tomato paste
black pepper
3⅓ cups/800ml water
9 tbsp/135ml heavy cream
2¼ oz/60g pecorino, finely grated
2¼ oz/60g Parmesan, finely grated
¼ cup/5g basil leaves, finely chopped
½ cup/10g parsley leaves, finely chopped, plus 1 tsp
9 oz/250g dried lasagne sheets (about 14 sheets)

This lasagne contains one of two epic ragù recipes in this book—the other is the ultimate roasting-pan ragù, page 101—that, we believe, give any meat ragù a terrifically good run for its money.

This particular ragù pays homage to penne all'Aconese, the first dish that Ixta fell madly in love with. It's served at Ristorante Pizzeria Acone, a community-run restaurant in the Tuscan village of Acone, perched at the top of the mountain on which she spent her formative childhood years. The recipe is a closely guarded secret, but the complex, earthy, and deeply umami flavor of dried porcini mushrooms is impossible to miss. This is our meatless take on that mythical sauce.

The ragù can easily be made vegan if you lose the cream. It can also be made ahead and refrigerated, ready to be served with pasta or polenta, saving yourself the trouble of constructing the lasagne if you're short on time.

Pull back on the black pepper and lose the chile for a child-friendly version. If you want to get ahead, the lasagne can be assembled, refrigerated, and then baked the next day (once it has come back up to room temperature). *Pictured on pages 230–231.*

1. Preheat the oven to 450°F/220°C fan. Line a large, rimmed baking sheet with parchment paper.

2. Put the button mushrooms and oyster mushrooms into the bowl of a food processor, in three or four batches, and pulse each batch until finely chopped (or finely chop everything by hand). Toss the chopped mushrooms in a large bowl with 3 tbsp of the olive oil and 1 tsp salt and spread out on the prepared baking sheet. Roast for 30 minutes near the top of the oven, stirring three times throughout, until the mushrooms are golden brown; they will have reduced in volume significantly. Set aside. Decrease the oven temperature to 425°F/200°C fan.

3. Meanwhile, combine all the dried mushrooms, the chiles, and hot stock in a large bowl and set aside to soak for 30 minutes. Strain the liquid into another bowl, squeezing as much liquid from the mushrooms as possible to get just under 1½ cups/340ml–if you have any less, top up with water. Very roughly chop the rehydrated mushrooms (you want some chunks) and finely chop the chiles. Set the stock and mushrooms aside separately.

4. Put the onion, garlic, and carrot into the food processor and pulse until finely chopped (or finely chop everything by hand). Heat ¼ cup/60ml olive oil in a large sauté pan or pot on medium-high heat. Once hot, add the onion mixture and fry for 8 minutes, stirring occasionally, until soft and golden. Pulse the tomatoes in the food processor until finely chopped (or finely chop by hand), then add to the pan along with the tomato paste, 1½ tsp salt, and 1¾ tsp pepper. Cook for 7 minutes, stirring occasionally. Add the rehydrated mushrooms and chiles and the roasted mushrooms and cook for 9 minutes. Resist the urge to stir; you want the mushrooms to be slightly crisp and browned on the bottom. Stir in the water and reserved stock and, once simmering, decrease the heat to medium and cook for about 25 minutes, stirring occasionally, until you get the consistency of a ragù. Stir in 7 tbsp/105ml of the cream and simmer for another 2 minutes, then remove from the heat.

5. Combine both cheeses, the basil, and ½ cup/10g parsley in a small bowl. Spread one-fifth of the sauce in the bottom of a round 12-inch/30cm baking dish (or a 9 x 13-inch/23 x 33cm rectangular dish), then top with a fifth of the cheese mixture, followed by a layer of lasagne sheets, broken to fit where necessary. Repeat these layers three more times in that order, and finish with a final layer of sauce and cheese; that's five layers of sauce, five layers of cheese, and four layers of pasta.

6. Drizzle with 1 tbsp cream and 1 tbsp olive oil, then cover with aluminum foil and bake for 15 minutes. Remove the foil, increase the temperature to 450°F/220°C fan, and bake for another 12 minutes, rotating the dish halfway through. Turn the oven to the broil setting and broil for a final 2 minutes, until the edges are brown and crisp. Set aside to cool for 5 minutes or so, then drizzle with the remaining 1 tbsp cream and 1 tbsp olive oil. Sprinkle with the 1 tsp parsley and finish with a good grind of pepper. Serve at once.

NOODLE SALAD WITH MUSHROOM AND PEANUT LAAB

SERVES FOUR
As a main

2 tbsp basmati rice
7 oz/200g dried vermicelli rice noodles
1 qt/1L boiling water
table salt
10½ oz/300g green beans, trimmed and cut in half crosswise
½ large cucumber (7 oz/200g), quartered lengthwise, seeded, and cut into ⅟₁₆-inch/2mm-thick slices at an angle
2 red chiles, seeded and julienned (¾ oz/20g)
½ red onion (2¼ oz/60g), peeled and thinly sliced
5 tbsp/70g store-bought tamarind paste (double if you're extracting it yourself from pulp; see page 20)
¼ cup/60ml maple syrup
3 tbsp fish sauce (optional; use 2 tbsp light soy sauce, if you like)
2 tbsp soy sauce
5 tbsp/75ml lime juice (from 4–5 limes)
9 tbsp/135ml peanut oil
10½ oz/300g brown button mushrooms, finely chopped
10½ oz/300g oyster mushrooms, roughly torn
1 tsp red chile flakes
scant **1 cup/120g raw peanuts,** lightly roasted and finely chopped
¼ cup/5g mint leaves
¼ cup/5g Thai basil leaves
½ cup/10g cilantro leaves

We use mushrooms and peanuts here for a vegan (if not including the fish sauce, which is optional) take on laab, a ground meat dish from Thailand and Laos. Our laab is mixed with rice noodles to create a fresh salad that is rich and complex enough to make a wholesome meal in itself.

The noodles and laab can be made up to 3 hours before, if you want to get ahead, but don't add the herbs or assemble until you're ready to serve.

1. Put the rice into a small pan on medium heat and toast for 10 minutes, or until the rice begins to color and smell nutty. Remove from the heat and, once cool, grind to a fine powder in a mortar and pestle or spice grinder. Set aside.

2. Put the noodles into a heatproof bowl, top with the boiling water, and then cover with a large plate or lid and let soften for 10 minutes. Drain, rinse under cold water, and drain again.

3. Meanwhile, bring a small pot of water to a boil. Add 1 tsp salt and the green beans and boil for 3 minutes. Drain and rinse under cold water, to stop the beans from cooking more, then drain again.

4. In a large bowl, toss the drained noodles with the green beans, cucumber, chiles, onion, and ¼ tsp salt and set aside.

5. In a separate bowl, whisk together the tamarind paste, maple syrup, 2 tbsp of the fish sauce (if using), 1 tbsp of the soy sauce, 3 tbsp of the lime juice, and 6 tbsp/90ml of the peanut oil and set this dressing aside.

6. Heat the remaining 3 tbsp peanut oil in a large sauté pan on high heat. Add all the mushrooms and cook for 12 minutes, stirring occasionally, until the liquid from the mushrooms has cooked away and the mushrooms have browned. Add the chile flakes and cook for 2 minutes more. Remove from the heat and stir in the peanuts, ground rice, remaining 1 tbsp fish sauce, 1 tbsp soy sauce, and 2 tbsp lime juice. Keep this laab warm.

7. When ready to serve, add all the herbs to the noodle salad along with half the tamarind dressing and toss to combine.

8. Pour the remaining dressing over the mushroom laab and mix well. Spread the laab out on a platter, then top with the noodles so the laab can still be seen around the edges.

SERVES FOUR
As a side or as part
of a mezze spread

CONFIT GARLIC HUMMUS WITH GRILLED MUSHROOMS

GRILLED MUSHROOMS
5 oz/140g brown button mushrooms, quartered
4¼ oz/120g shiitake mushrooms, roughly torn in half
1 garlic clove, crushed with the side of a knife
¼ cup/60ml olive oil
1 lemon: finely shave the peel to get 3 strips, then juice to get 2 tbsp
¼ oz/5g thyme sprigs
1½ tsp maple syrup
1½ tsp flaked sea salt
black pepper
1 dried cascabel chile

CONFIT GARLIC
HUMMUS
2 heads of garlic, top fifth cut off to expose the cloves
2 tbsp olive oil
flaked sea salt and black pepper
3 tbsp ice-cold water
2 tbsp lemon juice
2 tbsp tahini
scant 2 cups/300g Basic Cooked Chickpeas (page 79) or canned chickpeas

1 tbsp dill, roughly chopped
1½ tsp parsley, finely chopped

The hummus will keep for up to 3 days in the fridge, covered with a little oil so the surface doesn't form a crust. The mushrooms, however, are best grilled on the day of serving, as they become limp and less meaty when they spend time in the fridge.

1. For the mushrooms: Heat a large grill pan on high heat and add all the mushrooms, spread out (you may need to do this in batches, depending on the size of your pan). Grill for about 8 minutes, turning throughout, until all sides have dark char marks. Add the mushrooms to a medium bowl with the crushed garlic, olive oil, lemon strips, lemon juice, thyme, maple syrup, salt, and a generous grind of pepper. Mix well.

2. Add the dried chile to the grill pan and cook for 4 minutes, until fragrant. Roughly chop the chile and add it, along with its seeds, to the bowl with the mushrooms and set aside to marinate for 1–2 hours.

3. For the hummus: Preheat the oven to 425°F/200°C fan.

4. Drizzle the heads of garlic with 1 tbsp of the olive oil and sprinkle with a little salt and pepper. Wrap tightly in aluminum foil and place in the oven for 40 minutes, until the cloves have softened and are golden brown. Remove the foil and, when cool enough to handle, squeeze out the cloves, discarding the papery skins.

5. In a food processor, combine the cooked garlic, water, lemon juice, tahini, chickpeas, remaining 1 tbsp olive oil and ¾ tsp salt. Blitz until smooth, scraping down the sides of the bowl as you go, if necessary.

6. Spread the hummus in a shallow bowl, creating a large well in the center with the back of a spoon. Stir the dill and parsley into the mushrooms, then spoon into the well, along with the oil and aromatics. Serve at once.

BROWN RICE AND SHIITAKE CONGEE

SERVES FOUR
As a main

⅓ cup/80ml
sunflower oil
6 green onions, finely
chopped (¾ cup/60g)
1½ oz/40g fresh ginger,
peeled and very finely
chopped
6 garlic cloves, very finely
chopped (3 tbsp)
table salt
¾ cup plus 2 tbsp/
180g short-grain
brown rice
1¾ oz/50g dried shiitake
mushrooms, roughly
chopped
6⅓ cups/1.5L water
5¼ oz/150g rainbow or
breakfast radishes,
thinly sliced
2 tbsp rice vinegar
½ tsp superfine sugar

RAYU
2 tbsp red bell pepper
flakes (or 1 tbsp
Aleppo chile flakes
or Gochugaru Korean
hot pepper flakes)
½ tsp regular chile flakes
4½ tsp white sesame
seeds, toasted
1 tbsp black sesame
seeds, toasted
2½ tsp finely grated
tangerine zest
7½ tsp soy sauce
½ batch fried green
onion–oil mixture
(reserved from above;
see step 1)

2 green onions, julienned
(¼ cup/20g)
1¾ oz/50g crispy shallots

Congee is a rice porridge enjoyed across Asia and Southeast Asia. This congee—"like an amazing mushroom risotto, but more exciting," to quote Claudine, our recipe tester—can be served for a weekend brunch or an autumn supper. Soft-boiled egg or grilled or smoked fish are great served on top, if you are looking for a more substantial meal, as well as sautéed Asian greens served alongside.

Rayu is a Japanese chile oil often enjoyed with rice, ramen, or gyoza. Our variation includes tangerine zest (you can use orange instead), which sweetens and enriches it. You can make it even if you are not preparing the congee, and keep it in the fridge for whenever you need a bit of additional spice over your food. If you choose to do that, use all the sautéed green onions, ginger, garlic, and oil mixture and stir it together with double the other rayu ingredients, along with another ¼ cup/60ml of warm sunflower oil. It will keep in a sealed jar in the fridge for up to 2 weeks.

Make the congee the day before, if you want to get ahead. You may need to add a splash of water to loosen it when you reheat.

1. Put the sunflower oil, chopped green onions, ginger, garlic, and ¼ tsp salt into a large, high-sided sauté pan on medium heat. Fry for about 12 minutes, stirring often, until soft and very aromatic. Decrease the heat if the green onion mixture begins to color or sizzle too much. Remove from the heat and strain through a sieve, reserving the oil. Return half the green onion mixture to the pan. Put the oil and remaining green onion mixture into a small bowl and set aside.

2. In two batches, blitz the brown rice in the bowl of a small food processor, pulsing until the grains become roughly broken but not powdery. Set aside.

3. Add the shiitake mushrooms to a spice grinder or food processor, in two or three batches, and pulse until chopped into roughly ½-inch/1cm pieces. Add the rice and shiitake to the sauté pan with the green onion mixture and return to medium-high heat. Add the water and 1¼ tsp salt and bring to a simmer, then decrease the heat to medium. Cook the rice for 30 minutes, stirring often, until soft and the consistency of a wet porridge.

4. While the rice is cooking, put the radishes into a small bowl with the vinegar, sugar, and ¼ tsp salt and set aside to lightly pickle.

5. For the rayu: Add the bell pepper flakes, chile flakes, all the sesame seeds, tangerine zest, and soy sauce to the reserved green onion–oil mixture and stir to combine.

6. When the rice is cooked, divide it among four bowls and top each with the rayu. Garnish with the pickled radishes, julienned green onions, and crispy shallots. Serve at once.

OYSTER MUSHROOM TACOS WITH ALL (OR SOME OF) THE FIXIN'S

MAKES TWELVE TACOS
Serves four as a main

PICKLED ONIONS
1 red onion, finely sliced into rounds on a mandoline, if you have one, or by hand (1¼ cups/150g)
2 oranges: finely shave the peel to get 6 strips, then juice to get ¼ cup/60ml
2 hibiscus tea bags, or ¼ oz/5g dried hibiscus flowers (optional)
10 allspice berries
¼ cup/60ml white wine vinegar
1 tsp superfine sugar
¼ tsp table salt

AVOCADO CREMA
1 medium avocado, pitted and peeled
⅓ cup/90g coconut cream
½ cup/10g cilantro, roughly chopped
1 tsp water
¼ tsp table salt

PICKLED KOHLRABI
1 small kohlrabi (or a large radish), peeled and cut into wide matchsticks (1 cup/120g)
4½ tsp lime juice
¼ tsp table salt

1 lb 8 oz/680g oyster mushrooms, roughly torn
2 garlic cloves, crushed
3 tbsp soy sauce
4½ tsp maple syrup
7 tbsp/105ml olive oil
table salt
1 tsp cumin seeds
4 dried cascabel chiles or ancho chiles, stems removed, roughly broken
½ tsp allspice berries

A taco meal has an elasticity to it that appeals both to diners, who get to "make" their own food as they assemble their tacos, and to the cook, who can choose how much effort he or she would like to put in. Here, you can prepare your own tortillas, which will make you feel as though you'd conquered a substantial Mexican summit, or use store-bought corn tortillas instead. Jarred pickles and a tub of guacamole are reasonable alternatives to our homemade (yet super-quick) versions. The only essential bit, which you won't regret adding to your repertoire, is the roasted oyster mushrooms, which are crispy, chewy, and soft all at once, and soak up flavors like little sponges. The mushrooms also pair wonderfully with our fresh corn polenta (see page 140) or Esme's rough squash mash (page 136).

The pickles can be made the day before, as can the tortillas. The tortillas should be kept covered with a kitchen towel and warmed through in a pan or a hot oven just before you serve. *Pictured on pages 240–241.*

1. Preheat the oven to 425°F/200°C fan. Line two large rimmed baking sheets with parchment paper.

2. For the pickled onions: In a small serving bowl, mix together the red onion, orange peel, orange juice, tea bags (if using), allspice, vinegar, sugar, and salt and set aside.

3. For the crema: In the bowl of a small food processor, combine the avocado, coconut cream, cilantro, water, and salt. Blitz until smooth, scraping down the sides of the bowl as you go. Transfer to a small serving bowl and set aside.

4. For the kohlrabi: In a small serving bowl, mix together the kohlrabi, lime juice, and salt and set aside.

5. In a large bowl, mix the mushrooms with the garlic, soy sauce, maple syrup, 5 tbsp/75ml of the olive oil, and ¾ tsp salt. Blitz the cumin seeds, chiles, and allspice to a powder in a spice grinder or a mortar and pestle. Put 1½ tsp of the spice mix into a small bowl with the remaining 2 tbsp olive oil and set aside. Stir the rest of the spice mix into the bowl of mushrooms.

6. Transfer the mushrooms to the prepared baking sheets, spread out as much as possible, and roast for 20 minutes. Combine all the mushrooms on one sheet, mix well, and continue to roast for another 8 minutes, until crisp and browned.

TORTILLAS
1 cup plus 2 tbsp/125g masa harina, plus more as needed
table salt
1 cup/240 ml boiling water

2 limes, cut into wedges

7. For the tortillas: While the mushrooms are roasting, put the masa harina and a good pinch of salt into a medium bowl and pour in the boiling water, stirring with a spatula until the dough comes together, and then set aside. Once the dough is cool enough to handle, knead into a smooth ball that has the texture of play-dough (this should take less than a minute). The dough shouldn't be wet or come off in your hands, so you may need to add a bit more masa harina (depending on the brand you are using, as they can absorb water differently). Divide the dough into twelve pieces weighing about 1 oz/30g each. With lightly greased hands, roll each piece into a smooth ball. Keep any dough you're not working with covered with a clean damp cloth.

8. Get a clean kitchen towel ready and cut out six 6-inch/15cm pieces of parchment paper, which you'll need to help you press the dough. Place a large, nonstick frying pan on high heat. Place one piece of dough between two sheets of parchment, then, using a heavy-bottomed pan (or a tortilla press, if you have one), press down evenly and firmly on the dough to spread it out into a circle 4–5 inches/10–12cm wide. Remove the top sheet of parchment and use the bottom sheet to transfer the tortilla to the hot pan. Cook for 90 seconds until nicely browned, then flip and cook for another 1 minute to brown the other side. Transfer the cooked tortilla to the kitchen towel, fold it over to cover, and repeat with the remaining dough (cook as many tortillas at a time as will fit in the pan).

9. Warm the mushrooms in a hot oven for a few minutes if they have cooled, then pile onto a large platter and drizzle with the reserved chile oil. Serve with the tortillas, lime wedges, crema, and both pickles (discard the tea bags from the onions) alongside.

SERVES SIX TO EIGHT
As a starter

NEIL'S GRILLED ONIONS WITH GREEN GAZPACHO

GREEN GAZPACHO
2 green bell peppers, halved lengthwise and seeded (8½ oz/240g)
½ small cucumber, roughly chopped (1⅓ cups/200g)
1 green chile, roughly chopped
¾ cup/20g chives
½ cup/10g cilantro leaves
¼ cup/5g tarragon leaves
¼ cup/5g parsley leaves
4½ tsp apple cider vinegar
1 tbsp olive oil
2 tbsp water
¼ tsp table salt

8 Tropea onions, papery outer layers removed, trimmed, halved lengthwise, leaving the shoots intact (or 4 red onions, peeled and quartered)
4 tsp olive oil
2 tsp lemon juice
table salt and black pepper
4½ oz/120g feta, roughly broken
⅓ cup/80g Greek-style yogurt
¾ oz/20g croutons, roughly chopped
¼ tsp nigella seeds

This elegant starter was created by Neil Campbell, the charming and creative head chef at ROVI, as a true celebration of the humble onion. When we can, we use Calabrian Tropea onions in the restaurant, which are light red, sweet, and wonderfully mild, but other varieties of mild onion are fine, too, including regular red onions.

The gazpacho will keep for 3 days in a sealed container in the fridge, as will the whipped feta yogurt, if you want to get ahead. You'll make more gazpacho than you need. Whatever's left, serve in shot glasses to kick-start a summery supper.

Serve as part of a mezze spread (see page 304), or as an elegant starter, individually plated.

1. Preheat the oven to 450°F/220°C fan. Line a baking sheet with parchment paper.

2. For the gazpacho: Place the bell peppers on the prepared baking sheet, skin-side up, and roast for 25–30 minutes, until the skin has blackened a little. Transfer to a small bowl, cover with a plate, and let rest for 20 minutes, then peel off and discard the skin. Put the peppers into a blender with the cucumber, chile, chives, cilantro, tarragon, parsley, vinegar, olive oil, water, and salt. Blitz for a few minutes, until you get a smooth, green sauce, then set aside in the refrigerator.

3. Decrease the oven temperature to 400°F/180°C fan. Heat a large, nonstick frying pan on high heat. Toss the onions with 2 tsp of the olive oil, lemon juice, ¼ tsp salt, and some pepper. Place the onions, cut-side down, in the hot pan, then decrease the heat to medium-high. For halved Tropea onions, cook for 5–6 minutes, undisturbed, until the cut side is well charred. For quartered red onions, cook for 5–6 minutes on each cut side, until well charred. Place the onions in a baking dish, cover with aluminum foil, and bake until soft and cooked through but still holding their shape. This can take anywhere between 30–40 minutes, depending on the type of onion.

4. Put the feta and yogurt into the bowl of a small food processor and blitz until as smooth as possible (some small lumps will probably remain, which is fine).

5. Spread the whipped feta on a large platter, creating a dip in the middle with the back of a spoon. Pour about one-fourth of the gazpacho into the dip, then arrange the onions haphazardly on top. Finish with the croutons and nigella seeds and drizzle with the remaining 2 tsp olive oil. Serve at once.

SWEET AND SOUR ONION PETALS

SERVES FOUR
As a starter or as part
of a mezze spread

**1 lb 2 oz/500g golf
ball–size red onions**
(about 12), peeled,
then halved lengthwise

5 tbsp/75ml olive oil

table salt

**1⅔ cups/400ml
pomegranate juice**
(100% pure)

⅓ cup/10g chives, finely
chopped

**2½ oz/70g young and
creamy rindless goat
cheese,** broken into
¾-inch/2cm pieces
(optional)

⅔ tsp Urfa chile flakes
(or the same amount
of crushed ancho or
chipotle chiles)

These onions—sweet inside, charred at the edges, and swimming in a tart pomegranate syrup—started their life at Testi, a north London Turkish restaurant that we love, where a similar dish is made by charring onions next to lamb on the grill, then tossing them in şalgam, a juice made from the sour-salty brine of fermented purple carrots and turnips, and finally sweetening them with pomegranate molasses. The bittersweet onions are served alongside the meat, cutting through its fattiness like a sharp knife.

Our onions are made with reduced pomegranate juice instead of molasses and şalgam. They would obviously sit well alongside grilled meats, but we find them totally delicious also in a vegetarian context, with or without the goat cheese, which is optional. They will go really well with hummus (like our hummus with lemon, fried garlic, and chile, page 79), an eggplant salad (see eggplant with herbs and crispy garlic, page 251), and some bread.

1. Preheat the oven to 425°F/200°C fan. Line a baking sheet with parchment paper.

2. Heat a large nonstick frying pan on high heat until very hot. Toss the onions with 2 tbsp of the olive oil and ¼ tsp salt and place them, cut-side down and spread apart, in the hot pan. Place a saucepan on top to weight the onions down and create an even char, then decrease the heat to medium-high and cook, undisturbed, for about 6 minutes, or until the cut sides are deeply charred. Transfer the onions to the prepared baking sheet, charred-side up, and bake for about 20 minutes, or until softened. (If your onions are larger than golf ball–size, this may take longer.) Set aside to cool.

3. Meanwhile, put the pomegranate juice into a medium saucepan on medium-high heat. Bring to a boil, then simmer for about 12 minutes, or until the liquid has reduced to about 5 tbsp/75ml and is the consistency of a loose maple syrup. Set aside to cool; it will thicken as it sits.

4. Combine the chives with the remaining 3 tbsp olive oil and a good pinch of salt and set aside.

5. Pour the pomegranate syrup onto a large platter with a lip and swirl it around to cover most of the plate. Use your hands to loosely separate the onions into individual petals, then place them haphazardly over the syrup. Dot with the goat cheese, if using, then spoon on the chive oil and finish with the Urfa chile flakes before serving.

OLIVE OIL FLATBREADS WITH THREE-GARLIC BUTTER

FLATBREAD DOUGH
1½ cups/200g bread flour
1 tsp fast-acting dry yeast
1 tbsp olive oil, plus more as needed
½ tsp table salt
½ cup/120ml lukewarm water

THREE-GARLIC BUTTER
1 head of garlic, top fifth cut off to expose the cloves
1 tsp olive oil
flaked sea salt and black pepper
1 small garlic clove, roughly chopped
4 black garlic cloves, roughly chopped (optional)
½ cup/10g parsley, finely chopped
1½ tsp caraway seeds, toasted and crushed
7 tbsp/100g unsalted butter, softened

2 ripe plum tomatoes
2 black garlic cloves, thinly sliced (optional)
1 tsp thyme leaves
1 tsp oregano leaves
olive oil to drizzle
flaked sea salt and black pepper

Some things are impossible to resist and, indeed, shouldn't be resisted. This three-garlic butter is the best example we can think of. Made with mellow slow-roasted garlic, sweet black garlic, and pungent raw garlic, it is totally glorious and you'll want it over everything. Luckily, the recipe makes more butter than you'll need here (and we'd even make double). It will keep in the fridge for up to 2 weeks, ready to be smothered on toast, melted over roasted vegetables, or stuffed into baked potatoes.

On top of the layer of butter, we also spoon freshly grated tomato, which adds freshness and acidity to the flatbreads and turns them into a very good stand-alone snack. Without the tomatoes, however, they can be served alongside lots of dishes in the book, such as spicy berbere ratatouille with coconut sauce (page 209) and tofu meatball korma (page 268).

Wrapping a whole head of garlic in aluminum foil and roasting it, as we do here, is an accelerated way of getting results close to confit garlic. It's a nifty trick we use to add sweet-savory depth to lots of other dishes, such as our butternut, orange, and sage galette (page 132); barley, tomato, and watercress stew (page 68); Romano pepper schnitzels (page 146); and charred peppers and fresh corn polenta with soy-cured yolk (page 140). Roast three or four heads at a time, if you like; squeeze the cooked cloves into a jar and cover them with olive oil—they'll keep in the fridge for up to 2 weeks. The soft garlic is great to ramp up your soups, stews, and sauces, and the fragrant oil can be used to finish dishes.

Make the dough up to 2 days in advance and keep it refrigerated in a large, sealed container, if you want to get ahead. *Pictured on pages 248–249.*

1. Preheat the oven to 425°F/200°C fan.

2. For the flatbread dough: Put the flour, yeast, olive oil, and table salt into a large bowl. Pour in the water and use a spatula to combine the mixture. Transfer to a lightly oiled work surface and then, with lightly oiled hands, knead the dough for 5 minutes, until it's soft and elastic. You may need to add more oil if the dough starts to stick to your work surface. Return to the bowl, cover with a slightly damp clean kitchen towel, and let rise in a warm place for at least 1 hour (preferably 2 hours), until nearly doubled in size. Cut the dough into four equal-size balls and set aside, covered with a clean kitchen towel.

3. For the garlic butter: While the dough is rising, drizzle the head of garlic with the olive oil and sprinkle with a little flaked sea salt and pepper. Wrap tightly in aluminum foil and bake for 40 minutes, until the cloves have softened. Remove the foil and, when cool enough to handle, squeeze out the cloves, discarding the papery skin. Increase the oven temperature to 500°F/240°C fan.

4. Put the cooked garlic, raw chopped garlic, and black garlic (if using) into a mortar and pestle with 1½ tsp flaked sea salt and a generous grind of pepper. Pound to a rough paste, then transfer to a bowl and add the parsley, caraway seeds, and butter. Mix everything together and set aside.

5. Coarsely grate the tomatoes, discarding the skin. Transfer the tomatoes to a sieve set over a bowl and set aside to drain a little.

6. Place a large baking sheet on the middle rack of the oven to heat up.

7. Transfer the dough balls to a lightly oiled work surface and use your hands to stretch each piece into a rough circle, about 7 inches/18cm wide and ¼ inch/½cm thick.

8. Remove the hot baking sheet from the oven and quickly place two flatbreads on the sheet, spaced apart. The dough will be very thin but should have enough elasticity not to break. If you do get a hole in the dough, don't worry; this just adds to the homemade look.

9. Quickly return the sheet to the oven for 7–8 minutes, until the dough is golden brown and crisp. Continue with the remaining two flatbreads in the same way.

10. Spread each flatbread with about 1 tbsp of the garlic butter and top with the drained, grated tomatoes and the black garlic slices, if desired. Sprinkle with the herbs and finish with a drizzle of olive oil, a generous pinch of flaked sea salt, and a good grind of pepper. Serve at once.

SERVES SIX
As a side or as part
of a mezze spread

EGGPLANT WITH HERBS AND CRISPY GARLIC

4 medium eggplants
(2½ lb/1.2kg)
7 tbsp/105ml olive oil,
plus ⅓ cup/80ml
table salt and black pepper
6 garlic cloves, finely
sliced on a mandoline,
if you have one, or
by hand
7½ tsp white wine vinegar
1 green chile, finely
chopped
¾ cup/15g mint leaves,
finely sliced
¾ cup/15g cilantro leaves, finely sliced
¾ cup/15g dill, finely
chopped
1 tsp lemon juice

This is somewhere between a salad and a condiment, perfect as part of a spread, or equally delicious stuffed into sandwiches and wraps. You'll have some oil left over from frying the garlic, which can be happily tossed with pasta or salad.

The eggplant can be prepared the day before, up to the point where the herbs are added, if you like, finishing with the herbs, lemon juice, and crispy garlic when you're ready to serve.

1. Preheat the oven to 450°F/210°C fan. Line two large baking sheets with parchment paper. Line a plate with a double layer of paper towel.

2. Cut the eggplants into 1¼-inch/3cm chunks and put them into a large mixing bowl with the 7 tbsp/105ml olive oil, ¾ tsp salt, and a good grind of pepper. Toss together and spread out on the prepared baking sheets. Roast for 35 minutes, stirring the eggplants and swapping the sheets halfway through so the eggplants cook evenly, until a dark golden brown. Remove from the oven and let cool.

3. While the eggplants are roasting, heat the ⅓ cup/80ml olive oil in a small saucepan on medium-high heat. Once very hot, add the garlic and fry, stirring to separate the slices, until pale golden, about 1 minute. Watch that you don't cook it further, or it may burn and go bitter. Use a slotted spoon to transfer the garlic to the prepared plate, reserving the oil. Sprinkle the fried garlic with a little salt and set aside.

4. Put the eggplant into a large bowl and add the vinegar, chile, and 3 tbsp of the garlic frying oil. Toss together, then add all the herbs and mix well. Transfer to a serving plate, drizzle with the lemon juice, and serve with the fried garlic scattered on top.

SERVES FOUR
As a side

DIRTY RICE

1 cup/200g **basmati rice table salt**
1⅔ cups/400ml **hot water**
5 tbsp/75ml **olive oil**
7 **garlic cloves,** peeled:
  4 finely sliced, 3 crushed
¼ cup/50g **unsalted butter** (or another
  ¼ cup/60ml olive oil,
  to keep it vegan)
3 **onions,** finely chopped
  (2½ cups/350g)
1¼ cups/180g **pre-cooked and peeled chestnuts,** finely
  chopped
¼ cup/25g **black garlic,** finely chopped
  (optional)
4½ tsp **Creole spice blend**
  (we like Tony Chachere's
  Creole seasoning)
⅔ cup/160ml **vegetable stock or water**
½ cup/10g **parsley,** finely
  chopped
1 tbsp **lemon juice**

Yotam first fell in love with dirty rice in New Orleans, where the famous Herbsaint restaurant does an insanely delicious version of this Creole dish. With the help of Rebecca Wilcomb, chef de cuisine at Herbsaint at the time, we then re-created it in London. Rebecca taught us the importance of getting bits stuck to the bottom of the pan in order to boost the flavor and get the "dirty" look, which is also helped by the ground meat and offal that are part of the original dish. In this meat-free version, we use deeply caramelized onions, black garlic, and chestnuts to create a similar effect. We think, hand on heart, that it is just as good as the real thing.

Louisiana spice blends vary in levels of heat, so you may need to adjust how much you add, according to your taste. Some will also contain salt as the first ingredient, so do bear that in mind when seasoning the dish.

The rice can be made up to 2 days before, but don't add the parsley, garlic slices, lemon juice, or reserved oil until you are ready to serve.

1. Put the rice, ¼ tsp salt, and hot water into a medium saucepan, for which you have a lid, on medium-high heat. Bring to a boil, then decrease the heat to low, cover, and let cook for 12 minutes. Remove from the heat and leave covered for 10 minutes, then fluff up with a fork.

2. While the rice is cooking, line a plate with a double layer of paper towel. Heat 3 tbsp of the olive oil in a very small pan on medium heat. Once hot, add the sliced garlic (not the crushed!) and fry, stirring to separate the slices, until pale golden, 2–2½ minutes. Watch that you don't cook it further, or it may burn and go bitter. Use a slotted spoon to transfer the garlic to the prepared plate, reserving the oil. Sprinkle the fried garlic with a little salt and set aside.

3. Add the butter, remaining 2 tbsp olive oil, onions, and crushed garlic to a large, nonstick sauté pan on high heat. Fry for about 12 minutes, resisting the urge to stir too often, until the onions are a very deep golden brown—they should catch on the bottom of the pan every now and then but shouldn't burn, so decrease the heat if necessary. Decrease the heat to medium-high, then add the chestnuts, black garlic (if using), Creole spices, and ½ tsp salt and continue to fry for 7 minutes, stirring every now and then, until the whole thing is a deep, dark brown, but not burnt.

4. Stir the rice into the mixture until fully combined and increase the heat to high. Once the rice at the bottom of the pan begins to crisp up a little, 2–3 minutes, add the stock and cook, undisturbed, until the liquid has evaporated, another 2 minutes. Remove from the heat; stir in the parsley, fried garlic slices, lemon juice, and reserved garlic oil; and serve.

FRIED ONION RINGS WITH BUTTERMILK AND TURMERIC

DIPPING SAUCE
¼ garlic clove, peeled
¼ oz/5g fresh turmeric, peeled and roughly chopped (optional)
⅛ tsp flaked sea salt
7½ tsp mirin
1 tbsp lime juice
1 red chile, finely chopped

1 cup/240ml buttermilk
7½ tsp white wine vinegar
scant 1 oz/25g fresh turmeric, peeled and finely grated (or ½ tsp ground turmeric)
2½ cups plus 2 tbsp/325g all-purpose flour
7½ tsp nigella seeds
4½ tsp caraway seeds
1 lime: finely zest to get 2 tsp, then cut into wedges
1 tsp table salt
1 onion, cut into ¾-inch/ 2cm-thick pinwheels, then separated into individual rings (1 cup/150g)
10 green onions, trimmed
3¾ cups/900ml sunflower oil
flaked sea salt

Deep-fried onion rings are an irresistible treat, and we found out that deep-fried green onions are equally delicious, so we added some here. We serve them—to kick-start a party or as a fine snack—with a dipping sauce made with turmeric, mirin, and lime. This punchy combination is perfect with the rich fried onions, but you can easily do without it and serve them with just wedges of lime.

A couple of suggestions. Kitchen gloves are useful when grating the turmeric, to prevent stubborn yellow marks. Have your dipping sauce prepped, your vegetables battered, and your work surfaces ready before you start frying, so you don't get distracted away from the frying pan and can tuck in as soon as you're done.

1. For the dipping sauce: Pound the garlic, chopped turmeric (if using), and flaked sea salt to a rough paste in a mortar and pestle. Transfer to a small serving bowl; stir in the mirin, lime juice, and chile; and set aside.

2. In a medium bowl, stir together the buttermilk, vinegar, and grated turmeric and set aside.

3. Mix together the flour, nigella seeds, caraway seeds, lime zest, and table salt in a high-sided dish or wide container.

4. Set up two large racks on two baking sheets, lining one rack with plenty of paper towels.

5. Working in batches, coat the onion rings and green onions in the flour mixture, then in the buttermilk mixture. Lift them out, shaking off any excess, then coat once more in the flour and place, spaced apart, on the unlined rack.

6. Heat the sunflower oil in a large, high-sided sauté pan on medium-high heat. Once hot (355°F/180°C if you have a thermometer), add the onion rings and green onions in three or four batches and fry for 2–3 minutes, turning them over halfway through, until crisp and golden. Use a slotted spoon to transfer to the lined rack. Sprinkle with plenty of flaked sea salt, then arrange on a platter and serve with the dipping sauce and the lime wedges alongside.

12 medium leeks
(4½ lb/2.1kg)

MISO AND CHIVE
SAUCE
½ oz/15g fresh ginger, peeled and roughly chopped
¼ tsp flaked sea salt
4½ tsp mixed black and white sesame seeds, very well toasted
½ oz/15g chives, finely chopped
4½ tsp white or other miso paste
¼ cup/60ml mirin
2 tbsp rice vinegar

1¼ cups/300ml sunflower oil
1¼ tsp cornstarch
flaked sea salt
4 garlic cloves, finely sliced on a mandoline, if you have one, or by hand
1 tbsp olive oil
½ tsp finely chopped chives

LEEKS WITH MISO AND CHIVE SAUCE

The punchy sauce is the star here, pairing wonderfully well with the mild sweetness of the leeks. You can also use it to dress new potatoes, or to drizzle over tofu, fish, or chicken. The fried leek tops and garlic add aroma and crunch, but, if you want to avoid deep-frying, you can leave them out and simply serve the leeks with the sauce. They go well with turnip cake (page 270) or alongside fried tofu or roasted meats.

The sauce can be made up to 3 days before and kept in a sealed jar in the fridge. Don't steam the leeks too far in advance, as they can lose their color.

1. Remove and discard the tough outer layers of the leeks, then wash the leeks well to remove any grit. Cut off and reserve the darker green tops so each leek is about 8½ inches/22cm long.

2. Finely slice 2¼ oz/60g of the reserved green leek tops into 3¼-inch/8cm-long, thin strips. Rinse very well to remove any grit, then dry thoroughly and set aside.

3. For the sauce: Pound the ginger and salt into a paste using a mortar and pestle (or with the side of a knife). Put into a small bowl along with the sesame seeds, chives, miso, mirin, and vinegar; stir well to combine; and set aside.

4. Half-fill a pot (large enough to fit the length of the leeks lying down) with lightly salted water and place on medium-high heat. Once simmering, add the leeks and decrease the heat to medium. Place a lid smaller than the pot on top of the leeks, weighting them down so they don't float above the surface of the water. Simmer gently for 20 minutes, or until a knife goes through a leek easily but they still hold their shape. Transfer the leeks to a colander and stand them vertically so they drain thoroughly.

5. While the leeks are draining, line a plate with paper towels. Put the sunflower oil into a medium, high-sided saucepan on medium-high heat. Toss the dried, sliced green leek tops with 1 tsp of the cornstarch. Once the oil is very hot (340°F/170°C if you have a thermometer), add the leek tops and fry for about 2 minutes, stirring with a fork, until golden and crispy. Transfer to the prepared plate with a slotted spoon and sprinkle with some salt. Toss the garlic with the remaining ¼ tsp cornstarch and fry for about 1 minute, stirring frequently to separate the slices, until crisp and golden brown. Add to the fried leeks and sprinkle with salt.

6. Arrange the leeks on a large plate and spoon the sauce over them. Drizzle with the olive oil and top with the fried leeks and garlic. Sprinkle with the chives and serve.

MISO BUTTER ONIONS

8 small onions or
   8 large shallots
   (about 5¼ oz/150g
   each; 2⅔ lb/1.2kg total)
7 tbsp/100g unsalted
   butter, melted
⅓ cup plus 1 tbsp/100g
   white or other miso
   paste
1 qt/1L warm water

These onions are a bit of a revelation, and the very definition of low effort/high impact, where just a few ingredients come together to create something truly spectacular.

Still, the effort we save you on mise en place we take back by asking for a roasting pan that is *just* the right size. This is important. The pan should be just big enough to fit the halved onions in a single layer, without them overlapping. The onions will then shrink as they cook, creating the space the sauce needs to evaporate and thicken into a glorious gravy. If your pan isn't big enough to fit the onions (that's sixteen halves), then roast fewer, decreasing the rest of the ingredients proportionally (the cooking method and time stay the same).

The size of your onions is also important; they should be small, weighing about 5¼ oz/150g each. If you can't get hold of small onions, use large shallots instead.

Last, saturate each onion (or shallot) half very well every time you baste, spooning the sauce over them several times so the cut sides remain moist. This is to ensure that the onions caramelize rather than burn.

These are best eaten straight out of the oven, but if you are making them ahead, warm the sauce up before serving, thinning it with a bit of water. Serve spooned over toast, rice, or mashed potatoes. Roasted chicken, predictably, is also a great match.

1. Preheat the oven to 500°F/240°C fan.

2. Halve the onions or shallots lengthwise, discarding the papery skin, as well as the layer beneath if it is tough or dry. Trim the tops and a little off the bottom (not too much—you want to ensure the onion halves stay held together at the base).

3. In a medium bowl, whisk together the melted butter, miso, and warm water until fully combined.

4. Place the onion halves, cut-side down and spaced apart, in a 9 x 13-inch/23 x 33cm high-sided baking dish or pan and pour in the miso water. Cover tightly with aluminum foil and bake for 35 minutes, then remove the foil and turn the onions over so they are cut-side up (take care to ensure they remain intact). Baste the onions very well, then return to the oven, uncovered, for another 45–50 minutes, basting every 10 minutes, until the onions are very soft, deeply browned on top, and the sauce has reduced to a gravy consistency.

5. Carefully transfer the onions to a platter, pouring the sauce over and around them, and serve at once.

SERVES FOUR
As a side

KOHLRABI "NOODLE" SALAD

1 tbsp white or black sesame seeds, or a mixture of both, toasted

1 tsp poppy seeds, toasted

1 tsp nori sprinkles (or finely blitz ½ sheet of nori in a spice grinder and use 1 tsp)

1½ tsp Aleppo chile flakes or Gochugaru Korean hot pepper flakes (or ¾ tsp regular chile flakes)

½ tsp Szechuan peppercorns, finely crushed

1 tbsp roasted and salted peanuts, roughly chopped

flaked sea salt

2–3 medium kohlrabi, trimmed and peeled (1 lb 4 oz/570g)

3 tbsp lime juice

¾ oz/20g fresh ginger, peeled and roughly chopped

1 tbsp rice vinegar

6 green onions, finely chopped (¾ cup/60g)

¼ cup/60ml sunflower oil

Heat, acidity, and the numbing effect of ginger and Szechuan pepper create an intensity in this salad that can flavor an entire meal. We would serve it with a bowl of rice and some simply fried tofu (see page 172), seafood, or meat.

The nut-seaweed-chile-seed sprinkle is very special, so make extra to dust over salads, noodles, and rice. It will stay crunchy in a sealed container for up to 3 days.

If you can't get kohlrabi, this will also work with a large radish, such as daikon, or with green papaya. The salad can discolor and get a bit soggy, so it is best to toss it together just before serving.

1. In a small bowl, combine the sesame seeds, poppy seeds, nori sprinkles, chile flakes, peppercorns, peanuts, and ½ tsp salt.

2. Slice the kohlrabi as thinly as possible, on a mandoline if you have one (or use the appropriate attachment on a food processor). Stack the slices on top of each other in manageable piles and slice into ¾-inch/2cm-wide strips (to resemble short flat noodles). Put into a bowl with the lime juice and 1 tsp salt, toss together, and set aside for 10 minutes.

3. Meanwhile, put the ginger and ¾ tsp salt into a mortar and pestle and pound to a paste. Place in a small bowl with the vinegar and two-thirds of the green onions. Heat the sunflower oil in a small pan on medium heat until warm, then add to the bowl of ginger and green onions. Set aside for 20 minutes for the flavors to meld.

4. Drain the kohlrabi to get rid of most of the liquid that will have collected, then toss with the ginger mixture. Transfer to a platter, sprinkle with the mixed seeds and nuts, and finish with the remaining green onions. Serve at once.

RADISH AND CUCUMBER SALAD WITH CHIPOTLE PEANUTS

CHIPOTLE PEANUTS
1 chipotle chile, stemmed (or ½ tsp chipotle flakes)
⅔ cup/90g unsalted blanched peanuts
pinch of cayenne pepper
4½ tsp golden syrup (or maple syrup)
¼ tsp flaked sea salt
2 tsp lime zest
1½ tsp lime juice
1½ tsp olive oil

1 cucumber, cut into ⅛-inch/¼cm-thick half-moons on a mandoline, if you have one, or by hand (3 cups/300g)
1 daikon, peeled and cut into ⅛-inch/¼cm-thick half-moons on a mandoline, if you have one, or by hand (2½ cups/300g)
1¾ oz/50g breakfast radishes, thinly sliced on a mandoline, if you have one, or by hand
1 cup/20g cilantro, leaves picked with some of their stems
1 garlic clove, crushed
¼ jalapeño, seeded and finely chopped (1 tbsp)
1 tsp cumin seeds, toasted and roughly crushed in a mortar and pestle
2–3 limes: finely zest to get 1 tsp, then juice to get 3 tbsp
2 tbsp olive oil
flaked sea salt and black pepper

If you're in the mood for an all-out Mexican feast, serve this salad alongside cheese tamales (see page 158) or oyster mushroom tacos (see page 238), or both (see our Mexican feast, page 303)! Less taxing would be pairing it with just the roasted mushrooms from the taco recipe, making this a meaty salad fit for a midweek supper. Jicama, a crunchy Mexican root, can happily replace the daikon if you can get your hands on it.

Double up on the chipotle peanuts, if you like. They are very snack-friendly and will stay crunchy in a sealed container for up to 3 days. The salad, however, will lose its crispness if it sits around for too long, so is best served at once.

1. For the peanuts: Line a baking sheet with parchment paper. Blitz the chile in a spice grinder until you have a fine powder, or finely crush in a mortar and pestle. Measure out ½ tsp (reserving the rest for another recipe) and place in a small sauté pan along with the peanuts, cayenne, golden syrup, salt, lime zest, lime juice, and olive oil. Place the pan on medium-high heat and cook, stirring often, for about 8 minutes, or until the peanuts are sticky and well coated. Transfer to the prepared baking sheet and let cool completely. Break apart into bite-size pieces and set aside.

2. Put the cucumber, daikon, radishes, and cilantro into a large bowl. In a small bowl, combine the garlic, jalapeño, cumin seeds, lime zest, lime juice, olive oil, 1¼ tsp flaked salt, and a good grind of pepper. Whisk well and pour this mixture over the vegetables. Transfer to a large serving platter and top with half the peanuts, serving the rest in a bowl alongside.

SERVES FOUR
As a snack or as a starter

CORN RIBS

**BLACK LIME AND
PUMPKIN SEED BUTTER**
3 tbsp pumpkin seeds
**¼ cup/60g unsalted
butter,** very well
softened
1–2 dried black limes
(see page 18), roughly
broken, then finely
blitzed in a spice
grinder to get 2¼ tsp
(alternatively, use
grated lime zest)
1 tsp flaked sea salt

3 ears fresh corn,
husks removed
(1 lb 8 oz/680g)
**5½ cups/1.3L
sunflower oil**
1½ tsp honey
½ tsp flaked sea salt

We got the idea for corn-as-ribs for our restaurant ROVI from Max Ng and the team at Momofuku Ssäm, New York. These deep-fried corn quarters, which magically curl up to look like ribs, worked phenomenally well at ROVI, with its ethos of treating vegetables like meat. So much so, that a few diehard fans canceled their reservations abruptly when corn went out of season and we had to take it off the menu.

For home cooks who aren't endowed with the muscles or the knives of our hardy chefs, the biggest challenge is preparing the corn, cutting through its hard core. Make sure you start with a big sharp knife and make decisive, powerful cuts (keeping fingers well away). A blunt knife won't do the job and is more likely to cause an accident.

Double up on the black lime and pumpkin seed butter. It's seriously delicious spread on toast with a drizzle of honey, and will keep in a sealed jar in the fridge for up to 1 week.

1. For the butter: Preheat the oven to 350°F/160°C fan. Place the pumpkin seeds on a small baking sheet and toast until they are fragrant and golden brown and the skins are beginning to split, about 10 minutes. Coarsely blitz in a spice grinder (or finely chop them) and let cool for 10 minutes.

2. In a medium bowl, use a spatula to whip the butter with 2 tsp of the ground black lime, the pumpkin seeds, and salt until fully combined. Keep refrigerated, if getting ahead, removing it from the fridge 30 minutes before it's needed, to soften.

3. Use a large, sharp knife to carefully cut the corn in half crosswise, then cut each half lengthwise into quarters. This is easiest with the corn standing upright, so you don't squash the kernels.

4. Line a baking sheet with a double layer of paper towel. Heat the sunflower oil in a medium, high-sided saucepan on medium-high heat. Once very hot (around 355°F/180°C if you have a thermometer; or test by lowering in the end of one of the pieces of corn, it should sizzle but not brown straight away.) Add the corn in three batches and fry for 6–7 minutes (take care, the oil may spit!), turning them a few times until they have curled slightly and turned golden brown. Remove from the oil using a slotted spoon and set aside on the prepared baking sheet while you continue with the rest in the same way. Transfer to a bowl and toss with the honey and salt.

5. Pile the corn onto a platter, sprinkle with the remaining ground black lime, and serve the butter alongside.

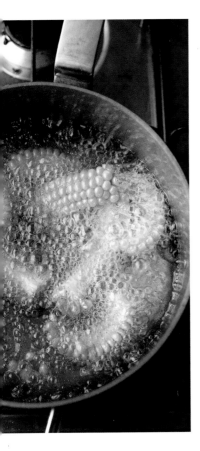

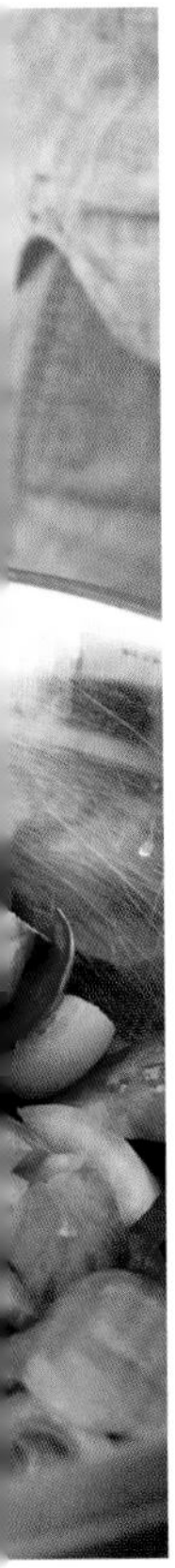

TOMATO AND PLUM SALAD WITH NORI AND SESAME

SERVES SIX
As a side

DRESSING
1¼ tsp fish sauce
(optional)
2 tsp superfine sugar
2 tbsp rice vinegar
2 tsp soy sauce
2 tbsp peanut oil
¼ oz/5g fresh ginger,
peeled and julienned
½ garlic clove, crushed
¼ tsp finely grated
orange zest
½ tsp flaked sea salt

NORI AND SESAME SALT
½ sheet nori
4½ tsp white or black
sesame seeds, or a
mixture of both, toasted
½ tsp chile flakes
½ tsp flaked sea salt

1¾ lb/800g mixed ripe
tomatoes (beef, plum,
tiger, green, yellow,
and cherry), large ones
cut into ½-inch/1cm-
thick wedges, cherry
tomatoes halved or
quartered
3 ripe plums, pitted
and cut into ½-inch/
1cm-thick wedges
(2 cups/250g; or more
tomatoes instead, see
headnote)
4 green onions,
finely sliced
¼ cup/5g cilantro
leaves, roughly
chopped

It's very 2020 to ditch chips and snack on dried nori sheets instead. This can only be a good thing, because they are delicious and nutritious and it means you can get them easily and use them to ramp up the flavor in all kinds of dishes, from roasted vegetables and salads to rice and noodles. So double (or quadruple!) the amount of nori and sesame salt, if you like, and keep as handy seasoning for all these instances.

The plums are glorious with the tomatoes but, if they aren't in season, substitute them with more tomatoes; the salad will still taste great without them. Toss the tomatoes and plums together with the herbs and dressing just before you're ready to serve, so the salad doesn't become too soggy.

1. For the dressing: In a medium bowl, whisk together the fish sauce (if using), sugar, vinegar, soy sauce, peanut oil, ginger, garlic, orange zest, and salt and set aside to let infuse.

2. For the salt: Roughly break up the nori sheet, then blitz to a rough powder (a spice grinder is best for this). In a small bowl, mix the nori with the sesame seeds, chile flakes, and salt. Set aside.

3. In a large bowl, toss the tomatoes with the plums, green onions, cilantro, and dressing. Transfer to a platter, sprinkle with the nori and sesame salt, and serve.

MAKES SIXTEEN BALLS
Serves four as a main

TOFU MEATBALL KORMA

½ red onion, thinly sliced
  (½ cup/60g)
2 tbsp lemon juice
⅛ tsp table salt
¼ cup/40g cashews
2 tbsp blanched almonds

TOFU MEATBALLS
2 tbsp olive oil
9 oz/250g brown button
  mushrooms, sliced
  ¼ inch/½cm thick
7 oz/200g extra-firm tofu,
  patted dry and crumbled
  into large chunks
3 garlic cloves, crushed
5¼ oz/150g silken tofu
2 tbsp tahini
1 tbsp soy sauce
¼ cup/30g panko
  breadcrumbs
1½ tsp cornstarch
8 green onions, thinly
  sliced (1 cup/80g)
½ cup/10g cilantro,
  finely chopped
table salt and black
  pepper

6 cardamom pods, pods
  discarded, seeds reserved
2 tsp cumin seeds
2 tsp coriander seeds
3 tbsp olive oil
1 onion, roughly chopped
  (1 cup/150g)
2¾ cups plus 2 tbsp/
  680ml water
4 garlic cloves, crushed
½ oz/15g fresh ginger,
  peeled and grated
1 green chile, seeded
  and finely chopped
1 cinnamon stick
¾ tsp ground turmeric
2 plum tomatoes, grated
  and skins discarded
  (1 cup/180g)
table salt and black
  pepper
2 tbsp cilantro leaves,
  finely sliced

If you don't have time to make the meatballs, you could just make the sauce to serve with roasted cauliflower or sweet potato. It will keep for 3 days in the fridge and up to 1 month in the freezer. The meatballs can be cooked the day before, just warm them together with the sauce in a pan before serving.

The flatbreads on page 246 will make an excellent side here, outshining any store-bought garlic naan. Both the korma and the flatbreads make up part of our korma feast (see page 303), if you're up to the challenge.

1. Preheat the oven to 425°F/200°C fan. Line a baking sheet with parchment paper. Combine the red onion, lemon juice, and salt in a small bowl and set aside, up to overnight.

2. Put the cashews and almonds into a small saucepan on medium-high heat. Cover with water, bring to a boil, then decrease the heat to medium and simmer for 20 minutes. Drain and set aside.

3. For the meatballs: Heat the olive oil in a large sauté pan on high heat, then add the mushrooms and extra-firm tofu and cook until lightly golden, about 8 minutes. Stir in the garlic for 30 seconds, then remove from the heat. Place in a food processor and pulse until roughly chopped. Transfer to a large mixing bowl with the silken tofu, tahini, soy sauce, panko, cornstarch, green onions, cilantro, ¾ tsp salt, and a good grind of pepper. Mix very well to combine. With oiled hands, form into sixteen Ping-Pong-size balls, about 1½ oz/40g each, compressing them as you go so they hold together. Place on the prepared baking sheet, spaced apart, and bake for 25 minutes until lightly golden. Set aside.

4. While the meatballs are in the oven, finely crush the cardamom seeds, cumin seeds, and coriander seeds in a mortar and pestle and set aside. Put 4½ tsp of the olive oil into a large sauté pan, for which you have a lid, on medium-high heat. Add the onion and cook for 10 minutes, or until softened and deeply browned. Transfer to a blender along with the nuts and ¾ cup plus 2 tbsp/200ml of the water and blend until completely smooth, about 2 minutes.

5. Put the remaining 4½ tsp olive oil into the same pan on medium-high heat. Add the garlic, ginger, and green chile and cook for 1 minute, then add the spices and cook for 1 minute more. Add the tomatoes and cook for 4 minutes, stirring occasionally, until thickened. Add the puréed onion-nut mixture, remaining 2 cups/480ml water, 1½ tsp salt, and a good grind of pepper. Bring to a simmer, then decrease the heat to medium and cook for 25 minutes, until reduced by a third. Add the meatballs to the sauce, cover, and heat for 5 minutes, until the meatballs are warmed through. Sprinkle with the cilantro and sliced red onion. Serve at once.

TURNIP CAKE

SERVES FOUR
As a main

SOY MAPLE NUTS

½ oz/15g dried shiitake
   mushrooms, soaked
   in boiling water for
   20 minutes

¼ cup/30g pine nuts,
   roughly chopped

⅓ cup/50g pre-cooked
   and peeled chestnuts,
   roughly chopped

1 tbsp white or black
   sesame seeds, or a
   mixture of both

1 small garlic clove,
   crushed

¼ tsp peeled and finely
   grated fresh ginger

3 tbsp soy sauce

¼ cup/60ml maple syrup

⅛ tsp table salt

1⅓ cups/130g Thai
   white rice flour
   (not glutinous variety,
   or regular rice flour)

1 tbsp cornstarch

2½ tsp superfine sugar

1 small garlic clove,
   crushed

¼ tsp peeled and finely
   grated fresh ginger

2 tsp sesame oil

1 cup/240ml water,
   plus 2 tbsp

1 tsp table salt

1–2 large daikon,
   trimmed, peeled,
   and roughly grated
   (1 lb 5 oz/600g)

7 tbsp/105ml
   sunflower oil

SOY MAPLE SAUCE

⅓ cup/80ml water

7½ tsp soy sauce

4 tsp maple syrup

1 tsp toasted sesame oil

4½ tsp finely chopped
   chives

A mild obsession and a pet peeve came together here, in a dish that we are especially proud of. The obsession is turnip cake—which isn't really a cake and isn't made of turnips but of daikon—served as part of Chinese dim sum. The pet peeve is nut loaf, the traditional centerpiece offered to vegans and vegetarians at holidays when no one can think of anything better to serve them. The challenge was to combine both, to create a festive vegan dish that is both special and truly satisfying. We like to think that our cake, in which the traditional Chinese sausage and dried shrimp are replaced with sweet and salty clusters of shiitake mushrooms, pine nuts, chestnuts, and sesame seeds, can sit respectfully both at the center of any festive spread (see page 304) and on the tables of the best restaurants in every Chinatown.

If you don't have a 9 x 13-inch/23 x 33cm high-sided pan, use another dish or pan with a similar surface area; the main objective is that the cake is ¾ inch/2cm thick. The dish or pan needs to be high-sided, as it sits in a water bath and you don't want the water spilling over the sides.

Thai white rice flour is available in specialty Asian supermarkets, and it is not interchangeable with the glutinous variety, or with regular rice flour.

Make the cake the day before, to get ahead, and keep refrigerated, ready to be fried just before serving. Keep the soy maple nuts loosely covered at room temperature, if you've made them the day before as well. The cake is best pan-fried on both sides but, to save time, you can brush the slices with oil and broil them for about 7 minutes, or until golden brown on top. *Pictured on pages 272–273.*

1. For the nuts: Line a baking sheet with parchment paper. Drain the mushrooms, squeezing them until dry, then finely chop and set aside.

2. Put the pine nuts and chestnuts into a large, nonstick frying pan and place on medium-high heat. Toast for 3–4 minutes, stirring, until golden and fragrant, then add the sesame seeds, toasting for 1 minute, followed by the chopped mushrooms, garlic, ginger, soy sauce, maple syrup, and salt. Continue to cook, stirring, until the liquid bubbles, reduces, and coats the nuts and mushrooms, 4–5 minutes. Spread out on the prepared baking sheet and set aside.

3. In a large bowl, whisk together the flour, cornstarch, sugar, garlic, ginger, sesame oil, 1 cup/240ml water, and salt until smooth, then set aside.

4. Place a large sauté pan on medium heat, add the grated daikon and remaining 2 tbsp water, and cook for 15 minutes, stirring every now and then, until all the liquid has evaporated (take care not to brown the daikon). Let cool for 10 minutes.

5. Preheat the oven to 450°F/220°C fan. Line and grease a 9 x 13-inch/ 23 x 33cm high-sided baking pan and set aside. Bring a kettle of water to a boil.

6. Transfer the daikon to the bowl, add about half of the soy maple nuts, and stir together. Spoon the mixture into the prepared pan, smoothing the top as you go, then seal tightly with aluminum foil and place the pan in a high-sided baking dish that is slightly larger than the pan. Pour enough boiling water into the baking dish to rise three-fourths of the way up the sides of the pan and bake for 35 minutes. Remove the pan from the water bath, discard the foil, and set aside to cool to room temperature. Transfer to the fridge for 40 minutes, or up to overnight, until completely chilled.

7. Turn the cake out onto a chopping board, then cut into eight even slices. Brush the slices on each side with 4 tbsp (total) of the sunflower oil.

8. Heat a large, nonstick frying pan on medium-high heat, then add 4½ tsp sunflower oil. Fry the slices in two batches (or more batches, if you can't fit four slices into the pan), spread apart, for 2–3 minutes on each side, until crisp and golden brown. Keep the first batch warm while you fry the rest with the remaining 4½ tsp sunflower oil.

9. For the sauce: Put the water, soy sauce, maple syrup, and sesame oil into a small saucepan on medium-high heat, stir together, and warm through, about 3 minutes.

10. Arrange the turnip cake slices on a large platter, overlapping each other. Pour half the sauce over the slices, then sprinkle with the chives and the remaining nuts. Serve at once, with the remaining sauce on the side.

POTATO SALAD WITH THAI BASIL SAUCE

SERVES FOUR
As a side

1 lb 5 oz/600g Jerusalem artichokes, peeled and cut into 1¼-inch/3cm pieces (optional)

1 lb 5 oz/600g small-to-medium yellow or red potatoes (or 2 lb 7 oz/1.1kg, if you're not using Jerusalem artichokes), peeled and cut into 1¼-inch/3cm pieces

5 tbsp/75ml olive oil

1½ tsp table salt

1¾ oz/50g breakfast radishes, thinly sliced on a mandoline, if you have one, or by hand

3 limes: finely zest to get 4½ tsp, then juice to get 3 tbsp

flaked sea salt

1 small garlic clove, roughly chopped

1 tbsp peeled and roughly chopped fresh ginger

1 cup/20g Thai basil, roughly chopped, plus a few whole leaves

1 large green chile, finely sliced into rounds

¼ cup/30g smoked, roasted, and salted almonds, roughly chopped (or regular roasted almonds)

This is as fresh as a potato salad will get, thanks to the large quantities of lime, garlic, chile, and Thai basil that are poured over it. It will make a good light supper with broccoli two ways (see page 186) and will also partner really well with salmon or roasted chicken.

If you can't get hold of Thai basil, an equal combination of cilantro and regular basil is a very good alternative. The sauce won't stay bright green for long, so make it just before you're ready to serve.

When Jerusalem artichokes are in season, we like to roast them and add them to this salad. We appreciate, however, that not everyone is a fan, so you can easily substitute them with the same amount of potatoes (in which case they'll all be boiled, so no need to turn on the oven).

1. If using Jerusalem artichokes, preheat the oven to 450°F/210°C fan and line a baking sheet with parchment paper.

2. Put the potatoes into a large saucepan, cover with cold salted water, bring to a simmer, and cook for about 10 minutes, or until the potatoes are cooked through but still holding their shape. Drain and set aside to cool for 15 minutes.

3. Meanwhile, mix the Jerusalem artichokes with 1 tbsp of the olive oil and table salt, and spread them out on the prepared baking sheet. Bake for 18–20 minutes, tossing them halfway through, until golden brown and cooked through. Let cool for a few minutes, then put into a large bowl with the cooled potatoes.

4. While the artichokes are roasting, mix the radishes with 1 tbsp of the lime juice and ¼ tsp flaked sea salt and set aside.

5. In a spice grinder or the bowl of a small food processor, blitz the lime zest, garlic, ginger, and chopped basil with 1 tsp flaked sea salt and the remaining ¼ cup/60ml olive oil to get a bright green paste. Scrape into the bowl of potatoes, along with the remaining 2 tbsp lime juice. Gently stir in the radishes (including the liquid) and whole Thai basil leaves. Finish with the chile and almonds and serve.

SPICY ROAST POTATOES WITH TAHINI AND SOY

SERVES FOUR
As a side

2 lb/900g red and yellow
  potatoes, skin on, cut
  into 1-inch/2½cm cubes
¼ **cup/50g rose harissa**
  (adjust according to
  the brand you are using;
  see page 20)
1 garlic clove, crushed
3 tbsp olive oil
**table salt and black
  pepper**

TAHINI SOY DRESSING
¼ **cup/60g tahini** (stir
  very well before using,
  to combine the solids
  and fat)
2 tbsp soy sauce
4½ tsp mirin
  (or maple syrup)
4½ tsp rice vinegar
1 tbsp water

**4½ tsp finely chopped
  chives**
**4½ tsp black or white
  sesame seeds,**
  preferably a mixture
  of both, toasted

There are different schools of roast potatoes. The English school, which calls for peeling, parboiling, and roasting in scalding fat, is one that Yotam endorses proudly and Ixta opposes strongly. They both, however, come together in adoration of the Italian school, which involves minimal fuss and maximum olive oil (two good things), yet still gives a great crisp result. The toppings here—tahini, soy, sesame, and chives—may seem a little unorthodox but add a nutty savoriness that the potatoes soak up.

Double or triple the tahini soy dressing, if you like; it's great as a salad dressing (see cucumber salad à la Xi'an Impression, page 113), drizzled over rice and noodles, or as a dipping sauce for tofu or chicken skewers. It will keep in a jar in the fridge for up to 2 weeks.

1. Preheat the oven to 500°F/240°C fan. Line a large baking sheet with parchment paper.

2. In a large bowl, mix together the potatoes, harissa, garlic, olive oil, ¾ tsp salt, and a generous grind of pepper until well combined. Transfer to the prepared baking sheet and spread out as much as possible, then cover tightly with aluminum foil and roast for 15 minutes.

3. Remove the foil, decrease the temperature to 425°F/200°C fan, and roast for another 25 minutes, stirring halfway through, until the potatoes are cooked and nicely browned.

4. For the dressing: While the potatoes are roasting, whisk together the tahini, soy sauce, mirin, vinegar, and water in a medium bowl until smooth.

5. Transfer the potatoes to a large, shallow serving bowl and drizzle with the dressing. Finish with the chives and sesame seeds and serve.

TANGERINE AND ANCHO CHILE FLAN

SERVES SIX

½ cup plus 1 tbsp/120g
superfine sugar

CUSTARD
1 large ancho chile,
soaked in boiling water
for 10 minutes, then
drained (and seeded if
you prefer less heat)
¾ cup plus 2 tbsp/270g
condensed milk
1⅔ cups/400ml whole
milk
7 tbsp/105ml heavy
cream
3 eggs
1 tsp vanilla bean paste
or vanilla extract
1 tsp finely grated
tangerine zest
generous pinch of
flaked sea salt

1 tbsp tangerine juice

Flan is the most traditional Mexican dessert, consisting of caramel with custard set on top (or below, once flipped). The method here couldn't be simpler! Once you've made the caramel, all the custard ingredients are thrown into a blender and blitzed until smooth. It's as easy as that.

This recipe was originally developed with blood oranges, which pair wonderfully with ancho chile. If they are in season, do use them instead. And by all means experiment with other dried chiles and fruit juices!

The flan will keep for up to 3 days in the fridge.

1. Preheat the oven to 350°F/150°C fan. Bring a kettle of water to a boil. Place an 8 x 8-inch/20 x 20cm nonstick pan, or a similar-size ovenproof dish, in the oven to keep warm until required. Make sure your pan is not springform; you don't want the caramel to escape.

2. Put the sugar into a large saucepan on medium heat and cook for about 8 minutes. Resist the urge to stir; instead swirl the pan until the sugar has melted. Continue swirling slowly until this caramel turns dark amber, then carefully and quickly remove the pan from the oven and pour in the caramel, tilting the pan as you go so the caramel covers the base evenly. Let the caramel set.

3. For the custard: Squeeze the chile very well to remove any liquid. Discard the stem, then put the chile and its seeds, condensed milk, whole milk, cream, eggs, vanilla, tangerine zest, and salt into a blender and blitz on high speed for about 30 seconds, or until well combined.

4. Tap the caramel to make sure it has set hard, then place a fine-mesh sieve over the pan. Pour the custard through the sieve into the pan, discarding any larger bits of chile that collect in the sieve.

5. Carefully transfer the pan to a larger, high-sided baking dish and place in the oven, keeping the oven door open. Carefully pour enough boiling water into the larger dish to come halfway up the sides of the flan pan. Bake for 40–50 minutes, or until the surface is set and golden brown but the flan still has a good wobble to it (it will set in the fridge). Remove from the water bath and set aside to cool slightly, then refrigerate for at least 3 hours, or overnight.

6. Remove the flan from the fridge 30 minutes before you want to serve it. Carefully run a small knife around the edges of the flan to release it. Place a large plate (larger than your flan dish, and with a lip to catch the liquid caramel) on top of the flan pan. Holding both the plate and the pan together, quickly flip the whole thing over. Gently lift off the pan—the flan should have released itself onto the plate. Drizzle the tangerine juice over the flan and serve at once.

MAKES FIFTEEN
FRITTERS
Serves four

TAPIOCA FRITTERS WITH ORANGE SYRUP AND STAR ANISE

⅔ cup/90g small pearl
tapioca
1¾ cups/420ml whole
milk
½ cup/120ml heavy
cream
1 tsp vanilla bean paste
or vanilla extract
½ tsp ground star anise
3 tbsp superfine sugar
¼ tsp flaked sea salt
1 egg, separated, plus
1 egg yolk
3 oranges: finely zest
to get 1½ tsp, then
juice 2 oranges to get
⅓ cup/80ml
¼ cup/75g honey
2 tbsp water
2 whole star anise
2 tbsp tapioca flour
2 cups/480ml
sunflower oil
1 tbsp confectioners'
sugar

Even if you think that you don't like tapioca, please try these fritters. They are sweet, soft, crisp, and very difficult to stop eating once you get started. They can be prepared a day in advance, up until the stage when you chill the raw mix, ready to fry when you need them. The syrup can also be prepared a day ahead.

1. In a medium, heavy-bottomed saucepan, combine the pearl tapioca, milk, cream, vanilla, and ground star anise and let soak for 20 minutes. Place the pan on medium-high heat and bring to a simmer. Add the superfine sugar and salt, then decrease the heat to medium and cook for another 12 minutes, stirring often, until the tapioca has become translucent and chewy and the pudding has thickened. In a small bowl, whisk the egg yolks with 3 tbsp of the tapioca mixture and add back to the saucepan. Remove from the heat and stir continuously for about 1 minute, until the yolks have blended into the pudding but have not scrambled. Stir in the orange zest and transfer the mixture to a bowl to cool, about 15 minutes.

2. Beat the egg white until medium-firm peaks form. Fold this into the cooled pudding, then cover the surface with plastic wrap to prevent a skin from forming. Transfer to the fridge to set, about 1½ hours or up to overnight.

3. Using a sharp knife, trim the top and tail off the unjuiced orange. Cut down along its round curves, removing the skin and white pith. Slice between the membranes to release the segments, then cut each in half. Set aside.

4. Put the orange juice, honey, water, and whole star anise into a small saucepan and place on medium-high heat. Allow to bubble away for 10–12 minutes, or until it has reduced by half. Remove from the heat, stir in the orange segments, and set the syrup aside to cool completely.

5. Stir the tapioca flour into the pudding mixture until well combined.

6. Line a baking sheet with a double layer of paper towel. Heat the sunflower oil in a medium saucepan on medium-high heat. Once hot, pick up about 1¼ oz/35g of the tapioca mixture shaping it into a rough ball the size of a golf ball; the mixture will be very sticky, so you might want to use gloves. Gently drop the ball into the hot oil and continue in this way, working quickly, frying about five balls at a time, until deeply golden on the outside and warmed through the center, 4–5 minutes. Transfer them to the prepared baking sheet while you continue with the rest. You should make fifteen balls.

7. Divide the syrup and orange segments among four plates, top each with three of the fritters (saving any extra for seconds), dust with confectioners' sugar, and serve.

SERVES FOUR

POACHED APRICOTS WITH PISTACHIO AND AMARETTI MASCARPONE

POACHED APRICOTS
7 tbsp/105ml Sauternes, or other light dessert wine
2½ tbsp water
1 lime: finely shave the peel to get 3 strips, then juice to get 1 tbsp
¼ tsp vanilla bean paste or vanilla extract
¼ cup plus 1 tbsp/60g superfine sugar
6 medium apricots, halved and pitted (9¾ oz/280g)
1 tsp orange blossom water

⅔ cups/80g pistachios
3 oz/80g amaretti cookies (the hard variety), roughly crumbled
2 tbsp superfine sugar
½ cup plus 1 tbsp/120g mascarpone
½ cup/120ml heavy cream
1 tsp finely grated lime zest

Pesche ripiene—stuffed peaches—is a typical dessert from Piemonte, Italy. It is a lesson in simplicity, where just a few great ingredients—namely ripe peaches, amaretti cookies, mascarpone, sugar, and eggs—are needed to create something quite spectacular. Perhaps because it is so easy, it was one of the first desserts Ixta ever made, from the first recipe book she ever had, *Italy: The Beautiful Cookbook* by Lorenza de' Medici. A few Ottolenghi twists and turns later, we have this recipe, inspired by pesche ripiene, using apricots instead of peaches, and with the addition of pistachios, orange blossom water, and lime zest.

This dessert is both rich and wonderfully refreshing, and requires very little effort. Make sure, though, that you use apricots that are at their very best. If your apricots aren't ripe, add them to the saucepan of hot syrup *before* you take it off the heat, allowing them to simmer gently for a couple of minutes before setting the pan aside. You can poach them the day before serving, if you want to get ahead. The amaretti cream can also be made a day ahead; the cookies in it will soften a bit, but that's okay—you'll get the crunch factor from the remaining cookies with which you'll top the dessert. *Pictured on page 284.*

1. For the apricots: Put the Sauternes, water, lime peel, lime juice, vanilla, and sugar into a medium saucepan on high heat and cook until the sugar has melted and the liquid is simmering. Remove from the heat and place the apricots, cut-side down, in the hot liquid. Let them poach in the residual heat until they are soft but still hold their shape, anywhere between 20–40 minutes depending on how ripe the fruit is. Remove the apricots and discard the lime peel, then cover the apricots to prevent discoloration and set aside. Return the saucepan of syrup to medium-high heat and simmer until reduced to 5 tbsp/75ml, 5–6 minutes. Stir in the orange blossom water and set aside at room temperature.

2. Preheat the oven to 375°F/170°C fan.

3. Place the pistachios on a baking sheet and roast for 10 minutes until very fragrant. Once cool, finely chop the pistachios and put into a bowl with the amaretti and 2 tbsp sugar.

4. Put the mascarpone and cream into the bowl of a stand mixer with the whisk attachment in place, or use a handheld mixer, and whip for 1–2 minutes, until smooth and fluffy (take care not to overwhip). Fold in three-fourths of the amaretti-pistachio mixture and set aside.

5. Divide the apricots and the amaretti cream among four bowls. Pour the syrup over the apricots and sprinkle the remaining amaretti-pistachio mixture over the cream. Finish with the lime zest and serve.

WATERMELON AND STRAWBERRY SORBET

SERVES EIGHT

1 small watermelon
(3 lb/1.4kg), rind and
seeds removed, flesh
cut into ¾-inch/2cm
chunks (4⅔ cups/700g)

**10½ oz/300g ripe
strawberries,** hulled
and roughly chopped

**⅓ oz/10g fresh makrut
lime leaves,** stems
removed, blitzed in a
spice grinder or very
finely chopped (or
3 rooibos tea bags)

¾ cup/180ml corn syrup

8 limes: finely zest to
get 4 tsp, then juice
to get 6 tbsp/90ml;
cut the remainder into
wedges (you'll need
an additional 1 tsp lime
zest if using rooibos tea)

¼ cup/60ml vodka

**1 tbsp plus 1 tsp
superfine sugar**

This sorbet is made without an ice-cream machine but it's still remarkably smooth. You can thank the vodka and corn syrup for that; they work together to prevent large ice crystals from forming.

You can choose to flavor your sorbet with fresh lime leaves or rooibos tea. Though very different, they both work really well. Fresh makrut lime leaves, which are becoming more readily available in supermarkets, deliver an intense citrus fragrance that pairs wonderfully with the watermelon and strawberry.

If you can't find lime leaves, or want to try something different, we found that rooibos tea—made from the leaves of the South African "red bush"—is an equally wonderful flavor pairing, bringing with it floral and ever-so-slightly bitter notes. If you're going with rooibos, which is available in any supermarket, simply steep three tea bags in the warm corn syrup, in place of the lime leaves. You can then use 1 tsp of regular lime zest in the finishing sugar, rather than the fresh makrut lime leaves.

Take the sorbet out of the freezer 5–10 minutes before serving, to make it easier to scoop. It will keep in the freezer for up to 1 month. *Pictured on page 285.*

1. Put the watermelon chunks and strawberries into a large container that will fit in your freezer, and freeze until solid–about 2 hours.

2. Meanwhile, put two-thirds of the lime leaves (or all the tea bags) into a medium saucepan with the corn syrup, lime zest, lime juice, and vodka and heat gently on medium heat until the corn syrup has melted and is warm. Set aside for 30 minutes to infuse, then pour through a sieve set over a blender, discarding the aromatics. Add the frozen fruit to the blender and blitz until completely smooth and slushy.

3. Transfer the slush to a wide freezer-proof container, cover with a lid, and freeze until set, about 5 hours.

4. Mix the remaining lime leaves (or 1 tsp lime zest if using rooibos) with the sugar. Divide the sorbet among eight glasses or bowls and serve with the sugar sprinkled on top and the lime wedges alongside.

SERVES SIX

COCONUT ICE CREAM WITH LYCHEE AND PASSION FRUIT

2 cups/180g dried coconut flakes

1¾ cups plus 2 tbsp/560g coconut cream (not coconut milk!)

1½ cups/300g superfine sugar

1 tsp vanilla bean paste or vanilla extract

¾ tsp ground star anise

1 tsp flaked sea salt

½ cup plus 1 tbsp/ 140ml aquafaba (the liquid drained from a 15-oz/425g can of chickpeas; use the drained chickpeas to make One-Pan Orecchiette Puttanesca, page 139)

15 fresh lychees, peeled, pitted, and roughly torn in half (canned is fine, 1⅓ cups/250g)

½ cup/90g passion fruit pulp (from 4–5 passion fruits)

3 tbsp lime juice

This is a dessert to impress, and it doesn't even require an ice-cream machine. It gets its volume and smooth texture from aquafaba—the viscous water you find in a can of chickpeas—which can (incredibly) be whipped up like egg whites.

You'll make enough ice cream and coconut chips (dubbed coconut "crack" in the test kitchen, for reasons that will become quite obvious when you make them) for about twelve portions. Both will keep for a good while, so you can always go back for more. The fruit will be enough to serve six, so increase or decrease depending on how many mouths you're feeding.

The ice cream melts very quickly, so take it out of the freezer just before you serve, and return it to the freezer very soon afterward.

1. Preheat the oven to 400°F/180°C fan. Line a large baking sheet with parchment paper. Spread the coconut flakes on a second baking sheet and bake for 7 minutes, stirring halfway through, until golden and fragrant.

2. Put the coconut cream into a medium saucepan on medium heat and stir in the sugar, vanilla, and star anise. Bring to a simmer and cook until the sugar dissolves into the cream, about 5 minutes. Remove from the heat, add the toasted coconut flakes, and let steep for 1 hour. Strain the liquid into a large bowl, compressing the flakes with a spoon to ensure all the liquid goes through. Set the cream aside. Transfer the strained coconut flakes to the prepared baking sheet and sprinkle with the salt. Mix well, and spread them out as much as possible. Set aside at room temperature for at least 2 hours. If making the day before, cover loosely with parchment paper but do not refrigerate.

3. Put the aquafaba into the bowl of a stand mixer with the whisk attachment in place (or use a handheld mixer). Whisk on high speed for about 8 minutes, until you get semistiff peaks. Gently fold the aquafaba into the coconut cream until well combined. Pour the mixture into a large container, then cover with a lid or wrap tightly with plastic wrap and freeze for 5 hours, or overnight, stirring the mixture two or three times during that time.

4. Preheat the oven to 350°F/160°C fan. Bake the coconut flake mixture for 15 minutes, stirring twice, until deeply golden. Set aside for 10 minutes to cool and crisp up.

5. Mix together the lychees, passion fruit, and lime juice in a medium bowl.

6. Scoop the ice cream into each of six bowls, spoon in the fruit mixture, and finish with a small handful of coconut chips. Serve at once.

MAX AND FLYNN'S LEMON SORBET

8 large lemons
1 cup/200g superfine
sugar
3 hibiscus tea bags
(or ⅓ oz/10g dried
hibiscus flowers)
1½ cups/360ml water
½ cup/10g mint, stems
and leaves

Some might think this hibiscus and lemon sorbet served in a lemon peel is a little garish—the sorbet is such a bright shade of pink from the hibiscus—but we love both the color and the old-school Italian presentation. Yotam's sons, Max and Flynn, proclaimed it the best dessert they'd ever had, "better than custard." It was probably the color that so enchanted them, but it is undeniably delicious, albeit very sour, in a wholly enjoyable, face-inverting kind of way.

Feel free to set the sorbet in a regular container if you don't want to carve out the lemons. If you don't have an ice-cream machine, churn by pouring the unfrozen sorbet into a plastic container and freezing it over a few hours, breaking down the ice crystals with a fork every now and then. The filled lemons will keep in a sealed container in the freezer for up to 1 month.

1. Cut the top third off each lemon. Juice both parts to get 1½ cups/360ml juice and pulp combined. Use a spoon to hollow out the lemons, discarding the remaining flesh and pith and being careful not to puncture the skins. Don't worry if you can't get it all out. Shave a little off the bottom half of each lemon so they can sit upright (again, taking care not to puncture the skin) and arrange them in a baking dish, open-side up, so they are snug and balanced. Freeze the bottoms and their lids on separate trays, while you make the sorbet.

2. Put the lemon juice and pulp, discarding the seeds, into a medium saucepan and add the sugar, hibiscus (tea bags or flowers), and water. Place on medium-high heat and simmer for about 6 minutes, stirring occasionally, until the sugar has melted and the liquid is hot. Remove from the heat, add the mint, and let steep for 15 minutes, until the liquid is bright pink.

3. Strain the liquid through a sieve into a wide container and discard the aromatics. Refrigerate until completely chilled, 1–2 hours. Pour the chilled liquid into an ice-cream machine and churn for 25–30 minutes, or until frozen and smooth. Transfer the sorbet into a piping bag or a zip-top bag and seal it closed. Freeze for 3–4 hours, until firm, crushing the bag with your hands a couple of times to break the ice crystals.

4. Remove the dish of hollowed-out lemon bottoms from the freezer. Cut the tip of the piping bag or zip-top bag to create a 1-inch/2½cm-wide opening. Pipe the sorbet into the lemons to come about 2 inches/5cm above the rim (you may need to hold the piping bag with a kitchen towel, as it gets very cold). Top each with a lemon lid, pushing them down so they are stable, and return to the freezer for 1 hour before serving.

SERVES FOUR

CRÊPES WITH ROASTED BANANAS AND BARBADOS CREAM

CRÊPE BATTER
6 tbsp/50g all-purpose flour
1 tsp light brown sugar
⅛ tsp table salt
1 egg
⅔ cup/160ml whole milk

BARBADOS CREAM
½ cup/100g mascarpone
½ cup/150g extra-thick Greek-style yogurt (such as Total)
½ tsp vanilla extract or vanilla paste

ROASTED BANANAS
2 tbsp unsalted butter
7½ tsp light brown sugar
¼ tsp ground ginger
4 ripe bananas, peeled, halved crosswise and then lengthwise
table salt

2 tbsp unsalted butter
1 tbsp spiced dark rum
3 tbsp light brown sugar
¼ cup/20g sliced almonds, lightly toasted

Barbados cream, introduced to us by Ixta's Aunt Rose (via Nigella Lawson), is extremely dangerous: creamy, boozy, sweet, and, with the sugar stirred into the rum just before serving, crunchy as well.

You'll make enough batter for about seven crêpes, three more than you will actually need. These are to account for those "missing in action," when the cook just can't resist temptation. Make the crêpe batter the day before if you want to get ahead, or, like Yotam, triple the batter, fry lots of crêpes, and keep them in the freezer, separated with parchment paper, ready to be quickly defrosted whenever you have a hankering. The cream mixture can also be made the day before, but hold off on roasting the bananas and mixing the rum with the sugar until just before serving. *Pictured on page 292.*

1. For the crêpe batter: In a medium bowl, whisk the flour with the brown sugar and salt. Add the egg and whisk together, then add the milk gradually, whisking until you have a smooth, thin batter. Set aside for 20 minutes.

2. Preheat the oven to 475°F/230°C fan.

3. For the cream: In a medium bowl, mix together the mascarpone, yogurt, and vanilla until smooth and set aside.

4. For the bananas: Place a medium, ovenproof frying pan on medium-high heat and add the butter. Once melted, add the brown sugar and ginger and stir until melted and combined, 1–2 minutes. Remove from the heat, add the bananas, and mix gently so they are coated, then arrange so they are cut-side up. Transfer to the oven for 12 minutes, or until softened and browned. Sprinkle with a little salt. Set aside.

5. Put 1 tsp of the butter into a medium frying pan and place on medium-high heat. Once melted and bubbling, add about 3 tbsp batter, swirling the pan to form a thin crêpe about 6½ inches/16cm in diameter. Cook for 1–2 minutes, then, using a spatula, flip over. Cook for another 30–60 seconds, until nicely browned on both sides, and then set aside. You may need to decrease the heat to medium if the pan gets too hot. Continue with the remaining butter and batter until you have four good crêpes (the first few may not be perfect). Cover and keep warm.

6. Just before serving, in a small bowl, stir together the rum and brown sugar.

7. Divide the crêpes among four plates, then top each with one-fourth of the bananas. Fold the crêpe over and spoon some of the Barbados cream alongside. Drizzle with the rum sugar, finish with the almonds, and serve.

SERVES FOUR

COFFEE AND PANDAN PUDDINGS

1¾ oz/50g **fresh pandan leaves,** roughly cut into 1½-inch/4cm pieces (or 1 vanilla pod, halved lengthwise)

1¼ cups/300ml **whole milk**

1¼ cups/300ml **heavy cream**

2 tbsp **cornstarch**

1¼ tsp **instant espresso powder**

5 **egg yolks**

¼ cup/50g **superfine sugar**

1 tsp **cocoa powder**

¼ tsp **flaked sea salt**

2 tbsp **unsalted butter,** at room temperature, cut into ½-inch/1cm cubes

COFFEE SYRUP

⅔ cup/160ml **strong brewed coffee**

¼ cup/50g **superfine sugar**

¼ cup/30g **salted macadamia nuts,** well roasted and roughly chopped

Brilliantly fragrant, pandan leaves are used in Asian cooking to flavor all sorts of sweet and savory dishes. Their aroma is somewhere between grass and vanilla, and they work particularly well with tropical fruit, in cakes, and when paired with coffee, as we have here. They are easily found in Asian supermarkets, but if you can't get hold of them, substitute with a whole vanilla pod.

The coffee syrup can be made a day ahead of time, but it tends to seep into the pudding if it is left to sit, so be sure to pour it on just as you serve. It takes 2 hours to infuse the milk with the pandan, and about 6 hours for the puddings to set, so you'd probably want to make them a day ahead as well. *Pictured on page 293.*

1. Put the pandan leaves (or vanilla pod), milk, and cream into a medium saucepan, for which you have a lid, and place on medium heat. Cover and allow to gently heat and steam, pressing down on the leaves a few times to release their flavor, about 20 minutes. Remove from the heat and let infuse, covered, for 2 hours. Strain through a sieve set over a bowl, pushing down to extract as much liquid as possible, discarding the leaves (or pod). Measure out ⅓ cup/80ml of the milk into a medium bowl and add the cornstarch, whisking until smooth. Pour the remaining strained milk back into the saucepan, add the espresso powder, and whisk to combine. Set both aside.

2. In a medium bowl, whisk together the egg yolks, sugar, cocoa powder, and salt until smooth.

3. Return the saucepan of infused milk to medium heat and bring to a simmer. Slowly pour half the warm milk mixture into the egg yolk bowl, whisking continuously until the bowl is warm to the touch. Add the cornstarch-milk mixture and whisk until smooth. Slowly pour the now tempered mixture back into the saucepan and whisk continuously, until it's the consistency of a thick but pourable custard, about 5 minutes. Remove from the heat and whisk in the butter until incorporated.

4. Divide the pudding among four martini glasses (or something similar) and let cool slightly before covering with plastic wrap and refrigerating until set, about 6 hours or up to overnight.

5. For the syrup: Put the coffee and sugar into a small saucepan on medium-high heat. Bring to a boil and let bubble away for 6–7 minutes, or until reduced by about half and is the consistency of maple syrup. Set aside to cool; it will thicken more as it sits.

6. Top each pudding with 2 tsp of the syrup, then sprinkle with the macadamia nuts and serve with any additional syrup alongside.

SERVES SIX

BERRY PLATTER WITH SHEEP MILK LABNEH AND ORANGE OIL

——————

LABNEH

3⅔ cups/900g sheep milk yogurt or cow milk yogurt

½ tsp table salt

7 tbsp/105ml good-quality olive oil

⅓ oz/10g lemon thyme sprigs, plus a few whole thyme leaves

1 orange: finely shave the peel to get 6 strips

1⅓ cups/200g blackberries

2 cups/250g raspberries

3 cups/300g strawberries, hulled and halved lengthwise (or quartered if they're larger)

¼ cup/50g superfine sugar

1 lime: finely zest to get 1 tsp, then juice to get 1 tbsp

1¼ cups/200g blueberries

⅔ cup/150g cherries, pitted

This display of the season's best can double up as a light dessert or as a brunch centerpiece. You can make your own labneh but it requires draining the yogurt for a good 24 hours, or you can make everything easily on the day using store-bought labneh or some Greek-style yogurt mixed with a little heavy cream. The berries you use are totally up to you, depending on what's good and not too expensive. You can use fewer types, or some frozen berries, if you like, especially for those that get blitzed in the recipe. You'll make more oil than you need; store it in a glass jar to drizzle over salads or lightly cooked vegetables.

1. For the labneh: Line a colander with a piece of muslin large enough to hang over the sides and place the colander over a bowl. Put the yogurt and salt into a medium bowl and mix well to combine. Transfer the yogurt to the muslin and fold over the sides to completely encase the yogurt. Place a heavy weight over the muslin (a few cans or jars will do) and transfer to the fridge to drain for at least 24 hours or up to 48 hours.

2. Meanwhile, put the olive oil into a small saucepan, for which you have a lid, on medium heat. Heat gently for about 7 minutes, or until tiny air bubbles form. Remove from the heat, add the lemon thyme sprigs and orange strips, and then cover and let infuse, ideally overnight, though 30 minutes will also do the job.

3. Put ⅓ cup/50g of the blackberries, ¾ cup/100g of the raspberries, and ⅓ cup/100g of the strawberries into the bowl of a small food processor along with the sugar and lime juice and blitz until completely smooth. Put all the remaining berries and the cherries into a large bowl along with the blitzed fruit and gently combine. (You can serve straight away or leave in the fridge for a few hours, bringing back to room temperature before serving.)

4. Spread the labneh out on a large platter. Spoon in the berries, then sprinkle with the lime zest. Drizzle with 2 tbsp of the infused oil, dot with a couple of the orange strips and whole thyme leaves, and serve at once.

FLAVOR BOMBS

We had various working titles for *Flavor* throughout the course of writing it. One of them was "The Ottolenghi F-Bomb." It was never going to fly, we knew, but the idea of "flavor bombs" is one that was with us every step of the way. Stocked up with a little arsenal of flavor-packed condiments, sauces, pickles, salsas, infused oils, and so forth, a meal full of flavor will only ever be just a few steps away. This list is our arsenal. They're all recipes-within-recipes from the book but useful to reference on the following spread as well, to see how stand-alone and versatile they can be. You don't need to make all of them, but having one or two or three in your fridge at any one time is really useful. Five-minutes-made scrambled eggs will never be the same once you've drizzled them with smoked cascabel oil or served them with a bit of charred chile sauce alongside.

A couple of practicalities: If you are making a batch of something for a recipe, it's often worth doubling or tripling the quantities so that you have some at the ready. Shelf lives and keeping notes vary depending on what you are making, so see each recipe for details. If you are scaling up a recipe, you'll probably need to increase pan or bowl size and cooking time accordingly. We always give a visual description of what you are looking for, so use those as a guide if quantities have been increased, rather than sticking religiously to times given. As always, trust your instincts and have the confidence to be your own judge. If you think something is looking, smelling, and tasting delicious and ready, then, chances are, it *will* be.

Oils, butters, and marinades

1. Black lime and pumpkin seed butter (PAGE 264)
2. Chile butter (PAGE 205)
3. Chile oil (PAGE 159)
4. Fenugreek marinade (PAGE 63)
5. Lime leaf butter (PAGE 50)
6. Numbing oil (PAGE 196)
7. Rayu (PAGE 237)
8. Smoked cascabel oil (PAGE 41)
9. Three-garlic butter (PAGE 246)

Sauces, salsas, and dressings

10. Blood orange nam jim (PAGE 202)
11. Chamoy (PAGE 187)
12. Charred chile salsa (PAGE 45)
13. Cilantro chutney (PAGE 193)
14. Nam prik (PAGE 44)
15. Quick chile sauce (PAGE 151)
16. Sweet tamarind dressing (PAGE 193)
17. Tahini and soy dressing (PAGE 113)

Condiments and pickles

Nuts and sprinkles

MEAL SUGGESTIONS AND FEASTS

Vegetable-focused meals are flexible by their very nature. There isn't a natural hierarchy or a clear order in which things need to appear at the table. The notion of a main course and sides, on which so many of us rely, simply doesn't lend itself so easily to a meal in which meat or fish don't occupy center stage. Though we aren't big fans of any form of fixed meal structure, even when we serve meat or fish, we are aware that the freedom that comes with the plurality of options of a veggie menu can bring with it some confusion.

To help a little with choosing how to put together meals from *Flavor*, we have come up with some suggestions. These are ideas only, seeds we plant in your head so you can navigate between dishes you've never cooked before. We encourage you to pick and choose from our menus. They are not set in stone. Add if you need more in your meal, take away if you think it's too much.

We would also love you to serve our dishes alongside your old favorites. Cooking a new dish is a challenge, cooking two is double the challenge. Make your life easier by taking single steps, if you need to.

In fact, cooking a single dish from the book and serving it with one or two "sides" is something we recommend wholeheartedly. Most of the dishes in *Flavor* were designed with big flavors in mind. The "simple salad," "sautéed greens," or "simple rice" we mention are all code for your favorite dishes from the raw veg, cooked veg, or starch families. Make them to go with one of our more substantial dishes, and that's all you'll need.

Last, make ahead! Whenever we can, we give you an idea about which parts of a recipe can be prepared in advance; often it's the dish in its entirety. Please take advantage of this. There is nothing better than getting a meal on the table in a matter of minutes and with very little effort. It leaves you stress-free and with all the time in the world to enjoy your hard-earned efforts.

Everyday Cooking

ONE PAN, READY IN 30 MINUTES OR LESS

Potato and gochujang braised **eggs** (PAGE 99) + simple **salad**

Za'atar cacio e pepe (PAGE 104) + simple **salad**

One-pan **orecchiette** puttanesca (PAGE 139) + simple **salad**

Cardamom **tofu** with lime **greens** (PAGE 172) + sticky **rice**

Super-soft **zucchini** with harissa and lemon (PAGE 204) + **pasta** or **rice**

ONE PAN, READY IN 1 HOUR

Bkeila, **potato,** and **butter bean** stew (PAGE 75) + simply grilled **tofu** or **fish**

Polenta with fresh corn and braised **eggs** (PAGE 163) + simple **salad**

The ultimate roasting-pan **ragù** (PAGE 101) + pasta or polenta and simple **salad**

READY IN 1 HOUR

Steamed **eggplants** with charred chile salsa (PAGE 45) + **noodles** or **rice**

Spring vegetables in Parmesan broth with charred lemon sauce (PAGE 109) + **pasta** or **noodles**

Chickpea **pancakes** with mango pickle yogurt (PAGE 91) + simple **salad**

Kimchi and Gruyère **rice fritters** (PAGE 166) + simple **salad**

Udon **noodles** with fried **tofu** and orange nam jim (PAGE 202)

Noodle salad with mushroom and peanut **laab** (PAGE 233)

Mafalda and roasted **butternut** in warm yogurt sauce (PAGE 151) + sautéed **greens** or simple **salad**

Brown rice and shiitake **congee** (PAGE 237) + soft-boiled **egg** or grilled **tofu** and sautéed **greens**

Spicy berbere **ratatouille** with coconut sauce (PAGE 209) + **rice** and/or **flatbreads**

Coconut and turmeric **omelette** feast (PAGE 145) + fried **tofu** or **prawns**

Sweet potato in tomato, lime, and cardamom sauce (PAGE 131) + **rice** and sautéed **greens**

LOW-EFFORT/ HIGH-IMPACT MEALS

Curry-crusted **rutabaga** steaks (PAGE 63) + **rice** or **flatbreads**

Sweet and sour **sprouts** with chestnuts and grapes (PAGE 93) + grilled **tofu** and **rice**

Cauliflower roasted in chile butter (PAGE 205) + **rice** and sautéed **greens**

Portobello steaks and butter bean mash (PAGE 210) + sautéed **greens** or simple **salad**

LOW-EFFORT/ HIGH-IMPACT SIDES

Cucumber salad à la Xi'an Impression (PAGE 113)

Oven **fries** with curry leaf mayonnaise (PAGE 89)

Tomato salad with lime and cardamom yogurt (PAGE 164)

Braised **greens** with yogurt (PAGE 175)

Sweet and sour **onion** petals (PAGE 245)

Miso butter **onions** (PAGE 258)

Grilled **figs** with Shaoxing dressing (PAGE 110)

Tomato and plum salad with nori and sesame (PAGE 267)

Kohlrabi "noodle" salad (PAGE 260)

Spicy roast **potatoes** with tahini and soy (PAGE 276)

Roasted **carrot** salad with chamoy (PAGE 187)

MAKE-AHEAD MEALS

The ultimate roasting-pan **ragù** (PAGE 101) + **pasta** or **polenta**

Rainbow **chard** with tomatoes and green olives (PAGE 183) + **rice** or **pasta**

Spicy **mushroom lasagne** (PAGE 228) + simple **salad**

Stuffed **eggplant** in curry and coconut **dal** (PAGE 152) + **rice** and/or **flatbreads**

Eggplant dumplings alla parmigiana (PAGE 156) + **pasta** and sautéed **greens**

Tofu meatball korma (PAGE 268) + **rice** and/or flatbreads and simple **salad**

Brown rice and shiitake **congee** (PAGE 237) + soft-boiled **egg** or grilled tofu and sautéed **greens**

Spicy berbere **ratatouille** with coconut sauce (PAGE 209) + **rice** and/or **flatbreads**

Portobello steaks and butter bean mash (PAGE 210) + sautéed **greens** or simple **salad**

Feasts

BRUNCH SPREADS

Potato and gochujang braised **eggs** (PAGE 99) or Coconut and turmeric **omelette** feast (PAGE 145) + Radish and cucumber **salad** (see PAGE 263) + **Crêpes** with roasted bananas and Barbados cream (PAGE 290)

Polenta with fresh corn and braised **eggs** (PAGE 163) + **Tomato salad** with lime and cardamom yogurt (PAGE 164) + **Butter beans** in smoked cascabel oil (PAGE 41) + Super-soft **zucchini** with harissa and lemon (PAGE 204)

THREE-COURSE MEALS

Pappa al pomodoro with lime and mustard seeds (PAGE 85) + **Za'atar cacio e pepe** (PAGE 104) + Poached **apricots** with pistachio and amaretti mascarpone (PAGE 282)

Corn ribs (PAGE 264) + Rutabaga **gnocchi** with miso butter (PAGE 94) + Coconut **ice cream** with lychee and passion fruit (PAGE 286)

Roasted and pickled **celery root** with sweet chile dressing (PAGE 55) + Cardamom **tofu** with lime greens (PAGE 172) and simple **rice** + Coffee and pandan **puddings** (PAGE 291)

Herb and charred **eggplant soup** (PAGE 42) + One-pan **orecchiette** puttanesca (PAGE 139) + Max and Flynn's lemon **sorbet** (PAGE 289)

ROVI SPREAD

Tempura stems, leaves, and herbs (PAGE 184) + Hasselback **beets** with lime leaf butter (PAGE 50) + Charred **peppers** and fresh corn polenta (see PAGE 140) + Rainbow **chard** with tomatoes and green **olives** (PAGE 183) + Tangerine and ancho chile **flan** (PAGE 278)

KORMA FEAST

Tofu meatball korma (PAGE 268) + Spicy berbere **ratatouille** with coconut sauce (PAGE 209) or Curry-crusted **rutabaga** steaks (PAGE 63) + Olive oil **flatbreads** with three-garlic butter (without the tomatoes) (PAGE 246) or simple **rice**

MEXICAN FEAST

Cheese tamales with all (or some of) the fixin's (PAGE 158) or Oyster **mushroom tacos** with all (or some of) the fixin's (PAGE 238) or both + Radish and cucumber **salad** with chipotle peanuts (PAGE 263) + Tangerine and ancho chile **flan** (PAGE 278)

EAST ASIAN FEAST

Cabbage with ginger cream and numbing oil (PAGE 196) + Asparagus and gochujang **pancakes** (PAGE 102) + Fusion caponata with silken **tofu** (PAGE 135) + **Cucumber salad** à la Xi'an Impression (PAGE 113) + Coffee and pandan **puddings** (PAGE 291)

FESTIVE SPREADS

Turnip cake (PAGE 270) + Sweet and sour **sprouts** with chestnuts and grapes (PAGE 93) + **Leeks** with miso and chive sauce (PAGE 257) + Esme's rough **squash mash** (PAGE 136) + Dirty **rice** (PAGE 252)

Cauliflower roasted in chile butter (PAGE 205) + Lime and coconut **potato gratin** (PAGE 72) + Roasted **carrot** salad with chamoy (PAGE 187) + Slow-cooked charred **green beans** (PAGE 49) or simple steamed **green beans**

SUNDAY ROAST

Celery root steaks with Café de Paris sauce (PAGE 60) + Cucumber, za'atar, and chopped lemon **salad** (PAGE 191) + Oven **fries** (without the curry leaf mayonnaise) (PAGE 89)

OUTDOOR SUMMER FEAST

Melon and buffalo mozzarella salad with kasha and curry leaves (PAGE 80) + **Tomato and plum salad** with nori and sesame (PAGE 267) + **Potato salad** with Thai basil sauce (PAGE 275) + Olive oil **flatbreads** with three-garlic butter (PAGE 246) + Super-soft **zucchini** with harissa and lemon (PAGE 204)

MEZZE

Eggplant with herbs and crispy garlic (PAGE 251) + Sweet and sour **onion** petals (PAGE 245) or Neil's grilled **onions** with green **gazpacho** (PAGE 242) + Confit garlic **hummus** with grilled mushrooms (PAGE 234) + **Tomato salad** with lime and cardamom yogurt (PAGE 164) + Olive oil **flatbreads** with three-garlic butter (PAGE 246)

DIPS

Hummus with lemon, fried garlic, and chile (PAGE 79) + Mashed **sweet potatoes** with yogurt and lime (PAGE 192) + White **bean mash** with garlic aïoli (PAGE 76) + Curried **carrot mash** with brown butter (PAGE 67)

INDEX

ACKNOWLEDGMENTS

I am often asked how I carry on creating new recipes for home cooks after more than a decade of publishing cookbooks. The answer is that I don't. What I did create (with many others) is an environment that I am tremendously proud of: the test kitchen that sits under a railway arch in Camden, north London, and the Ottolenghi restaurants, including NOPI and ROVI. These are the places where new dishes are shaped, and it's the people who work in them that come up with the ideas that find themselves, in print, on people's kitchen counters.

In Camden, alongside Ixta and Tara, Team Test Kitchen is blessed with Noor Murad, who grew up in Bahrain and is the unofficial expert in Middle Eastern feasts, tamarind, and everything rice related, amongst countless other talents. I am also immensely grateful to Gitai Fisher, who's good at everything, and is often the one with the clever idea that helps us crack a "troublesome" dish.

Other constant contributors are Calvin Von Niebel, Verena Lochmuller, Paulina Bembel, Neil Campbell, Helen Goh, and Esme Howarth. I am grateful to them all. I am also grateful to Claudine Boulstridge for her priceless appraisals.

I would like to thank Jonathan Lovekin and Caz Hildebrand, my long-standing creative partners, for being so incredibly good at their jobs, Wei Tang for the props and honesty, and Nishant Choksi for the clever illustrations. Thanks also to Sam Carroll and Sytch Farm Studios.

Thanks to Felicity Rubinstein for standing by my side, often having to hold my hand, through old challenges and new, and to Lizzy Gray for her intelligence and infinite patience.

A massive thank-you to Noam Bar for his continual presence behind every single project, to Cornelia Staeubli for her unconditional support, and to Sami Tamimi for his friendship.

I am also extremely grateful to the team at Ebury: Joel Rickett, Sarah Bennie, Celia Palazzo, Stephenie Naulls, Catherine Wood, Vanessa Forbes, and Catherine Ngwong. Across the Atlantic, my deepest thanks to Kim Witherspoon, Aaron Wehner, Lorena Jones, Kate Tyler, Windy Dorresteyn, Sandi Mendelson, Jane Chinn, Kelly Booth, Emma Rudolph, Doug Ogan, Mari Gill, Robert McCullough, Lindsay Paterson, and Carla Kean.

Thanks also to Mark Hutchinson and Gemma Bell and her team, and to Bob Granleese and Tim Lusher.

Finally, but most important, thank you to the love of my life, Karl Allen, and to the two monkeys, Max and Flynn. Thanks also to Michael and Ruth Ottolenghi; Tirza, Danny, Shira, Yoav, and Adam Florentin; Pete and Greta Allen, Shachar Argov, Garry Chang, Alex Meitlis, Ivo Bisignano, Lulu Banquete, Tamara Meitlis, Keren Margalit, Yoram Ever-Hadani, Itzik Lederfeind, Ilana Lederfeind, and Amos, Ariela, and David Oppenheim.

YOTAM OTTOLENGHI

Thank you to my parents, Nicolas Belfrage and Maria Candida De Melo, for love that knows no bounds, and for the unforgettable adventures through Brazil, Mexico, and Italy that shaped the cook that I am today.

To my sister Beatriz Belfrage, for wisdom and support I can always turn to.

To my cousin Moby Pomerance, for nurturing a love of food in me.

Thanks to Claudia Lazarus, my partner in crime in most food-related endeavors outside of Ottolenghi. Thanks to NOPI restaurant, where I met Claudia across a crowded kitchen, and where my Ottolenghi adventure began.

Thank you to Alex Intas, for his unwavering love and support, and, more important, for his unwavering willingness to eat.

Thanks to Lauren and Felipe Gonzalez, for giving me a copy of *Plenty More* all those years ago with a message in it to the tune of "follow your dreams." I could never have dreamt of this!

To Noor Murad, thank you for being a constant source of light and inspiration.

To Jonathan, Lizzy, Celia, Annie, Caz, Wei, and Nishant, thank you for helping make this first venture into the world of book-making a joyous one.

And, most important, thank you to Yotam for the opportunity of a lifetime, and for being a fiercely patient, intelligent, and kind teacher.

IXTA BELFRAGE

Published in the United States by Ten Speed Press, an imprint of
Random House, a division of Penguin Random House LLC, New York.
www.tenspeed.com

Ten Speed Press and the Ten Speed Press colophon are registered
trademarks of Penguin Random House LLC.

Originally published in Great Britain by Ebury Press,
an imprint of Ebury Publishing, Penguin Random
House Ltd., London.

Library of Congress Cataloging-in-Publication Data is on file
with the publisher.

Library of Congress Control Number: 2020937975

Hardcover ISBN: 978-0-399-58175-5
eBook ISBN: 978-0-399-58176-2

Printed in China

Design by Here Design
Prop styling by Wei Tang
Cover design by Kelly Booth

10 9 8 7 6 5 4 3 2 1

First US Edition

OTTOLENGHI

FLAVOR

Yotam Ottolenghi
Ixta Belfrage

THE PERFECT INTERACTIVE COMPANION TO THE BOOK

A GIFT FROM YOTAM AND IXTA
All of the recipes at your fingertips, wherever you are

BROWSE
Access all the recipes online from anywhere

SEARCH
Find your perfect recipe by ingredient or browse through the chapters

FAVORITES
Create your own list of go-to recipes and always have them at hand, whether shopping on the way home or looking for recipe ideas during a weekend away

TO UNLOCK YOUR ACCESS, VISIT OTTOLENGHIBOOKS.COM
AND ENTER YOUR UNIQUE CODE: FD4E-FA53-3ED2-4DC8-96